THE
INSIDERS'®
GUIDE
TO

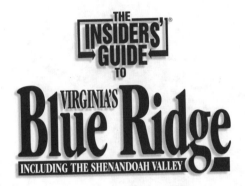

VIRGINIA'S
Blue Ridge

INCLUDING THE SHENANDOAH VALLEY

THE INSIDERS' GUIDE TO

VIRGINIA'S Blue Ridge

INCLUDING THE SHENANDOAH VALLEY

by
Lin Chaff
and
Dale Leatherman

The Insiders' Guides®, Inc.

Co-published and marketed by:
Richmond Times Dispatch
333 East Grace Street
Richmond, VA 23219
(804) 775-8079

Co-published and distributed by:
The Insiders' Guides® Inc.
The Waterfront • Suites 12 &13
P.O. 2057
Manteo, NC 27954
(919) 473-6100

•

FOURTH EDITION
1st printing

•

•

Printed in the United States
of America

•

ISBN 0-912367-84-9

Richmond Times Dispatch
Supplementary Publications

Manager
Ernie Chenault

Account Executives
Heidi Crandall,
Patricia Thingstad, John Wade

Project Coordination
Amy Patina

Artists
Susan Reilly,
Ronnie Johnson, Ben Schulte

The Insiders' Guides® Inc.

Publisher/Editor-in-Chief
Beth P. Storie

President/General Manager
Michael McOwen

Vice President/Advertising
Murray Kasmenn

Partnership Services Director
Giles Bissonnette

Creative Services Director
Mike Lay

Online Services Director
David Haynes

Sales and Marketing Director
Julie Ross

Managing Editor
Theresa Chavez

Project Editor
Eileen Myers

Project Artist
Mel Dorsey

Fulfillment Director
Gina Twiford

Controller
Claudette Forney

Welcome to our favorite place.

Many Americans still long for a simpler way of life in smaller towns. This is where they find it, trading in business suits for blue jeans. It's a privilege to live in the Blue Ridge of Virginia, pure and simple. Every day is a feast for the senses. And at night, you can drift off to sleep knowing that if your environment can impact upon your sense of well-being, you are one of the luckiest — and happiest — people around.

This is the nostalgic land of Earl Hamner's John-Boy and the Walton family. You can still find a lot of general stores like Uncle Ike's. You can still find clucking, blue-haired ladies preparing banana pudding and fried chicken for Sunday School picnics in the country and small congregations worshipping in white, clapboard chapels. You can still find the strong family values that compel generations of extended families to all live down the same country lane. You'll find neighbors who mind their own business but are ever willing to lend a helping hand.

Welcome to a place where people still wave to strangers on back country roads, and children and the family dog still swim with patched innertubes in pristine creeks under covered bridges. Welcome to life in the slow lane, with the same benefits but few of the hassles of life in the fast lane.

For sheer beauty and tranquility, nothing equals the Blue Ridge of Virginia's mountains, flora, fauna, rivers and lakes. We're a rhapsody of riotous yellow fuchsia and redbud in the spring. We're a sonnet of sunny meadows with hovering hummingbirds and singing songbirds in the summer. We're a painter's palette of colors in the autumn. We're an aria to the simple setting of the first Christmas as we celebrate with handwrought wreaths and the tree we just cut out back on the snow-covered mountain.

We revere our environment, realizing a covenant with the land. We pull our cars off our highways to watch the sun go down and are filled with a sense of awe that a pinpoint of light bursting through a cloud can make a mountain appear to be wrapped in red velvet.

Ours is a land of great dynamics. We are inventors, like Cyrus McCormick, whose Shenandoah Valley mechanical reaper revolutionized the world. We are the land of Thomas Jefferson, the quintessential Renaissance man, who invented not only the concept of democracy in America, but also the dumb waiter, the original mimeograph and the brave art of eating the "love tomatoe." We are the land of robots and fiber optics in Roanoke, smart road technology in the New River Valley and solar-powered SIRUS Earthship homes in Floyd County.

We are a land of great leaders. On our Natural Bridge, George Washington carved his initials and later bailed Washington and Lee University out of impending bankruptcy. Ours is a land where Robert E. Lee led troops to great valor and honor during a four-year Civil War that was supposed to last just a few weeks. Our Shenandoah Valley is where Stonewall Jackson exasperated his students at the Virginia Military Institute with his toughness and humorlessness and then went on to create a legend in military strategy still taught by U.S. military leaders.

We are a people who revere our history and honor our dead. We preserve our crumbling cemeteries and battlefields as hallowed ground. We build museums in the tiniest of communities as we welcome at least half a million people a year to Monticello and Montpelier in Charlottesville. We build monuments to every Civil War battle ever fought and museums to honor our fallen soldiers.

We are a land of great scholarship and creativity, where the slave Booker T. Washington grew up in Franklin County to become one of the great African-American thinkers and leaders of all time. Here, the great Harlem Renaissance poet Anne Spencer entertained Martin Luther King, Congressman Adam Clayton Powell, Justice Thurgood Marshall and singers Paul Robeson and Marion Anderson at her Lynchburg garden home.

This is also a land of enormous, diverse culture. We flatfoot on Friday nights in the Alleghany Highlands. We go to drive-in movies and eat buttered popcorn in Rockbridge County while celebrities fly in from around the world to see our American Film Festival in nearby Charlottesville. In Amherst County, near Lynchburg, we provide one of the largest residential colonies in the world for international artists and writers to stir their creative juices. At our colleges and cities, we display works of art and crafts equal to that of any metropolitan area in the country.

We're a big playground where you can camp, hike, bike, canoe, golf, boat, swim, horseback ride, hunt, fish, hang glide and soar until you drop!

We're a land of festivity looking for excuses to celebrate. We stage festivals to honor everything from apples, strawberries, garlic, dogwoods, ramps, wine and maple sugar to folklife and railroads.

This is also a land of superlatives. No matter which region of the Blue Ridge you visit, you'll find "the biggest," "the oldest," "the most important" or "nationally known" and "internationally acclaimed." Every region is a gem of multifaceted culture, like precious stones on a necklace, the common thread being the beauty of the Blue Ridge and our vast quality of life.

We are Charlottesville, land of Jeffersonian mystique and international chic. We are Staunton, heart of the Blue Ridge with our famous July Fourth picnics in Gypsy Hill, begun by the world-famous Statler Brothers. We are Harrisonburg, with fields of golden, waving grain and hills white with turkeys, and Roanoke, "Capital of the Blue Ridge," the largest metropolitan area off the Blue Ridge Parkway, voted by travel writers as the most beautiful road in the world. We are the intellectually stimulating New River Valley, home to gigantic Virginia Tech, as well as a tie-dyed counterculture that came to Floyd County and never left the '60s. We're the staid German Baptists at Smith Mountain Lake, the playground of western Virginia, and we still hunt for the cryptic, elusive Beale Treasure in nearby Bedford County. We're Jerry Falwell and the Moral Majority in Lynchburg, the home of one of the largest churches in America. We're the residents of the pastoral Alleghany Highlands, where the sheep outnumber the human population and life is as slow and sweet as the maple sugar trickling down the trees in the spring.

Welcome to our favorite place. Everywhere you travel you'll find beauty that stops you in your tracks, people who are courteous, trusting and kind, and the opportunity to be transformed by the goodness of your environment.

Visit with us awhile. Rock on our wide front porches and sit a spell. Join us in our favorite pastime of watching the sun set over the Blue Ridge of Virginia. Have some peach cobbler and Virginia-made wine to settle you for the night. And when the stars blanket the Blue Ridge of Virginia, pack away your worries and tough times and mount a carousel horse (you can buy one in Newbern) to ride through your dreams. Now, say good night to John-Boy Walton and the rest of the family. Dream of waking up to the warmth and promise of Blue Ridge sunshine and the goodness it will bring.

Good night, John-Boy.

Good night.

Photo: Lexington Visitor Center

Historic Lee Chapel in Lexington on the campus of Washington and Lee University.

About the Authors

Lin D. Chaff arrived in Blacksburg fresh out of West Virginia University in 1972, as the editor of the *Blacksburg Sun*. While in Blacksburg she fell in love with the Blue Ridge of Virginia and ever since has made it her life's mission to live and work there, taking time out to earn a graduate journalism degree at Northwestern University.

Before moving back in 1978 to become a reporter for the New River Valley Bureau of the *Roanoke Times*, she worked for Gannett newspapers and Associated Press and on Capitol Hill and received a string of journalism awards.

After the birth of her first daughter, she became manager of publicity for Dominion Bankshares Corp. (now First Union) in Roanoke. After the birth of her second daughter, she started her own public relations, marketing and advertising firm, in part to promote tourism in western Virginia. The firm's work was honored by Virginia's premier Public Relations Society of America competition for the best public relations campaign in the state of Virginia in 1995. The agency also won the 1995 American Advertising Federation "Addy" for advertising excellence.

Chaff belongs to numerous tourism marketing groups, including the Blue Ridge Commission's Marketing Committee, and is accredited by PRSA. She thanks her husband, John Wade, and her daughters, Elizabeth and Priscilla, for their patience, support and shared enthusiasm for this labor of love.

Dale Leatherman grew up near Martinsburg, West Virginia, and graduated from West Virginia University in 1966 with a degree in recreation. Her interest in horses drew her to New York, where for seven years she was a professional rider.

Returning to Martinsburg in the 1980s, she began writing for the local newspaper. In 1985 she became features editor for *Polo Magazine* and, later, *Spur Magazine*, two upscale national publications covering the equestrian lifestyle. During that time, her first travel articles began appearing in general magazines.

Today, Leatherman is a contributing editor for *Spur, Metro Golf, Mid-Atlantic Country* and *Links* magazines and writes freelance travel articles, primarily on the Caribbean. Her sports and adventure travel articles have appeared in *Town and Country, The New Yorker, Washingtonian, Caribbean Travel & Life, Snow Country, Golf for Women, Baltimore, Diversion* and others. Her *Mid-Atlantic Country* story on West Virginia was chosen best feature in the state's 1993 media awards.

In 1991 St. Martin's Press published *Courting Danger*, a book Leatherman wrote with the late 1930s tennis star and

World War II spy Alice Marble. It has since been optioned for a feature film. Leatherman is working on two other books and her first screenplay.

The author still owns a small horse farm in West Virginia but makes her home on a mountaintop overlooking the Shenandoah Valley near Front Royal, Virginia.

Acknowledgments

Lin acknowledges the Smith Mountain Lake Partnership; Andy Dawson, Shenandoah Valley Travel Association; Martha Doss, Lexington Visitors Center; Lynchburg Convention & Visitors Bureau; Nita Echols, the Vinton Messenger; Kitty Ward Grady, Town of Wytheville; Larry Hincker, Virginia Tech University Relations; Helen Looney, Craig County Historical Society; Martha Mackey, Catherine Fox and the entire staff, Roanoke Valley Convention and Visitors Bureau; Ned McElwaine and Donna Johnson, Botetourt County; Franklin County Chamber of Commerce; Franklyn Moreno, New River Valley Economic Development Alliance; Anne Piedmont, Roanoke Valley of Virginia Economic Development Partnership; Barbara Ring, Bedford County Chamber of Commerce; Heather Cormany, Lin Chaff Public Relations and Advertising; Prof. James Robertson, Virginia Tech; Martha Steger, Department of Economic Development, State of Virginia; Gary G. Walker, Civil War expert of Southwestern Virginia; Michelle Wright, Alleghany Highlands Chamber of Commerce; the New River Valley Hosts; the directors of the Southwest Virginia counties' Chambers and Economic Development groups; and a host of others who firmly believe the Blue Ridge of Virginia is the most beautiful, special place on earth.

Dale is grateful to Donnelle Oxley, who is always ready to join her on hiking, mountain biking, skiing, riding or rafting adventures in the mountains of Virginia's Blue Ridge. The travel writer/photographer team have spent a lifetime in these hills and are equally happy camping in a state park or living it up at luxury resorts such as The Homestead or Wintergreen. Dale also acknowledges the golf course managers of the region, who have given her another good reason to explore the area — some of the most scenic and challenging links in the country. Special thanks go to the folks at the Virginia Department of Tourism.

Dale dedicates her efforts to the Piedmont Environmental Council, the Nature Conservancy, the U.S. National Park Service, Upperville philanthropist Paul Mellon and the other groups and individuals who are vigorously committed to ensuring a green and open Virginia for generations to come.

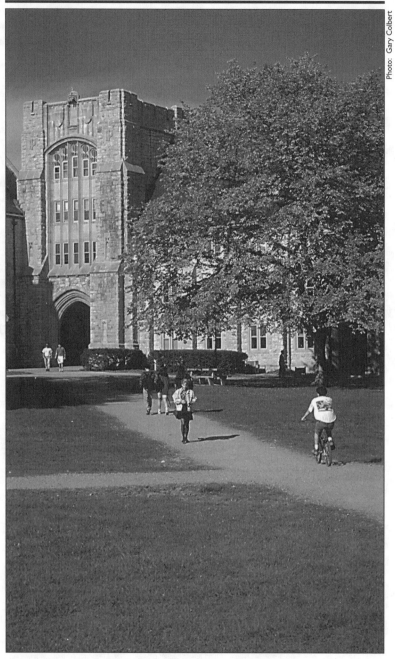

Photo: Gary Colbert

Students on the walk at Virginia Tech in Blacksburg.

Table of Contents

Directory of Maps

Photo: Lee Chichester

Snow-covered Slate Mountain Church in Floyd County.

How to Use This Book

When we decided to produce an *Insiders' Guide® to Virginia's Blue Ridge*, the most time-consuming discussions went into figuring out just how to present the material on such a large geographic area in a sensible and accessible way. It wasn't easy! If you are already familiar with this region, you'll sympathize with us.

We have a lot of ground to cover from roughly Winchester down through the New River Valley, then over to the Alleghany Highlands and Southwest Virginia. With so much to do and see in between, we hardly knew where to start recommending! But we think we've produced a guide that is organized so you can easily find what you're looking for.

Each chapter is presented geographically, in regional segments, from north to south and east to west. We've defined four regions: the Shenandoah Valley, East of the Blue Ridge (also sometimes referred to as the foothills), the New River Valley and the Alleghany Highlands. So, each chapter starts with a regional header to orient you, followed by information about towns and cities in that region, with the overall geographic traffic pattern flowing south from the top of the Blue Ridge area, zigzagging back and forth from east to west.

We begin the book by introducing, in a general way, the four main regions of the Blue Ridge, as noted earlier, and their cities and towns. Then come sections on such topics as Civil War sites, restaurants and accommodations, using the same geographical framework. In other words, if you're interested in visiting a winery in the Shenandoah Valley, look under that region's heading in the Wineries chapter. The same rule applies with nightspots, shopping, bed and breakfast inns and *almost* all the other topics we cover. The Recreation chapter is organized by type of activity, and Annual Events and Festivals by months, but the geographic flow continues under those headings.

One exception to this organization is the chapter on Skyline Drive and the Blue Ridge Parkway. Here, we let you know where you can eat and spend the night without departing from the two connecting mountaintop highways.

Some special chapters, such as Restaurants or Arts and Culture, will describe all the best restaurants or museums, galleries and dance groups in a given city in alphabetical order. In other chapters, such as Shopping, we let you know about our favorite stores in a given neighborhood or shopping center in every major city or town. But you still need to look first for the major region. For example, in the Shenandoah Valley region look under Lexington for a description of all the neat little boutiques and shops in its historic downtown district.

At the end of the book, we provide you with a look at some of the interesting places to see in the area known as Southwest Virginia. This huge region to the south and west of the New River Valley, including towns such as Marion and Wytheville and the vast George Washington and Jefferson National Forest, is made up of 14 counties, all distinct and interesting in their own right.

We've included maps to help you. It's a good idea, especially if you aren't familiar with the area, to spend some time studying them before you dive into the book. They will help you understand visually how the regions are divided and what towns and cities belong in each one.

This is not meant to be the kind of guide that you must read from beginning to end to reap the benefit of buying it.

But we do recommend that you start out by reading our introductions to each region; these will give you an indication of what the areas have to offer — what makes our cities, towns and little hamlets unique and worth visiting.

One important note to keep in mind as you use this guide: On July 15, 1995, the 703 area code that precedes many of the phone numbers in the Blue Ridge changed to 540.

We hope you have a good time exploring both this guide and the beautiful Blue Ridge area. Let us know what you think of the book, its organization and helpfulness. We really want your input. Write us at:

The Insiders' Guides® Inc.
P. O. Box 2057
Manteo, North Carolina 27954

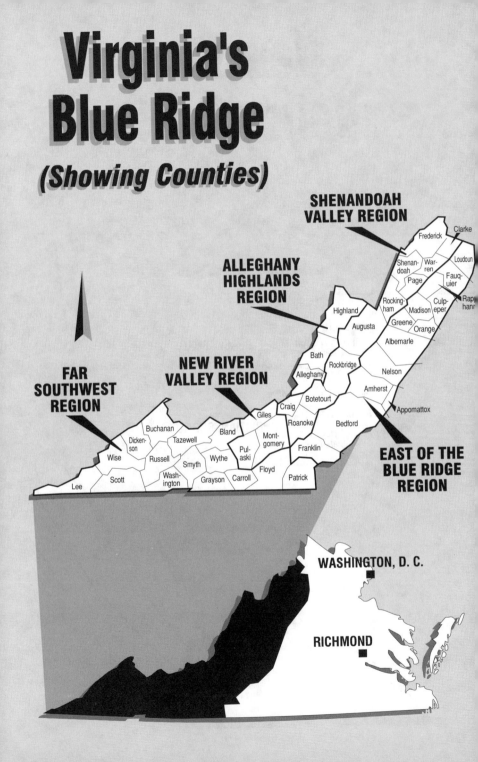

New River Valley Region

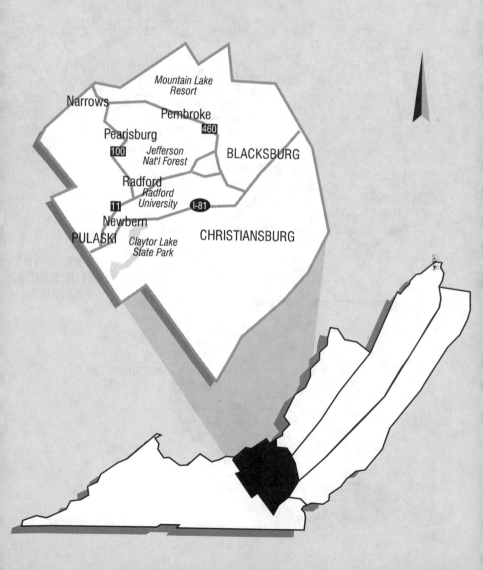

Narrows

Mountain Lake Resort

Pembroke

460

Pearisburg

100

Jefferson Nat'l Forest

BLACKSBURG

Radford

Radford University

I-81

11

Newbern

PULASKI

Claytor Lake State Park

CHRISTIANSBURG

Alleghany
Highlands Region

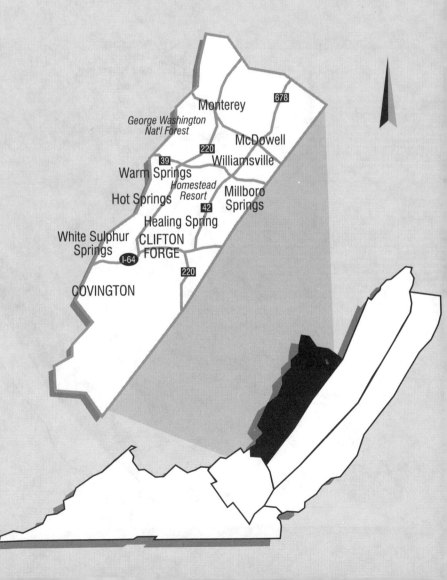

Monterey
678
George Washington
Nat'l Forest
McDowell
220
Williamsville
39
Warm Springs
Homestead
Resort
Millboro
Hot Springs
Springs
42
Healing Spring
White Sulphur
CLIFTON
Springs
FORGE
I-64
220
COVINGTON

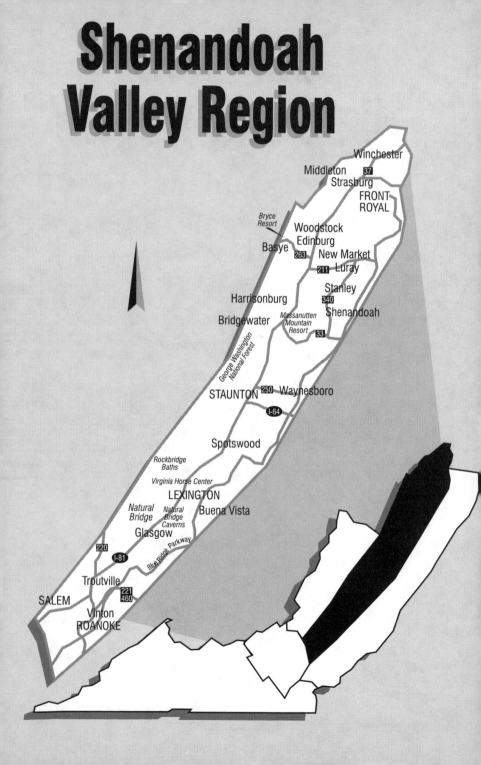

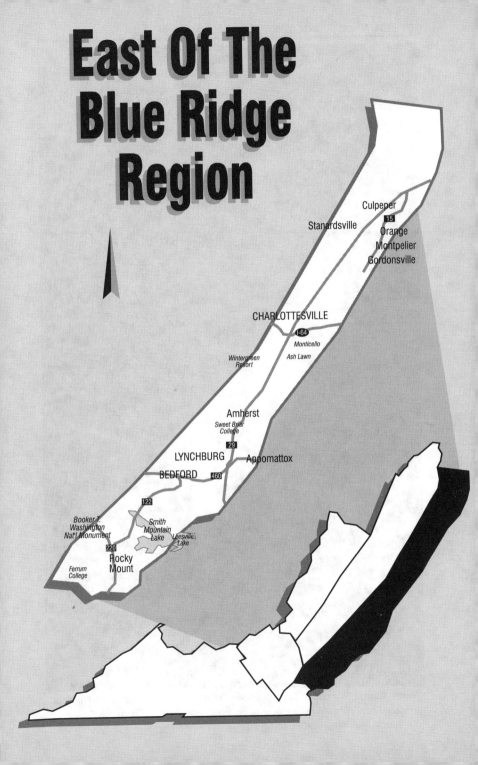

East Of The Blue Ridge Region

Culpeper
Stanardsville
15
Orange
Montpelier
Gordonsville

CHARLOTTESVILLE
I-64
Monticello
Ash Lawn
Wintergreen
Resort

Amherst
Sweet Briar
College
29
LYNCHBURG   Appomattox
BEDFORD   460

122
Booker T.
Washington   Smith
Nat'l Monument   Mountain
Lake   Leesville
Lake
220
Rocky
Ferrum   Mount
College

James Monroe, our nation's fifth president, made his home at Ash Lawn-Highland near Charlottesville to be closer to his friend and mentor, Thomas Jefferson.

City, Town and County
Overviews

Shenandoah Valley Region

Shenandoah — the name conjures up images of rolling green farmland, beautiful old barns and the legendary Shenandoah River that winds its way north to Harpers Ferry, West Virginia. The Native Americans called the river Shenandoah, meaning "daughter of the stars," for the sparkling points of light on its broad surface. The 200-mile-long valley that shares its path and its name stretches from Frederick and Clarke counties in the north almost to Roanoke in the south.

White explorers traveled through the valley as early as the mid-1600s, but it wasn't until the early 1700s that the first German and Scotch-Irish families began to put down roots here. They had migrated south from Maryland and Pennsylvania seeking rich, cheap land and greater freedom for themselves and their children. German families settled mainly in the area between Winchester and Staunton; the Scotch-Irish chose Staunton and the valley south for their homesites. This is only a general pattern of settlement; to some extent both groups were interspersed along the entire length of the valley.

Original barns and homesteads dot the landscape of the valley, and many museums along Interstate 81 — the Woodstock Museum in Shenandoah County, the lovely Virginia State Arboretum in Clarke County, the Cyrus McCormick Farm near Steele's Tavern and the Museum of American Frontier Culture in Staunton — give visitors a closer look at the daily lives of these rugged pioneers. All these offer glimpses into the Shenandoah's past with their early American farm equipment, pottery, furniture, Native American artifacts and Civil War exhibits. At the Museum of American Frontier Culture, visitors can even watch costumed interpreters perform such pioneer chores as churning butter, threshing grain and shearing sheep.

During the Civil War, the fertile, grain-producing Shenandoah Valley was known as the Breadbasket of the Confederacy until Union general Philip Sheridan began torching nearly all the barns and mills in the valley. Crops were destroyed and livestock and horses confiscated. One writer observed that "a crow flying across the valley would have to pack its lunch."

Some of the heaviest fighting of the Civil War took place in the valley, and many of the war's hardiest soldiers hailed from here. According to Lt. Col. C.F.R. Henderson, author of the two-volume *Stonewall Jackson and the Civil War*, " . . . no better material for soldiers ever existed than the men of the valley. . . . All classes mingle in the ranks, and all ages. . . . They were a mountain people, nurtured in a wholesome climate, bred to manly sports, and hardened by the free life of the field and forest. To social distinctions they gave little heed. They were united for a common purpose... and their patriotism was proved by the sacrifice of all personal consideration and individual interest."

The valley is also the burial place of many heroes of that terrible war. Robert E. Lee and Stonewall Jackson were laid to rest in Lexington. Lee was president of the city's Washington College (now Washington and Lee) after the war, and Jackson had taught natural philosophy at the Virginia Military Institute for years. Jackson's horse, Little Sorrel, remains close to his master in Lexington. Still standing in the VMI Museum, the preserved horse is a bit threadbare, but then, he's kept his vigil more than 100 years. Jackson is memorialized in a rollicking musical called *Stonewall Country*, performed under the stars every summer at Lexington's Lime Kiln Theater.

The Shenandoah Valley was home to other great leaders of our nation. Woodrow Wilson was born in Staunton, and a museum next to his birthplace tells all about his life and his vision for world peace. Also in Lexington is a museum honoring George C. Marshall, a VMI graduate who went on to lead the U.S. Army during World War II and later devise a plan to rebuild Europe after the war.

Visitors to the valley need not have a strong interest in history to enjoy themselves. Majestic caverns filled with ancient and colorful calcite formations await the curious. The magnificence of Natural Bridge, once owned by Thomas Jefferson, is another destination. Rivers invite you to take a lazy canoe trip or an action-packed whitewater run.

Antique lovers will delight in shops set in charming small towns and, in some cases,

the middle of nowhere. We're more sophisticated than anyone thinks!

If you time your visit right, you'll catch some of the East's finest fairs and festivals: Virginia's number one Agricultural Fair at Harrisonburg, the Maple Festival in Highland County and the popular Apple Blossom Festival in Winchester.

Downtown districts beg for exploration on foot, offering a concentration of beautiful architecture, fine restaurants, boutiques and galleries. You can spend hours exploring Roanoke's city market area or historic downtown Lexington or Staunton.

Modern accommodations are plentiful in the valley, and you'll discover quaint inns and bed and breakfasts in beautifully restored old homes. The Virginia Division of Tourism, (804) 786-4484, will recommend bed and breakfasts and make reservations. For other reservation services see our Bed and Breakfast and Country Inns chapter.

The Shenandoah Valley has many more villages and towns than we can highlight, but the following introductions will give you a taste of what each area has to offer. For more detailed information on restaurants, museums, accommodations, antiquing and more, read on.

Winchester

Once called Frederick Town after Frederick, father of King George III, Winchester is full of reminders of our nation's early history. The city and surrounding area was settled by Pennsylvania Quakers in 1732; soon after, Germans, Scots, Irish, English, Welsh and French Huguenots also followed the Great Wagon Road from Pennsylvania and put down roots here. Winchester was a thriving cen-

Photo: Wintergreen Resort

The Blue Ridge Mountains offer the ideal getaway for families.

ter of commerce during the settlement of our nation; pioneers obtained their wagons and provisions here for trips farther west and south.

The city saw much action during the Civil War. Five battles and many skirmishes were fought within or near Winchester, which changed hands more than 70 times. Stonewall Jackson used a home on Braddock Street for his headquarters during the war, and today his office remains much the way it was during his stay. The Kurtz Cultural Center downtown has a permanent exhibit, Shenandoah — Crossroads of the Civil War, which provides details on the major battles fought here.

When he was 16, George Washington started his career in Winchester as a surveyor for Lord Thomas Fairfax (owner of a 5 million-acre royal grant), who lived in nearby White Post. Later, the father of our country saw to the protection of Virginia's frontier, overseeing the construction of Fort Loudoun, today a museum in Winchester. He also was elected

to his first political office, as a member of the House of Burgesses, in Winchester.

Country music fans know Winchester as the birthplace of Patsy Cline, that spunky, honey-voiced singer made famous by her renditions of "I Fall to Pieces," "After Midnight" and "Sweet Dreams" in the early '60s. In 1963 the 30-year-old Cline was killed in an airplane crash. She was buried in a simply marked grave at the Shenandoah Memorial Cemetery on U.S. 522, also known as the Patsy Cline Memorial Highway, just south of U.S. 50. The singer's mother and sister still live in town.

On a literary note, the Winchester area was also the birthplace of another pioneering woman, novelist Willa Cather. Cather's family moved from Frederick County to Nebraska when she was 10.

Winchester is probably best-known for its annual Shenandoah Apple Blossom Festival. For four days every spring, the town plays host to more than 250,000 visitors who gather to enjoy the Grand Feature Parade, the queen's coronation, arts and crafts festivals, races, dances and a circus.

For more information about attractions, events and tours of the Winchester area, call the Winchester-Frederick County Visitor Center/Chamber of Commerce at (800) 662-1360 or write to them at 1360 S. Pleasant Valley Road, Winchester, Virginia 22601.

Middletown

This quaint town in southern Frederick County lies along U.S. 11, once the Great Wagon Road, the most important frontier highway in Colonial America. It has always been a favorite stopping place for valley travelers, and has settled into an unhurried pace since I-81 siphoned off the faster traffic. A tavern built on the roadside in 1797 later became a stagecoach relay station and an inn; it's still in operation as the Wayside Inn and Restaurant, a beautifully restored watering hole in the center of town. The inn is a paradise for antique lovers with its Colonial furnishings, rare antiques and historic paintings. It's also noted for its hearty regional American cuisine.

Middletown is home to Belle Grove plantation house, a large stone mansion built between 1794 and 1797 by Isaac Hite, who married James Madison's sister. The mansion served as Union general Philip Sheridan's headquarters during the decisive 1864 Battle of Cedar Creek, which occurred 2 miles south of town.

Every October the plantation grounds attract crowds for a major Civil War re-enactment hosted by the Cedar Creek Battlefield Foundation Inc. Surprisingly, it's one of the few re-enactments to take place on an original Civil War battlefield. The foundation is raising money to secure complete ownership of the 158-acre battlefield, which lies adjacent to the plantation.

Wayside Theatre in downtown Middletown is the second-oldest theater in the state and hosts dramas, comedies and mysteries from May through December. Some famous faces got their start here, including Susan Sarandon, Jill Eikenberry of *L.A. Law* and Peter Boyle.

For more information about Middletown attractions, contact the Winchester-Frederick County Chamber of

Photo: Alleghany Highlands Chamber of Commerce

Humpback Bridge, Virginia's oldest standing covered bridge, is part of a wayside on U.S. 60 in Alleghany County.

Commerce, (800) 662-1360, at 1360 S. Pleasant Valley Road, Winchester, Virginia 22601.

Front Royal

This northern Blue Ridge town was once known as Helltown for all the shootings, brawls and hard drinking that went on here in the mid-1700s. Today Front Royal and surrounding Warren County, only 57 miles from the Beltway, are fast becoming a bedroom community of Washington, D.C. But Front Royal is also the gateway to the wilderness of the Shenandoah National Park. The north and south forks of the majestic Shenandoah River come together here, and campgrounds and canoe outfitters abound.

Front Royal has a revitalized downtown district full of interesting boutiques and antique shops. An old-fashioned town clock sits in the Village Common, where a gazebo and picnic tables welcome tourists and downtown workers to sit for a spell.

The town has a Confederate Museum that documents how this important rail and river junction withstood numerous clashes during the Civil War. Belle Boyd, the beautiful aristocratic Confederate spy, stayed for awhile in Front Royal during the war. One night she was upstairs in a house while a Union general and his officers discussed maneuvers plans downstairs. Belle watched and listened through a small hole in the closet floor and heard every word of their plans. She wrote each plan down in cipher, stole down the back steps and rode horseback for 15 miles in the middle of the night to carry the message to Confederate troops.

Attractions in the Front Royal area include Skyline Caverns, Skyline Drive and two wineries offering tours and tastings: Oasis Vineyard and Linden Vineyards and Orchards.

Front Royal pulls out the stops every May for the Virginia Mushroom Festival. The fest features Virginia shiitake mushrooms, which are cultivated in the Warren County area, along with wine tastings, arts and crafts exhibits and cooking demonstrations.

For more information, write to the Chamber of Commerce of Front Royal and Warren County, 414 E. Main Street, Front Royal, Virginia 22630. You can call them at (540) 635-3185 or (800) 338-2576.

Strasburg

Staufferstadt is the original name of Strasburg, a busy little town just south of Middletown. German Mennonites and Dunkards who had migrated from York County, Pennsylvania, settled the village, and Peter Stover petitioned for a charter for the town in 1761. He then changed the name to Strasburg in honor of his home city in Germany.

Later the town was nicknamed Pottown for the high-quality pottery produced here during the antebellum period. The first potter came in 1761, and since then at least 17 potters have produced earthen and stoneware in Strasburg.

You can see some of this pottery in the Strasburg Museum and Gift Shop, which was originally a steam pottery built in 1891. Also in the museum are Civil War relics, Native American artifacts, blacksmith collections and displays from Colonial farms and businesses.

Antique lovers will have a heyday in Strasburg. Nearly 100 dealers of high-quality antiques are housed under one roof in the downtown Strasburg Emporium. You'll find not just furniture representing every American era, but also carriages, chandeliers, rugs, quilts, lace, old carousel horses and pottery.

A great place to stay overnight in town is the Hotel Strasburg, a renovated Victorian hotel where the rooms are decorated with antiques that are also for sale. The hotel's restaurant has a popular following among folks from nearby valley towns and is by far the best place to dine for miles around. For more information on towns such as Strasburg, Woodstock, New Market, Edinburg, Mt. Jackson, Basye and Orkney Springs, contact the Shenandoah County Travel Council, (540) 459-5522, at Woodstock 22664.

Woodstock

This charming valley town was originally called Muellerstadt after its founder Jacob Mueller, who arrived from Germany in 1749. In 1761 the frontier settlement was chartered by an act of the Virginia Assembly, sponsored by George Washington, a representative from Frederick County. Its name was then changed to Woodstock. The Woodstock Museum on W. Court Street has artifacts recalling the valley's early settlement. These include Native American tools, maps, ledgers, portraits, furniture, quilts, a moonshine still and Civil War memorabilia.

The museum sponsors a walking tour through town, where you can see examples of Federal, Greek Revival and Classic Revival architecture. The courthouse, the original section of which was built in 1795, is the oldest courthouse west of the Blue Ridge in continuous use as a court building.

Nearby Orkney Springs hosts the Shenandoah Valley Music Festival every spring and summer. Concerts are held in a covered, open-air pavilion and on the grounds of the historic Orkney Springs Hotel, a 19th-century mineral springs spa and resort.

New Market

Here you will find caverns, museums, golf, a battlefield historical park and an excellent tourist information center for the whole Shenandoah Valley.

New Market was settled later than other valley towns. English settlers from the North and East named their village after a horse-racing town in England, and in the early days there was actually a racetrack near New Market.

New Market is famous for the 1864 battle that involved 247 cadets fresh from the classrooms of the Virginia Military Institute (see our Civil War chapter). You can view a stirring account of the battle on film at the Hall of Valor Museum at the New Market Battlefield Historical Park. The museum also presents a nonpartisan view of major Civil War events with its artifacts, murals and life-size models. On the 220-acre battlefield stands the restored farm of Jacob and Sarah Bushong, whose home was used as a hospital and whose orchards became the killing fields of war. The farm has wheelwright and blacksmith shops, a loom house and a summer kitchen, typical features of a 19th-century valley farm.

New Market is also at the epicenter of valley caverns: Shenandoah, Endless, Luray and Grand caverns.

Historic buildings are features on a downtown walking tour. And, while it sounds like a "sleeper" of an attraction, you shouldn't miss the Bedrooms of America Museum on Congress Street (U.S. 11). There are 11 different rooms of authentic furniture showing every period of America's bedrooms from William and Mary (c. 1650) through Art Deco (c. 1930). The museum is housed in the same 18th-century building used by Gen. Jubal Early as his headquarters during the Civil War.

For shopping, don't miss Paper Treasures, also on Congress Street. The store has an extraordinary collection of old books, maps and magazines such as *Ebony*, *Collier's Weekly* and the *Saturday Evening Post*. The shop also sells framed, hand-tinted illustrations from some of these old magazines.

The River Farm is a working sheep farm near town that offers weekend workshops in spinning, weaving and dying, as well as lodging for students. A shop sells fleece, fibers, spinning wheels and looms.

For another taste of history, drive north of town to Meem's Bottom Bridge, which stretches 191 feet across the north fork of the Shenandoah River. Built in 1892, it is the longest covered bridge of the nine remaining in Virginia and the last remaining covered bridge across the Shenandoah.

Luray

There is no agreement as to how this town got its name. The best explanation is that the Huguenots who escaped from France and migrated to the valley named the new settlement Lorraine, and that Luray is a corruption of the former name.

Luray is a central gateway to the 105-mile-long Skyline Drive. The Shenandoah National Park borders Page County on the east and the George Washington National Forest on the west.

Luray, county seat of Page, is the home of the internationally famed Luray Caverns, a magical underground world of stalactites, stalagmites and crystal clear

pools, which can be explored in an hourlong guided tour. Housed in the same complex is the Historic Car and Carriage Caravan, an exhibit of antique cars, carriages, coaches and costumes dating back to 1625. Rudolph Valentino's 1925 Rolls Royce is here.

Shenandoah River Outfitters in Luray and the Down River Canoe Company in nearby Bentonville offer canoe trips on the south fork of the Shenandoah River, which travels the entire length of Page County. Guilford Ridge Vineyard is just a few miles out of town and offers tours and tastings of its wines by appointment. And would you believe one of the state's largest reptile collections is in Luray? The Luray Reptile Center and Dinosaur Park on U.S. 211 will keep your kids squealing for hours. Tame deer and llamas inhabit the petting zoo.

A good time to visit the area is Columbus Day weekend in October, when Page County throws its annual Heritage Festival. First held in 1969, it is one of the oldest arts and crafts shows in Virginia. Craft demonstrations range from quilt making, woodworking, wheel spinning and soap making to apple butter boiling and apple cider pressings. The festival features an antique tractor steam and gas engine show, mule train rides, country bands and clogging demonstrations.

For more information about attractions and events in Page County contact the Luray-Page Chamber of Commerce, (540) 743-3915, at 46 E. Main Street, Luray 22835.

Harrisonburg

Harrisonburg is a thriving city and the seat of one of the nation's leading agricultural counties. In fact, so valuable is poultry to Rockingham County's economy that a proud statue of a turkey stands alongside U.S. 11 south of town. Every May Harrisonburg hosts the week-long Poultry Festival, which includes a Friends of Feathers banquet.

There are more than 2,000 farms in the county, and nearly half of the land is classified as agricultural. The county is the state's leading producer of dairy, poultry and beef products. The city also is home to 20 major industries and serves as the financial and retail center for eight counties, including three in neighboring West Virginia.

Opportunities for higher education abound in the area. Bridgewater College, Eastern Mennonite College and Seminary and James Madison University are all here, so students and professors comprise a large part of the population.

In 1778 Virginia governor Patrick Henry named Rockingham County for the Marquis of Rockingham, one of the few friends Virginia had at the Court of London. The following year, a prominent farmer named Thomas Harrison donated 2½ acres for a courthouse, and the city of Harrisonburg was born.

During the Civil War productive farms in the area helped feed the Confederate army. Stonewall Jackson used Harrisonburg as one of his headquarters, and today his military strategies that so confounded Union officers are illustrated in an electric, wall-size map at the Shenandoah Valley Heritage Museum in nearby Dayton.

Testimony to earlier area battles are on exhibit at Dayton's Daniel Harrison House, also known as Fort Harrison. This beautiful stone house was built in the mid-1750s, when bands of Native Americans roamed the area threatening the settlers. The house served as a fort and had a stockade and underground passage to a nearby spring.

Dayton is also home to a wonderful indoor Farmer's Market where you can find fresh cheeses, baked goods, antiques, bulk grains and spices and a fantastic country restaurant run by a former Mennonite missionary. It's not unusual to see a black carriage or two with horses parked out front; about 1,000 Old Order Mennonites, easily identified by their simple style of dress, live in the area. Their horse-

Insiders' Tips

The tiny hamlet of Washington, Virginia, is actually older than its bigger "younger brother" to the east. In fact, the Rappahannock County community is the oldest of the 28 U.S. cities named after our first president. We'll go so far as to say it's also the prettiest.

Photo: Winchester-Fredrick Co. Chamber of Commerce

The Abram's Delight Museum, built in 1754, is the oldest house in Winchester.

drawn buggies and immaculate farms are a common sight in the southwestern region of the county.

More than 139,000 acres of George Washington National Forest lie in western Rockingham County. On the east, the county is bordered by the Shenandoah National Park. The Massanutten mountain range is just east of town and is home to Massanutten Resort, a year-round residential community known for its ski slopes, golf courses and impressive indoor sports complex. Guests can also fish, swim, hike and ride horses here.

Another recreational attraction near Harrisonburg (but in Augusta County) is Natural Chimneys, a place where huge rocks tower to heights of 120 feet. From one perspective, these rocks resemble a foreboding medieval-style castle with turrets and towers, and this may have inspired the creation of the Natural Chimneys Jousting Tournament more than 170 years ago. The tournament is the oldest continuously held sporting event in America, having begun in 1821. Modern-

day knights still match their skills in the ancient art of jousting here on the third Saturday in August every year.

The Natural Chimneys Regional Park has 120 campsites, a swimming pool, picnic area, camp store, nature and bike trails and more.

For more information about attractions in the Harrisonburg and Rockingham County area, contact the Harrisonburg-Rockingham County Convention and Visitors Bureau, (540) 434-2319, at 800 Country Club Road, Harrisonburg 22801.

Staunton

A great city to explore on foot, Staunton is full of Victorian architecture, unique shops, one-of-a-kind eateries and important historical sites. The city is the birthplace of President Woodrow Wilson, who was born in 1856 to a Presbyterian minister and his wife in a Greek Revival manse on Coalter Street. Today the manse is open for tours and sits next door to a museum where you can learn all about Wilson's life, his political views and his vision for world peace. The Woodrow Wilson Museum also houses the president's 1919 Pierce Arrow limousine.

Another major attraction in Staunton is the Museum of American Frontier Culture, an indoor-outdoor living museum that features four authentic working farms from Germany, England, Northern Ireland and early America. Children love this place, where lambs, chickens, cats and all kinds of farm critters animate the landscape. It recently won the Phoenix Award of excellence from the National Association of Travel writers.

Staunton is an appropriate place for a museum that documents life in frontier America. It is the seat of Augusta County, which once stretched all the way to Mississippi. Most early settlers in the area were Scotch-Irish, including John Lewis, the first white man to build a homestead here in 1732. In 1749 Lewis' son Thomas laid out lots and streets for the new town of Staunton, named in honor of Lady Rebecca Staunton, Gov. William Gooch's wife.

Staunton became Virginia's capital for 17 days in June 1781, as Gov. Thomas Jefferson and the General Assembly fled advancing British troops led by Tarleton. Those Redcoats had already captured seven Virginia delegates, including Daniel Boone, in nearby Charlottesville.

Nineteenth-century Staunton grew by leaps and bounds following incorporation as a town in 1801. Education became a priority, with the establishment of the Virginia Institute for the Deaf and the Blind in 1839, Augusta Female Seminary in 1842 (now Mary Baldwin College), Virginia Female Institute in 1844 (now Stuart Hall School) and Staunton Military Academy in 1884.

The railroad came to Staunton in 1854, which stimulated the city's growth as a center of commerce for the region. Today Amtrak serves the city, and the old C&O train station is a showcase of meticulous restoration work. There you'll find an authentic 1880s Victorian Ice Cream Parlor serving dense, Italian-style ice cream in a room with antique parlor and drug store furnishings from ceiling to floor. Next door, the Depot Grille boasts a gorgeous, hand-carved antique walnut bar, and in the same building, Depot Antiques sells fine collectibles, Victorian and country furniture.

The wharf area is undergoing much restoration work; the old mill buildings and warehouses already house antique shops, a pottery workshop and studio and a marvelous antique car dealership, and you can expect much more in the future. The Historic Staunton Foundation has a detailed brochure to guide visitors on a walking tour of the city, as well as a new guide to antique shops.

Other attractions in Staunton include the beautiful Gypsy Hill Park, which has tennis courts, softball fields, a lake and a duck pond. Right across the street is the Statler Brothers museum and office complex. Yes, these famous, down-home country music stars actually live and work in Staunton, and their children go to school here. For 25 years the Statler Brothers have thrown a huge Happy Birthday U.S.A. celebration in Gypsy Hill Park, complete with concerts, firework displays, free tours of their museum and patriotic speeches.

For additional information about Staunton, contact the Augusta-Staunton-Waynesboro Travel Information Center, Richmond Avenue at I-81, Staunton 24401. You can call them at (540) 332-3972 or (800) 332-5219.

Staunton, Waynesboro & Augusta County, Virginia

In the Heart of the Shenandoah Valley

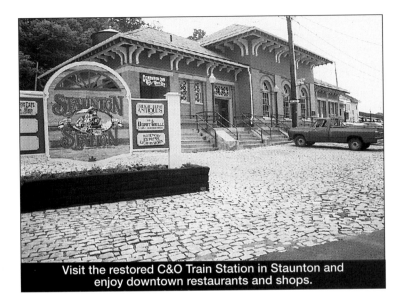

Visit the restored C&O Train Station in Staunton and
enjoy downtown restaurants and shops.

Staunton, Waynesboro & Augusta County: In the Heart of the Shenandoah Valley

Staunton (pronounced STAN-ton) was settled during the 1730s as one of the first Virginia settlements west of the Blue Ridge Mountains. It was named for Lady Rebecca Staunton, wife of Virginia Governor William Gooch. During the late 1850s the railroad made Staunton a major center for trade. It was a vital rail-link during the Civil War between the "breadbasket of the Confederacy" and the rest of Virginia.

After the war, Staunton experienced tremendous growth, resulting in an extraordinary collection of architectural treasures. These can be viewed on a walking tour of Staunton's five National Historic Districts. The downtown's historic railroad station is served by AMTRAK and a seasonal antique steam train.

Staunton's many attractions include the Woodrow Wilson Birthplace and Museum — dedicated to the achievements of our 28th president, and the Museum of American Frontier Culture, whose four working farms provide a living history of the synthesis of European culture into

Woodrow Wilson's Birthplace and Museum — Dedicated to the achievements of our 28th president.

the pioneer lifestyles of Virginia. Staunton's fire department has the last surviving 1911 Robinson pumper fire engine, called "Jumbo", on view, and the old Valley National Bank (now Crestar Bank) houses a small bank history museum. The famous Statler Brothers live and work in Staunton, and a museum highlighting these country music legends is open to the public.

Waynesboro was settled by Irish and German immigrants and named in 1797 to honor "Mad Anthony" Wayne. The community was known at an early date for its schools. These included the

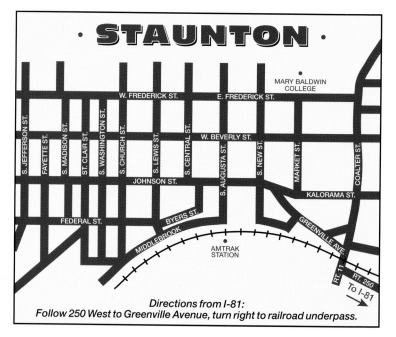

· STAUNTON ·

MARY BALDWIN COLLEGE

W. FREDERICK ST.   E. FREDERICK ST.

S. JEFFERSON ST.
FAYETTE ST.
S. MADISON ST.
ST. CLAIR ST.
S. WASHINGTON ST.
S. CHURCH ST.
S. LEWIS ST.
S. CENTRAL ST.
S. AUGUSTA ST.
S. NEW ST.
MARKET ST.
COALTER ST.

W. BEVERLY ST.

JOHNSON ST.

KALORAMA ST.

FEDERAL ST.   BYERS ST.

MIDDLEBROOK

AMTRAK STATION

GREENVILLE AVE.

RT. 11
RT. 250
To I-81

Directions from I-81:
Follow 250 West to Greenville Avenue, turn right to railroad underpass.

Waynesboro Academy which was the forerunner of present-day Fishburne Military Academy — one of the oldest military schools in the nation.

The nearby P. Buckley Moss Museum houses artwork by one of America's most popular artists. The Museum overlooks the Waynesboro Village Factory Outlets which boasts over thirty-famous-brand outlet stores.

Waynesboro's annual events include the popular Fall Foliage Festival, held during the first two weekends of October, and First Night Waynesboro, a family-oriented New Year's Eve celebration. The Civil War Battle of

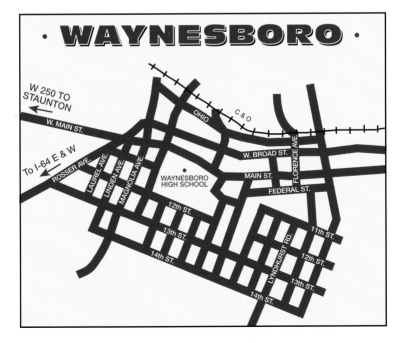

Waynesboro, an engagement between Generals Jubal Early and Philip Sheridan on March 1, 1865, is also commemorated annually.

For more information on Waynesboro, contact the **Afton Mountain Tourist Center** at (540) 943-5187.

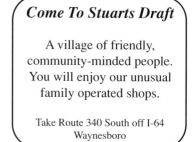

Antique buffs will enjoy exploring "Antique Alley" on Route 11, home to a large number of antique shops.

AUGUSTA COUNTY

Conveniently located in the heart of the Shenandoah Valley near the intersection of interstates I-81 and I-64, Augusta County has much to offer lovers of history, dining, shopping, recreation and relaxation.

Augusta County, named for the Princess of Wales, was founded in 1736, and once stretched westward to the Mississippi River. It included land which now comprises Ohio, Kentucky, Indiana, Illinois and part of West Virginia and western Pennsylvania.

Geographically the second-largest county in Virginia, Augusta County spans the entire width of the Shenandoah Valley from the Blue Ridge Mountains to the Alleghenies.

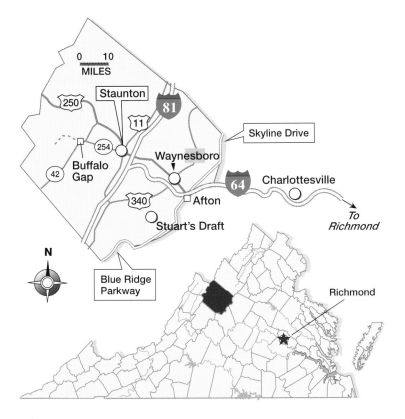

0   10
MILES

Staunton

250

81

11

254

Waynesboro

Skyline Drive

42

Buffalo Gap

340

Afton

64   Charlottesville

Stuart's Draft

To Richmond

N

Blue Ridge Parkway

Richmond

Make Your Trip Complete Visit Waynesboro Today!

Waynesboro, Stuarts Draft and Fishersville

Named in honor of Revolutionary War hero Gen. Anthony Wayne, Waynesboro thrived as an industrial community during the late 1800s, a trend that continues today. Thanks in part to its convenient location just 8 miles east of the intersection of I-81 and I-64, companies such as DuPont, Genicom and Hershey have plants here.

Waynesboro is also known for being a friendly town and a wonderful place to raise children. Nearby Stuarts Draft and Fishersville are also attractive communities for families.

Waynesboro extends to Afton Mountain, from which you can see clear to Charlottesville and beyond. The Shenandoah National Park's southern tip ends on that mountain, and the Blue Ridge Parkway begins its southern trek there. One note of caution: It's not a fun mountain to cross during foggy weather; many fatal accidents have occurred here during thick fog. So, park yourself in pleasant Waynesboro if such conditions exist.

In Waynesboro, the P. Buckley Moss Museum, named for "The People's Artist," is in a tall brick house surrounded by trees — a scene reminiscent of one of her watercolors. Since the early 1960s the world-renowned, multimillionaire artist and philanthropist has found her inspiration and much of her subject matter in valley scenery and in the Amish and Mennonite people of the area. The museum is within easy walking distance of the Waynesboro Outlet Village, a fantastic place to find bargains in designer clothing, leather goods, imported china and much more.

While in Waynesboro, you can also watch age-old techniques of brass molding at the Virginia Metalcrafters factory showroom. The Shenandoah Valley Art Center in downtown Waynesboro offers residents and visitors a place to enjoy the arts through exhibits, workshops, classes and performances.

Mennonites who live in the area have established some businesses that provide a refreshing alternative to standard grocery stores. Kinsinger's Kountry Kitchen, on Va. 651 off Va. 608, and The Cheese Shop up the road are two of the best. And Milmont Greenhouses, on U.S. 340, has grown from a Mennonite housewife's hobby nearly 20 years ago to a bustling business today. Speaking of green things, one of the leading perennial nurseries in the nation, Andre Viette Farm and Nursery, is based in Fishersville and is definitely worth visiting (see our Shopping chapter).

Recreational opportunities abound in the area. The Sherando Lake State Park is just outside Waynesboro, and Shenandoah Acres Resort is in Stuarts Draft. At the latter, you can swim, ride horses and play badminton, mini-golf, croquet and volleyball. Lodging is in the campsite or year-round cottages.

For more information about attractions in the Waynesboro-East Augusta County area, stop by the Augusta-Staunton-Waynesboro Travel Information Center, Richmond Avenue at I-81 or call (540) 332-3972 or (800) 332-5219.

Lexington

Perhaps more than any other place in the valley, downtown Lexington has retained the graceful beauty and genteel character of its prosperous past. And no other city or town in the Blue Ridge has a history that is so well-preserved and honored by its citizens. The town's heritage includes four of America's greatest generals. It seems that everywhere you go, you are walking on historic, hallowed ground.

Filmmakers agree. In 1992 tons of dirt were dumped on downtown streets along an unusual number of 19th-century buildings for scenes in the Civil War-era movie *Sommersby*, starring Richard Gere and Jodie Foster.

Throughout Lexington's history, the presence of its great military leaders has inspired its preservation efforts. They are George Washington; the great Confederate generals Robert E. Lee and Thomas J. "Stonewall" Jackson; and World War II hero Gen. George C. Marshall, the Nobel Peace Prize-winning creator of the Marshall Plan, which rebuilt wartorn Europe.

Lexington is the historic and cultural heart of Rockbridge County (population 32,000), where most prosperous residents enjoy a genteel country-estate way of life. Many are early retirees from New York, New Jersey, Connecticut and elsewhere who devote their considerable knowledge and energy to the community as volunteers and activists. Others are college professors at nearby Virginia Military Institute and Washington and Lee University.

The county boasts the breathtaking 3-mile-long Goshen Pass, a journey along the Maury River through rhododendron, laurel, ferns, mosses, magnificent pines, hemlocks, maples, dogwood and mountain ash.

Goshen Pass, a popular place for swimming, tubing, canoeing and picnicking, is so beautiful that one prominent Lexington citizen, Matthew Fontaine Maury, asked that, after he died, his body be carried through the pass when the rhododendron was in bloom. Complying with his request in 1873, Virginia Military Institute cadets formed an honor guard and gave their professor his last wish.

The roles that Lexington's world-famous universities, VMI and Washington and Lee University, have played in the area's historic culture cannot be underestimated. In 1796 George Washington saved W&L from bankruptcy with a gift of $50,000, which still receives dividends. VMI cadets are immortalized forever both on campus, with the statue "Virginia Mourning Her Dead," and at the New Market Battlefield Museum and Hall of Valor (an hour north of the city), for their role in the Civil War.

The Civil War Battle of New Market in 1864 was the first and only time in American history that an entire student body was recruited to fight a war. When the smoke cleared, 10 cadets lay dead, including Cadet Thomas G. Jefferson, 17, progeny of our nation's third president.

As a city that has had more than its share of encounters with famous presidents, it has had one rather unlikely encounter. Visitors

When considering trips to the Blue Ridge, think about a hub-and-spoke concept: Stay in a metropolitan area and take side trips to smaller towns and attractions. After your first day, you'll get a feel for how long it takes to get places.

can see the National Historic Landmark cadet barracks where actor Ronald Reagan's movie *Brother Rat* was filmed. The movie's premiere was held at Lexington's State Theatre.

VMI is now facing one of its toughest battles ever, answering the question why the college, supported by public tax dollars, should not become coed. The fight is expected to reach the highest court of the land. In the meantime, you can still see the all-male cadet corps and marvel at its precision during one of the formal dress parades.

Many of Lexington's attractions focus on its famous former citizens. There's the Stonewall Jackson House, where the tough general lived while teaching natural philosophy at VMI, and the Stonewall Jackson Cemetery, his final resting place after he was mistakenly killed by his own soldiers. You can see his bullet-pierced raincoat at the VMI Museum, along with the curious taxidermy display of his favorite war horse, Little Sorrel. Jackson's birthday is celebrated in Lexington every January 21 with a ceremony, cake and a free tour of the only home he ever owned.

Lee Chapel, still in use by W&L students, is another famous site. The famous striking white statue of the recumbent Lee by sculptor Edward Valentine is alone worth a visit to Lexington. The chapel also is the site of the famous Peale portrait of George Washington. You can see Lee's office as he left it in 1870 after assuming the presidency of W&L following his Civil War defeat. Lee's favorite mount, Traveller, also is buried on campus.

The third famous military landmark to see is the George C. Marshall Museum, where Marshall, VMI class of 1901, began a remarkable military career that led to his position as U.S. Army Chief of Staff and later recipient of the Nobel Prize in 1953. An electric map detailing the military march of World War II shows you the breadth of what this military genius accomplished and why the United States earned a reputation world wide as a country with a heart in the aftermath of the war.

Lexington's historic sites are well-documented by its history-loving populace. You can even see the troughs where its famous equestrian residents, Little Sorrel and Traveller, refreshed themselves. A walking tour map will keep you exploring enough bridges and locks, churches, cemeteries, houses, mills, baths and springs to quench even the most avid history buff's thirst for knowledge, inlcuding a nearby museum dedicated to Cyrus McCormick, inventor of the mechanized reaper. The pamphlet is available at the Visitors Center at 102 E. Washington Street or by calling (540) 463-3777.

Every summer day, the Lexington Carriage Company leaves its hitching post at the Visitors Center and carries passengers from 9:30 AM to 5:30 PM. You can ride the same streets as Jackson and Lee did on their famous horses.

Since the memory of two famous horses are awarded such places of honor in Lexington, it stands to reason the Commonwealth of Virginia saw fit to award Lexington its $12 million Horse Center, situated on 400 rolling acres. It is one of the top equine facilities in the United States with 4,000 spectator seats, 610 permanent stalls and a gigantic show arena. Its schedule of events includes everything from the Bonnie Blue Nationals to the Northeast Peruvian Horse Club Show. In 1992 the Center hosted the return of the Rockbridge Regional Fair after 50 years' absence following World War II. The 1995 fair was held July 25 through 29.

Photo: Lynchburg Chamber of Commerce

Poplar Forest, Thomas Jefferson's retreat in Bedford County.

Also bringing fame and visitors to the area is Lime Kiln Theatre, named by *Theatre Journal* as "the most unusual theater setting in the United States" because of its location in an abandoned kiln beside a craggy, wildflower-strewn hillside. Lime Kiln puts on an array of plays and musicals every summer that highlights the history and culture of the Southern mountains. The theater also offers a Sunday night concert series with an eclectic slate of musicians from across the country and around the world. Every year, Robin and Linda Williams of National Public Radio's *Prairie Home Companion* fame also perform at one of the concerts. They make their home in nearby Augusta County.

Going out into the countryside, there's the beautiful Chessie Nature Trail along the Maury River and numerous hiking paths in nearby mountains, among them the Appalachian Trail. If you'd like to see 100 years of nostalgia, stop by Olde Country Store on the way to Goshen Pass, in Rockbridge Baths. If you're into horseback riding, Virginia Mountain Outfitters, (540) 261-1910, will put together half-day or overnight trips that will take you along forest trails and trout-filled rivers to the tops of mountains.

If canoeing is your passion, the James River Basin Canoe Livery, (540) 261-7334, will outfit you with boats, supplies, maps and a shuttle service for a trip along with the mighty James River and the rushing Maury. Farther north, call Dick Pickle at Wildnerness Canoe Company at Natural Bridge, (540) 291-2295, for outdoor fun and adventure. You can choose from the early-bird shuttle at 8 AM to the sunset cruise at 2 PM.

The great outdoors should also include a visit to Hull's Drive-In, one of the premier mom-and-pop operations anywhere and one of the few surviving drive-in theaters in Virginia. It's open weekends mid-March through November.

In Buena Vista, six miles east of Lexington and the only other city in the county, you will find much of the county's manufacturing industry. You'll also find The General Store, a trip back in time for an unusual shopping experience. Every Labor Day, Buena Vista attracts huge crowds and state political leaders to a popular festival in Glen Maury Park.

Do not leave Rockbridge County without visiting Natural Bridge, one of the seven natural wonders of the world. The awesome limestone bridge is 215 feet high and 90 feet long (see our Attractions chapter).

Whether visiting the Lexington area for its history, beauty or attractions, you'll be impressed with its sense of historical importance, its gracious old homes and its vibrant downtown district with fine restaurants and one-of-a-kind shops.

Roanoke Valley Region

God lives here. You can tell from the scenery. So does Elvis, at least in miniature, at Miniature Graceland in Roanoke. The Roanoke Valley of Virginia, including the bedroom communities of Botetourt and Craig counties, is home to about a quarter million people who work and play in a cultured, historical place of incredible beauty.

Even I-81, which connects the Roanoke Valley, is beautiful. One of the first things visitors usually say is they can't get over the absence of potholes and rough pavement. Then they marvel at all the wildflowers, redbud, yellow forsythia and flowering orchards along western Virginia's main thoroughfare.

People usually don't set out to move to the Roanoke Valley. Instead, they are converted into relocating here. When you talk to people about how they came to live here, so many times the story starts out, "We were driving down the (fill in the blank with either A. Interstate or B. Blue Ridge Parkway), when we were so smitten that we moved here without even having jobs." Or else they discovered the Roanoke Valley while hiking on the Appalachian Trail, taking the Bikecentennial path coast to coast or vacationing at nearby Smith Mountain Lake. Inevitably, the conversation ends with, " . . . and we'd never go back home. We'll never leave this place."

Consider this: The Roanoke Valley of Virginia was the first in the state to have curbside recycling, mandatory comprehensive recycling and a downtown recycling program that also was a first on the North American continent. This should tell you something about Valley citizens' overwhelming sensitivity to their environment.

Parenting magazine calls the Roanoke Valley one of the 10 best places to raise a family in the United States. The U.S. Department of Education has recognized Roanoke Valley schools for being among the nation's best. *Inc.* magazine named the Roanoke Valley one of the country's top-100 hot spots for business development. The region is blessed with many community-minded businesses and industries, such as Cox Cable of Roanoke, a dynamic civic booster, and Signet Bank, which sponsors a number of benefit events in the area.

Whether they live in historic Botetourt County, the lush, forested Catawba Valley of Craig County, the energetic cities of Roanoke or Salem, suburban Roanoke County or the quaint town of Vinton, Roanoke Valley residents are always glad to come home — and most of them never leave.

Botetourt County

If Virginia can be referred to as the "Mother of States," then Botetourt could be called the "Mother of Counties." With a population of 25,000, the county is home to an independent, history-loving people who are smug in the fact that their county, a land grant to Lord Botetourt, once stretched the whole way to the Mississippi River. Historic Fincastle has been the county seat since 1770. This vast tract of land once included the entire present state of Kentucky and much of what is now West Virginia, Ohio, Indiana and Illinois.

George Washington, Patrick Henry and Thomas Jefferson either appeared in Fincastle or sent their agents to lay claim to tracts of wilderness lands. Jefferson designed a county courthouse. After the Lewis and Clark expedition west, William Clark returned to Fincastle to marry resident Judith Hancock. Thousands of English, German and Scotch-Irish pioneers passed through on their way down the great Valley Road that traversed the famed Shenandoah Valley to settle the western frontier country.

Combining the talents of German craftsmen and Scotch-Irish merchants and lawyers, Fincastle's founding fathers built a town of well-proportioned houses and public buildings, a substantial number of which still survive. These include the Old Jail Building, the Court House Complex, the Presbyterian Church, the Botetourt Museum Building and the Botetourt County Courthouse. Newer buildings, such as the historic Bank of Fincastle, a major force in the community, are designed to blend into the historic environment.

You can take a guided tour, by appointment, by contacting Historic Fincastle Inc. Write them at P.O. Box 19, Fincastle 24090. On your tour you will see beautiful wrought iron fences, balconies and gates, flagstone walks from the early 19th century, horse mounting stones in front of the Presbyterian Church and early gravestones in church cemeteries, with the oldest dating to 1795. Steeples contain bells, the focal point of a much publicized and honored tradition of ringing out the old and ringing in the New Year.

It stands to reason that Botetourt County residents love antiques. The Chamber of Commerce will send you a brochure listing 25 different shops, most of them clustered in Troutville and Fincastle. The Troutville Antique Mart has a plethora of these shops. The town of Buchanan is also a blossoming area for antiques and other shopping, thanks to its Main Street program. There are beautiful side trips. For a striking view of orchards in bloom, take Laymantown Road left past Troutville Baptist, a cut-through road to U.S. 220. Mounds of blooming apple trees against the setting sun are indeed a sight to behold. In the fall the fruit of the harvest is available for the picking at seven orchards, most of them huge operations that also offer seasonal items, such as acres of pumpkins for Halloween.

Agriculture is still a big industry, but farmland is at a premium. There are bounties on Botetourt County real estate, with people desperate to buy the scenic farmland, which has often been in the same family for generations.

If you seek the exotic, stop at the farm for emus and ostriches off Blue Ridge Road (T-652) between Troutville and Blue Ridge. Residents on the road love to exchange stories about the time an ostrich got loose, blocked the road and caused drivers to think they were losing their minds. It took a rodeo cowboy with a lasso to catch the errant fowl, truss it and carry it home in a flatbed truck.

Two scenic landmarks tourists especially enjoy are the unusual, huge, jutting Eagle Rock boulders off U.S. 220; they appear to be on the verge of falling at any moment into the gorge. Beyond on Route 220 is Eagle Rock's Roaring Run Furnace, part of the Jefferson National Forest and typical of the scores of iron furnaces that were scattered throughout the hills and mountains of western Virginia. The single-stack, hot-blast charcoal furnace, built of large, squared stones, was constructed in 1832, rebuilt in 1845 and rebuilt again early in the Civil War. Most of the pig iron produced was shipped to Richmond for the war effort.

A third landmark here on the National Register of Historic Places is Wilson Warehouse, built in 1839 at Washington and Lowe streets and now Buchanan's Community House. It is a relic of western Virginia's antebellum prosperity.

It stands to reason that Botetourt County's largest and most popular festival is Historic Fincastle Days in the autumn. Attending the festival, sponsored by Historic Fincastle Inc. and held in the charming, historic downtown, is serendipity to lovers of fine art and crafts, since Fincastle is home to several well-known Virginia artists including Mark Woodie and Harold Little. The show is hung in the historic town square.

Recreational opportunities abound, including hiking the Appalachian and Bikecentennial trails that pass by Blue Ridge Road in Troutville. Other major activities are canoeing or floating the James River and Craig's Creek and hunting, camping and fishing.

Although Botetourt County is a county with a past, it is definitely one with a bright future while it tries to hang on to its pastoral environment. For more information, contact the Botetourt County Chamber of Commerce, at P.O. Box 92, Fincastle 24090. Call them at (703) 473-8280.

Craig County

Just as Botetourt residents are trying to protect their pristine environment, the rural residents of pastoral Craig (population 4,500) fiercely guard their stake in God's Country. Tourism is a major industry in this county, which is more than half-covered by the Jefferson National Forest.

The county got its name from Robert Craig, delegate to the General Assembly from Roanoke County who was instrumental in legislation that formed Craig County in 1851. New Castle was desig-

Photo: Washington & Lee University

The front campus of Washington & Lee University is centered by Washington Hall, built in 1824. It is a designated National Historic Landmark.

nated the county seat, and the historic courthouse was erected the same year by slave labor. Its bell was cast at the same foundry as the Liberty Bell.

Early settlers probably first traveled up Craig's Creek, the county's major waterway, in the 1730s. By the end of the Indian Wars of 1756 to 1762, 45 families lived along the creek. George Washington reportedly passed through the junction of Craig's Creek and Meadow Creek, the site of New Castle.

The county seat contains several charming old buildings that have been designated historical landmarks, including the courthouse (which was miraculously spared during the Civil War), a jail, Central Hotel and Star Saloon (now official headquarters of the Craig County Historical Society), First National Bank and the G.W. Layman office building. You'll see several lovely old homes in the area, including the Layman house (c. 1901), on the corner of Va. routes 311 and 42, and the big, brick castle-like Todd house at the top of the hill going out of town on Route 42.

Also worth a visit is Tingler's Mill at Paint Bank. While this particular mill was built in 1873, grinding had been going on at the site since 1783. Henry Tingler was excused from military service in the Confederate Army because grinding meal was a higher war need. After 182 years of daily operation, the mill closed in 1965 but is now being restored.

Here's an interesting, little-known fact: Because of Civil War geographical boundary changes, the mill has been in two different states and five different counties without ever having been moved. In 1783 the land was part of Botetourt County, remaining so until 1792, when Monroe County, Virginia, was created. In 1851 Craig County was carved from

parts of Botetourt, Monroe, Roanoke and Giles counties. In 1863 that portion of the county joined Monroe County when West Virginia was formed during the Civil War, but was returned to Craig County after the war.

The route of Gen. David Hunter's retreat in the summer of 1864 still has natives talking. The Union soldiers burned marriage records and Deed Book 1 and spilled ink on all the others. Then they chopped up parts of the courthouse for kindling. However, an order to burn the courthouse was somehow overlooked.

This gentle beauty of a county, rich in history, is noted as one of the most popular playgrounds in western Virginia. The scenery is spectacular. If you want to see the epitome of a quaint country road, travel Va. 42 from New Castle to Giles County. This delightful road, which crosses the eastern Continental Divide, passes old farms with rail fences, graveyards of Civil War veterans and late 19th-century houses.

Va. 658 in the John's Creek area takes you to the sites of two now-defunct summer resorts where people would come to "take the cure," as they called it, of the orange sulphur mineral waters. The 1987 movie, *In a Shallow Grave*, used the site of Blue Healing Springs resort's crumbling dance hall.

Another site to see is Hebron Church, built in 1830, complete with its own slave balcony. Locked during the week, arrangements may be made to visit through the Craig County Historical Society (see the Arts and Culture chapter).

The Appalachian Trail is one of the county's major attractions. Thirty miles of the Maine-to-Georgia footpath pass through this area, and several shelters and camping facilities are scattered along the way. The Trout Branch to Dragon's

Tooth section is 7 rugged miles, but the views are spectacular (park in the lot off Va. 311 in Roanoke County).

For mountain-bike enthusiasts, hikers and horseback riders, Craig County is peppered with trails that range from the easy to challenging and all with scenic value. Some local favorites include Va. 179, the road over Bald Mountain, and Va. 177 over Potts Mountain. Va. 188, the road across the top of Brush Mountain, will take you past the monument where World War II hero Audie Murphy's plane crashed.

Camping enthusiasts can stay at Craig Creek Recreation area, Steel Bridge and the Pines. Some of the best information on Craig County can be obtained from the New Castle Ranger Office by calling (703) 868-5196 weekdays. It is located on Va. 615, 3 miles east of New Castle.

If you're looking for adventure, wildlife and blessed isolation and meditation, Craig County is the place to live or visit. For more information, contact the County of Craig, Corner of Court and Main streets, New Castle 24127; (703) 864-5010.

Roanoke

Capital of the Blue Ridge, Roanoke (population 96,400) has it all: history, culture, close-knit neighborhoods and a heady sense of environment. Its downtown was the first in North America to offer recycling, thanks to Downtown Roanoke Inc.

These happy environmental facts are the products of a cutting-edge grassroots environmental group, Clean Valley Council, gutsy government officials willing to take a stand and Cycle Systems, an 80-year-old, fourth-generation recycling firm that has led Virginia in the recycling effort. Just like at Disneyland, you can count the moments before a piece of dropped litter is whisked out of sight . . . that is, if anybody has the gall to drop a piece in this earth-conscious area.

You'll probably do a double take the first time you see Roanoke's Mill Mountain Star, visible for a radius of 60 miles. The 45-year-old, 100-foot-high star is a popular landmark for airplane pilots who frequently feel compelled to explain to passengers that what they think they're seeing below really is a gigantic, man-made star. The star has lured many people, including Elvis Presley, who donned a disguise to see it after a concert when his curiosity got the best of him. Beside the star are scores of contented, well-illuminated animals at Mill Mountain Zoological Park.

And, just in case you think Roanokers are the only ones who brag about their community, let's talk about awards. A University of Kentucky study calls Roanoke one of the nation's top 20 cities for quality of life. Zero Population Growth says Roanoke is one of the 10 least stressful cities for quality of life. Downtown Roanoke's revitalization has been touted as one of America's 10-best by the National Trust for Historic Pres-

Virginia ranks among the top 10 states in the production of turkeys and apples, which come primarily from the Blue Ridge area.

Insiders' Tips

ervation. And twice in the past decade Roanoke has received the All-America City designation.

Always a crossroads for commerce, Roanoke's story began in the early 17th century. Native resistance to settlers was fierce. The city, formerly called Big Lick for its salt marshes, was later named Roanoke. "Rawrenock," meaning white beads, actually shells with holes worn on strings around the neck and arms and passed as currency among Native Americans, was described early on by Capt. John White, who attempted to settle Roanoke Island in North Carolina.

Little towns were the foundation for what is now the city of Roanoke. New Antwerp appeared in 1802 followed by Gainesborough in 1825 and Old Lick in 1834. Big Lick, chartered in 1874 with 500 citizens, became a railroad crossroads. After Norfolk and Western Railroad came to town in 1882, Roanoke grew quickly. Its historic city market still functions and is the anchor of the revitalized City Market square downtown.

Roanoke is the largest metropolitan city in Virginia west of Richmond and off the widely traveled Blue Ridge Parkway. It is the major center for transportation, served by the Norfolk Southern Railway, the Valley Metro bus system and a modern airport with a $25 million airport terminal built in 1990. The city is also the medical center of western Virginia, with more than 2,400 hospital beds and a gigantic medical center, Roanoke Memorial Hospitals.

The Roanoke Valley has a culture all its own. The Roanoke Symphony has been featured on the *Today Show* and in the *New York Times* and *Wall Street Journal*. Cultural complements include Opera Roanoke and Center in the Square, a unique, multicultural institution that's home to five resident organizations of art, history, theater and science.

A national exhibition, To the Rescue, puts Roanoke on the map as the birthplace of the volunteer rescue squad movement. The Explore Project, open, but a work in progress, is a re-creation of an 18th-century pioneer village on nearly 1,500 acres.

Perhaps the most curious of Roanoke's attractions is Miniature Graceland, a private collection of tiny scale-model buildings built by Kim Epperly, the editor of the international Elvis newsletter and the Ultimate Elvis Fan (see our Other Attractions chapter). And a lighted fountain of recycled metal, which you can see off I-581, is a monument of sorts to Roanoke's devotion to recycling. It was a recent gift of Cycle Systems.

There's family entertainment a-plenty in Roanoke. Striving to live up to its nickname as Festival City of Virginia, Roanoke hosts the blockbuster, two-weekend-long Festival in the Park each May. Nearly 400,000 people attend this celebration of art, music and the human spirit that signals the start of summer in Roanoke. Other festivals include a celebration of African-American culture on Henry Street in the fall and the Chili Cook-off and Community School Strawberry Festival the first May weekend, when palates burning from flaming chili can get cooling ice cream and berries just down the block.

Roanoke is a great jumping-off point for side trips. The number of attractions within an hour's radius is unbelievable, and you'd need a good week's stay at a great place, such as the Roanoke Marriott, historic Radisson Patrick Henry Hotel or newly re-opened Hotel Roanoke just to have time to see and do even half of what's available. Be sure to stop by the Roanoke

Valley Convention & Visitors Bureau on the City Market, (800) 635-5535. An enthusiastic staff and a dynamic director will guide you to the many local attractions.

Roanoke County

Roanoke County (population 80,000) is a mostly affluent suburban area surrounding the city of Roanoke. It includes the placid, comfortable town of Vinton. The county is noted for its superior school system, network of top-notch recreational centers and willingness to finance a superior quality of life for its citizens.

In 1838 mountainous Roanoke County was carved out of the huge county of Botetourt. Many of its communities are named for its peaks; one of the most unique may be Twelve O'Clock Knob, so named because slaves west of Salem could look at the mountain and tell it was time for lunch when the sun was at a point just over the 2,707-foot peak. Underground springs, another of the area's natural resources, inspired other names, such as Virginia Etna Springs, site of a former water bottling plant, and Big Cook Spring in Bonsack, an area heavily touched by the Civil War because of several blanket factories there. Legend has it that one factory was burned to the ground by the Yankees but the other was spared because its owner, with fingers crossed, promised not to sell blankets to the Confederate merchants down the road in Roanoke City. Another spring, Botetourt Springs, became the site of Hollins College, one of the most prestigious undergraduate women's colleges in America (graduate programs are coeducational).

Bonsack, east of Vinton, was the home of Jim Bonsack, who quit Roanoke College to work on a competition to invent the first cigarette-rolling machine. Young Bonsack won the $75,000 competition, patented his machine in 1880 at the age of 22, made a fortune and spawned a national industry.

Roanoke County's pioneering spirit has extended to modern times. The county was the Roanoke Valley's pioneer in curbside recycling and has led the rest of the Valley in environmental concerns and issues. It also has been nationally recognized for governmental cooperation in a joint industrial park and library built with Botetourt County. In 1987 community leaders began the Blue Ridge Region economic marketing group, a legislative group targeting General Assembly action to improve the area's quality of life. In 1989 Roanoke County was named an All-America City for its governmental cooperation, quality of life and support of the Explore Project.

Explore, a unique recreational and educational experience, is the county's tourism focus. It opened to the public in 1994. Many events are being held there now including astronomy field trips, bird watching, Sierra Club hikes and Scout projects. The restored Hofauger Farmhouse, the focus of the park, is complete and available for use with advance reservations. Explore's three main parts include a frontier settlement, a North American wilderness zoological park and an environmental education center. The park will be completed in various phases, with a major emphasis on environmental preservation.

Recreation and historical preservation have been a longtime focus for Roanoke Countians. Green Hill Equestrian Park is the site of the annual autumn polo match benefiting the Roanoke Symphony. This year, again, the Park hosts a Civil War battle recreation, Gen. David Hunter's Retreat. It is one of 44 parks and recreational facilities in the Roanoke Valley.

Roanoke County is known for its family-oriented neighborhoods with a wide range of styles — urban townhouses, bucolic farmhouses and suburban subdivisions — and prices averaging $100,000. Families also like the county for its superior school system, which offers remedial education and classes for the gifted.

Major employers include ITT, manufacturer of night vision goggles, Ingersoll Rand and Allstate Insurance.

Tanglewood Mall, undergoing extensive renovation, is the county's busy shopping destination, and numerous family restaurants in the same area make this a magnet for the whole valley.

Most of all, however, Roanoke County is known as a desirable place to live because of the high quality and variety of suburban services it offers residents. For more information, contact the Roanoke County-Salem Chamber of Commerce at 7 S. College Avenue, Salem 24153; (540) 387-0267.

Salem

An old story has made its rounds in the *Roanoke Times* newspaper office about a cub reporter who, having just moved to Salem and feeling a sense of isolation, asks a veteran reporter just how long it would take to get accepted by her neighbors.

"Oh, about three," the old Salem native replied.

"Three years?" responded the incredulous cub.

"No, three generations, my dear!" was the reply.

To say the city of Salem (population 25,000) has a sense of its own history and self-sufficiency is an understatement. Salem, its name derived from "shalom," meaning peace, is the oldest and southernmost community in the Roanoke Valley. That historical fact pervades Salem's quaint, charming culture. Many of its historic downtown Victorian homes, with stained-glass windows, tin roofs and pointed towers, are on the National Historic Register.

Gen. Andrew Lewis started the settlement in 1768 when he acquired his estate,

Richfield. In 1806 a charter to James Simpson created the town of Salem out of the Lewis estate, bounded by Union Street, Church Alley and Clay and Calhoun streets. Salem, chartered as a city in 1968, has a downtown museum operated by the local historical society.

Salem also has an excellent sense of community, especially when it comes to sports. The Salem Civic Center is the site of the fabulous Salem Fair and Exposition, a real coup for Salem and the largest of its kind in Virginia. You can do everything there from bungee jump to watch pigs race. The Civic Center seats 7,500 and offers a wide and varied program of community events. For example, it's home to the Roanoke Valley Horse Show, one of the 10 largest in the country. Salemites' love for athletics borders on the fanatic and considerable emphasis is placed on recreation, with more opportunities

Credit: Roanoke Convention and Visitors Bureau

Center in the Square in Roanoke.

available than in most other areas of similar size. Facilities recently were expanded to include an 8,000-seat football stadium for the beloved Salem High Spartans.

Salem also provides exciting Class A professional baseball through the Salem Avalanche, a farm team that plays at Salem Municipal Field. The city has three golf courses. In 1995 Salem will once again host football's national Alonzo Stagg Bowl.

Salemites also have a collective heart that never stops beating for their own. When high school football star Chance Crawford was paralyzed by a spinal injury during a football game in the early '80s, the townspeople rallied to pay his medical expenses. Beyond that, an annual ball tournament was arranged to assure the Crawfords would have no financial worries. As a final tribute, Crawford was overwhelmingly elected to public office.

Festivals are especially popular. Old Salem Days in September features one of the largest antique car shows on the East Coast, as well as fine Salem art. One of the Roanoke Valley's best-known artists, Walter Biggs, lived here, and his legacy is carried on by Salem artists, such as Harriet Stokes.

Vigorous industries, such as General Electric, and the regional Veterans Administration Hospital are here. It is home to Roanoke College, a Lutheran-affiliated private liberal-arts school that lends enormous culture to the area's charm.

Salem's downtown shopping district has numerous antique stores and mom-and-pop operations; Roanoke College students enjoy the local hangouts, Mac & Bob's, Macados and the new Mill Mountain Coffee & Tea.

Many of Salem's citizens work, live and play within its boundaries and never feel the need to leave their beloved city, regardless of how long it really takes to become an Insider. For more information, contact the Roanoke County-Salem Chamber of Commerce at 7 S. College Avenue, Salem, Virginia 24153; (540) 387-0267.

Vinton

Vinton, a small, unpretentious town (population 7,665) east of Roanoke, must be doing something right. Over the past several decades, in the midst of its home-spun lifestyle, it has spawned and nurtured some of Virginia's most important modern leaders.

On any given day, Virginia House Majority Leader C. Richard Cranwell, called "the most powerful man in the Blue Ridge of Virginia," can be found having lunch downtown with his constituency, who call him "Dicky" and tell him how to run Virginia's Legislature. Fortune 500 Norfolk and Southern CEO David Goode still visits his wise dad, Ott, founder of Vinton's famous Dogwood Festival, at Ott's 50-year-old downtown real estate business to get advice.

Vinton also is an important leader in its own right. In 1990 it put other Virginia municipalities on notice when its forward-looking town council began the first mandatory comprehensive recycling program in the state, effectively reducing landfilled solid waste by 25 percent. Vinton is also proud of a school system ranked among the state's top 10, and its populace comes out in droves for the William Byrd High Terriors. Its school system has the highest average achievement scores in the Valley, and teachers' salaries rank ninth in the state.

Gish's Mill, built prior to 1838, provided a start for the town. David Gish sold his mill to Isaac White Vineyard in 1867, and by that time enough people had settled around the mill to form the basis of the town of Vinton. Although the mill burned, some of the brick walls still stand. The town was chartered in 1884 and relied on the railroad for employment. Moving into the future, the N&W Railway continued to be Vinton's most important industry. Today, Precision Weaving is Vinton's largest employer.

Vinton residents play as hard as they work, having easy access to recreation by the town's proximity to the Blue Ridge Parkway. Vinton's Folklife Festival and Farmer's Market are annual excuses to have a good time. And Vinton hosts the oldest festival in the Roanoke Valley, the Dogwood Festival, always a pageantry of queens, bands, floats and politicians that has attracted a number of celebrities over the past three decades. The first-class, All-American parade always ends at the Vinton War Memorial, Vinton's landmark building and cultural center.

An incredibly moving parade followed the Persian Gulf War, when Terry Plunk, the slain former William Byrd High School star athlete and straight-A VMI cadet, was honored with a dogwood tree planted at the War Memorial by the Kuwaiti ambassador. Vinton also received national recognition for its downtown Persian Gulf War information and support center, in the true spirit of Small Town, USA.

Vinton serves its citizens well with plentiful recreational and spectator sports activities. Its municipal pool is beautiful and its recreation department program and special events are second to none.

Insiders' Tips

Virginia's motto is *Sic semper tyrannis* (Thus always to tyrants). In the Blue Ridge, you'll see that motto reflected in its people's strength, independence and zeal to protect their way of life.

Vinton's untapped tourism potential is enormous as the center of the politically designated Blue Ridge Region of Virginia. In addition to being next to the well-traveled Parkway (9 million visitors a year travel the Virginia section), Vinton is the last commercial center before Smith Mountain Lake, Virginia's largest lake. It also is the gateway to Virginia's Explore Park.

In the meantime, it's the epitome of the best of small town living. The best is yet to come. For more information, contact the town of Vinton at 311 S. Pollard Street, Vinton, Virginia 24179, (540) 983-0613.

East of the Blue Ridge Region

This gorgeous stretch of land begins in Loudoun County, with its famous Hunt Country and landed gentry, and sweeps southward along the mountains all the way through Charlottesville and Lynchburg to Franklin County south of Roanoke.

For the most part, we are talking about rural territory with few glaring billboards, convenience stores and shopping malls. It's an area rich in history that has little in common with the Shenandoah Valley across the mountains. Whereas the valley was settled primarily by Scotch-Irish and Germans who migrated south from Pennsylvania and Maryland, the foothills east of the Blue Ridge, especially Charlottesville and lands to the north, became home to families moving west from Richmond and the Tidewater.

Though I-66 cuts across the region, there is no north-south interstate paralleling the Shenandoah Valley's I-81. Va. 29 is the major artery from Culpeper to Lynchburg, along which you will find wineries, splendid antique shops and quaint country stores. The secondary roads winding through the region will also carry you to gorgeous bed and breakfast and country

inns, vineyards, pick-your-own apple orchards and historic mansions open for tours.

It takes a little more effort to tour this region and do it right, but it's worth it.

Loudoun, Fauquier and Culpeper Counties

In the north, Loudoun, Fauquier and Culpeper counties claim some of the most productive pastures in America — places where thoroughbreds thrive and the economy is still largely driven by a multi-million dollar equine industry. The postcard-perfect villages of Waterford, Hillsboro and Middleburg in Loudoun County, Paris and Upperville in Fauquier County and Jeffersonton in Culpeper County afford some of the most scenic and historic real estate in the Old Dominion.

Middleburg, right on the line between Loudoun and Fauquier counties, is the acknowledged Hunt Country Capital and is surrounded by the estates of some of the country's wealthiest and most powerful people. Yet you'd be hard-pressed to identify some of them as they run errands in Middleburg dressed in jeans and gum boots. Until her death, Jackie Kennedy was a regular in Middleburg, foxhunting with the locals and browsing the town's elegant shops. Philanthropist Paul Mellon and Ambassador Pamela Harriman have estates in the area, as does actor Robert Duvall. Before her divorce from Sen. John Warner (who owned a farm nearby), Elizabeth Taylor shopped in the local grocery stores. Paul Newman still pops in for lunch at the Red Fox Tavern when he's racing cars at Summit Point in West Virginia.

Middleburg is a delightful anachronism, because life follows a centuries-old rhythm as unchanged as its stone walls and pre-Civil War mansions. Horses are a part of daily life and a great equalizer. Your status in the real world matters a lot less than your horsemanship. You can rub elbows with celebrities and the horsey crowd during races and horse shows at Glenwood Park, at the Red Fox Tavern or at Tutti's Back Street Cafe, one block off Main Street.

Most people are surprised Middleburg's town proper is so small and so uniformly historic. This is, of course, by design. If area property owners have anything to do with it, Middleburg will never see a 7-Eleven or McDonald's, nor will it give way to the wave of development working its way west from Washington, D.C. Very seldom does anything smaller than a 100-acre estate come on the market here. The locals opposed the Walt Disney Company when the entertainment giant planned to build a theme park in Haymarket, just east of Middleburg. Despite having the governor in its corner, Disney finally yielded to the powerful local forces and gave up the project.

For more information on Loudoun and Fauquier counties, contact the Loudoun County Conference/Visitor Bureau, 108-D South Street, Leesburg 22075, (800) 752-6118, and the Warrenton-Fauquier County Visitor Center, 183A Keith Street, Warrenton 22186, (540) 347-4414.

Rappahannock, Madison and Greene Counties

Rappahannock County to the south is home to one of the most charming, even Utopian, towns in America — "Little" Washington. It is the oldest of the 28 towns in the United States named for the Father of Our Country, who surveyed and laid out the town around 1749. Washington has its own internationally known five-star restaurant and inn, a performing arts center, an artists' cooperative and several classy galleries, boutiques and antique shops.

Rappahannock's county seat, historic Sperryville, sits below the entrance to Skyline Drive. It's a great little town to explore on foot, with antique stores, galleries, arts and crafts studios and a shop where you can buy Native American weavings, jewelry, quilts and crafts.

In the northern foothills are two entries into Shenandoah National Park: Thornton Gap at U.S. 211 near Sperryville and Swift Run Gap at U.S. 33, which passes through Greene County.

Madison County has no road into Shenandoah National Park, a source of long-standing frustration among many residents. The county lost more land to the national park than any other and was reportedly promised a gateway, but for some reason national leaders reneged. This history explains in large part the level of local outrage when park officials proposed expanding the national park's boundaries into the county. The officials eventually dropped the idea, realizing how ugly a battle it would be.

Ironically, Madison County has received national acclaim for one of its scenic roads, but not the Skyline Drive. The Va. 231 Scenic Byway, which runs through 50 miles of the Piedmont from Sperryville south to Shadwell, near Charlottesville, was named one of America's 10 Most Outstanding Scenic Byways for 1995. The recognition came from Scenic America of Washington, D.C., an organization which seeks to call attention to outstanding routes and preserve endangered ones.

Madison County's earliest settlers were German iron workers. When they had completed the terms of their indentured servitude at Lord Spotswood's Germanna mines in Orange County, the Germans set out to build new lives for themselves as craftsmen and farmers. That tradition continues in Madison County. Many craftspeople — furniture makers, potters, wood carvers, quilters and jewelry artisans — make this area their home.

The same can be said for Greene County, where you can drop by the Blue Ridge Pottery on U.S. 33 to Skyline Drive and chat with local potter Alan Ward as he works at his wheel. The store, which occupies the former Golden Horseshoe Inn built in 1827, is a kind of headquarters for arts and crafts made especially in Greene County (see our Shopping chapter).

Orange County

To the east, the rolling hills of Orange County hold many historical attractions, including Montpelier, the 2,700-acre estate that was the lifelong home of James Madison and his equally famous and more popular wife, Dolley.

Orange County is also home to the prestigious Barboursville Vineyards, situated on the bucolic grounds of what was once an imposing brick mansion designed by Thomas Jefferson. The ruins and surrounding towering boxwoods form the backdrop for summer Shakespeare productions by the Four County Players of Barboursville.

This Italian-owned winery is one of many in the foothills region, which is truly the heart of Virginia wine country. Within a couple of miles is the family-owned Burnley Vineyards. Linden, Oasis and Farfelu vineyards lie in the northern foothills near Front Royal. Farther south in Madison County, Rose River Vineyards hugs the mountains near Syria. The award-winning Misty Mountain Vineyards lies farther south in Madison, and Virginia's largest and most successful winery, Prince Michel Vineyards, is located off Va. 29 near Culpeper (see our Wineries chapter).

This beautiful, hilly land northeast of Charlottesville has a rich Colonial history. Lt. Gov. Alexander Spotswood used Germanna in Orange County as a base for exploring the Shenandoah Valley in the early 1700s. He and his fellow English adventurers scaled what is now called Swift Run Gap to see the fertile valley for the first time. Many on the trip suffered fevers, chills and no doubt a few hangovers (one of the explorers wrote about drinking to the Royal family's health in brandy, shrub, rum, champagne, canary, burgundy and many more spirits). In jest, the group decided to call themselves the Knights of the Golden Horseshoe.

Historians relate that when Spotswood returned to Williamsburg he promptly wrote a letter to His Majesty King George and told him of the wonderful country beyond the Blue Ridge. He also asked for a grant for the Order of the Knights of the Golden Horseshoe. In time, a proclamation arrived from England creating the Order, and included were 50 tiny golden horseshoes inscribed in Latin. King George must have had quite a sense of humor, because along with granting Spotswood the title of Knight, he sent him a bill for the golden horseshoes. Reportedly, Spotswood paid for them out of his own pocket without a complaint.

Today, visitors can see the Enchanted Castle at the Germanna Archeological Site, where Spotswood built an elegant brick mansion in the early 1720s. The house burned in about 1750, and the site is undergoing extensive archeological research. It's under shelter and open to visitors.

Orange County later became home to James Madison, the fourth U.S. president and the Father of the Constitution. Madison's grandparents settled Montpelier, a 2,700-acre estate now owned by the National Trust for Historic Preservation and is open for tours. This is a fascinating place to watch the restoration process unfold, as staff archeologists and architectural historians work on site to discover more about the vast property during Madison's time (see our Arts and Culture chapter).

The James Madison Museum is in nearby Orange, where you can also visit the only surviving example of Thomas Jefferson's design for church architecture, St. Thomas Episcopal Church.

Orange County contains reminders of the terrible war that nearly split our country in two. The Wilderness Battlefields in the eastern end of the county were the scene of the first clash between Robert E. Lee and Ulysses S. Grant in May 1864 in which 26,000 soldiers died. The battlefields are open for self-guided tours.

Nearby Gordonsville is home to the Exchange Hotel, a restored railroad hotel that served as a military hospital during the war. It now houses an excellent Civil War museum.

Closer to Charlottesville are the Barboursville Ruins, what's left of a mansion designed by Jefferson for James Barbour, governor of Virginia, U.S. senator, Secretary of War and minister to England.

Orange County boasts the most acres of grape production of any county in the Commonwealth. Along with the Barboursville Winery, which has been praised by *Wine Spectator* magazine, the county is home to the smaller Burnley Vineyards, one of the oldest vineyards in the region (see our Wineries chapter).

The Montpelier estate hosts a wine festival every May, featuring live music, crafts, food and local wines. Montpelier is also the scene of steeplechase races on the first Saturday every November. Since 1928 this hallowed tradition has drawn huge crowds of horse-lovers.

Orange County has a unique resident in Heidi McMurran, who operates Carriage Outings, Inc., (540) 832-2785. Heidi lives in Barboursville, but she and her network of cohorts will transport horses and carriages almost anywhere for weddings, anniversaries, wine tastings, picnic outings — you name it. Several clever fellows have proposed marriage in the romantic setting of a carriage ride. Heidi's carriages appear frequently in the Charlottesville area at the Boar's Head Inn, Keswick Hall, Prospect Hill and Ash Lawn-Highland.

For more information about these and other attractions and fine bed and breakfasts in Orange County, contact the Visitors Bureau, 154 Madison Road, Orange 22960; (540) 672-1653. The James Madison Museum, (540) 672-1776, at 129 Caroline Street in Orange, also has a visitors center.

Charlottesville and Albemarle County

Charlottesville is a crown jewel of a city, with so much beauty, history, culture and lively commerce that it's no wonder it is growing by leaps and bounds.

If he were alive, Thomas Jefferson, a native of the territory, would probably roll his eyes and sigh at the traffic congestion that now clogs such major arteries as U.S. 250 and U.S. 29. Such is the cost of the city's allure.

Fortunately, Albemarle County, which surrounds Charlottesville on all sides, remains largely rural, with rolling pastures, elegant horse farms and lush forests that lead up to the wilderness of the Shenandoah National Park. And the city itself contains many enclaves of natural beauty, from the lovely gardens along the colonnade at the University of Virginia to fine old homes surrounded by mounds of azaleas, rhododendrons and camellias.

Reminders of the nation's early history abound in the Charlottesville area. The city took its name from the popular Queen Charlotte, wife of King George III. Albemarle County dates back to 1744, when it was named in honor of William Ann Keppel, second Earl of Albemarle, who was governor general of the colony of Virginia. The Earl never laid foot in the county, but two U.S. presidents, Jefferson and James Monroe, made it their home.

Monticello, the architectural wonder Jefferson designed and never stopped tinkering with, remains the area's leading attraction. The mountaintop estate opens its doors to visitors seven days a week, inviting all to glimpse Jefferson's genius through his architecture, gardens and innovations. Another fascinating exhibit about Jefferson's domestic life at Monticello lies down the hill and next to I-64 at the Thomas Jefferson Visitors Center (see our Arts and Culture chapter).

Thanks to Jefferson's architectural abilities, the campus of the University of Virginia is considered one of the most beautiful in the nation. Jefferson designed the Rotunda of his academic village after the Roman Pantheon. The graceful Rotunda, the pavilions and their gardens and the whitewashed colonnade comprise the original university buildings. In 1976 the American Institute of Architects voted the original campus the most outstanding achievement in American architecture.

Not far from Monticello, on another mountain slope, is Ash Lawn-Highland, home of James Monroe, Jefferson's friend and America's fifth president. Strutting, showy peacocks grace the lawn at Ash Lawn-Highland, where visitors can witness Monroe's cultured lifestyle and learn about a working farm of the 19th century. The boxwood-covered grounds at Ash Lawn come to life in the summer, when light opera performances entertain guests under the stars (see our Arts and Culture chapter).

You'll find reminders of this rich history in the streets of downtown Charlottesville, especially around Court Square, where Jefferson and Monroe spent much of their leisure time. Here every building bears a plaque dating it to the early days of the city, making it easy to imagine what the city must have looked like when Jefferson practiced law here.

The Albemarle County Courthouse, built in 1762, served as the meeting place of the Virginia Legislature as the leaders fled Cornwallis' approaching army in 1781. State Legislator Daniel Boone was one of the seven men captured in a surprise raid on Charlottesville led by British Cavalry general Banastre Tarleton during that campaign. Tarleton failed at capturing then-governor Jefferson, but nabbed Boone at the corner of Jefferson and Park streets.

History buffs are not the only ones interested in the downtown historic district. Folks of all ages enjoy strolling along the pedestrian-only downtown mall, lined on both sides with specialty boutiques, antique stores, outdoor cafes, ice-cream shops and bookstores.

Also within easy walking distance are galleries, including McGuffey Art Center, a transformed elementary school where you can observe artists at work in their studios and buy fine handcrafts, pottery, paintings, photos and prints (don't miss the Second Street Gallery inside). Adjacent to the McGuffey Art Center and across the street is Vinegar Hill Theater, a place to see foreign films, documentaries and movies not usually shown in standard theaters. Within walking distance are museums, libraries and more than 25 restaurants from which to choose.

Speaking of food, the culinary scene in Charlottesville has become rather lively and diverse. If you want hot and spicy Southern barbecue or country ham and biscuits, you'll find it here. But you may also be tempted by the Indian, Vietnamese, French, German, Italian, Brazilian and American nouvelle cuisine in the area.

At the risk of sounding trite, we must not forget the famous figures of the film world who make Charlottesville their home. Charlottesvilleans are reportedly known for their ability to fake nonchalance at the sight of such figures as Sam

Shepard, Jessica Lange and Sissy Spacek. It is considered gauche to gawk or ask for an autograph, and this must be one reason why these famous folks and their families seem to have found such a comfortable life here.

Of course, Charlottesville's association with the rich and famous is nothing new. The area was the setting for part of *Giant*, the western film starring Elizabeth Taylor, Rock Hudson and James Dean. Randolph Scott, a leading star in *Ride the High Country*, one of the greatest westerns ever made, lived at Montpelier for a couple of years when he was married to Marion duPont.

Land has become very expensive in the Charlottesville, so it is nearly impossible for people of moderate means to purchase their own place. The gulf between the "haves" and "have-nots" in Charlottesville is widening so much even the local association of Realtors is disturbed, making the issue of affordable housing their highest priority. For instance, several developments are selling homes on lots no larger than three acres for between $300,000 and $800,000; homes that cost around $130,000 are considered low-end.

Among the high-end communities is Keswick, a private, gated enclave east of town owned by Sir Bernard Ashley of the Laura Ashley group. Membership (by invitation only) in the Keswick Club, a sports complex centered around an Arnold Palmer golf course, is $25,000 per person. An overnight stay at the posh Keswick Hall costs between $195 and $640 a night.

The new affluence of Charlottesville has its positive side: the backing of such cultural resources as the Virginia Festival of American Film. Patricia Kluge, ex-wife of the richest man in America, provided the primary means to establish the festival, which is held at UVA every October. Illustrious special guests have included Jimmy Stewart, Gregory Peck, Ann Margret, Charlton Heston and a host of screenwriters, critics and academics.

More than 2,000 accommodations are available in the Charlottesville area, ranging from economy motels to some of the most elegant inns and bed and breakfasts imaginable.

A trip to Charlottesville isn't complete without at least one stop at a local winery for a sample, a bottle, or a tour to learn how wine is made. Ten wineries sit within easy driving distance of Charlottesville, the wine capital of Virginia. Jefferson would be proud to know this; he often dreamed of producing fine Virginia wines and experimented with grape growing for more than 30 years. One of the region's finest wineries, Jefferson Vineyards Ltd., is situated on the same property near Monticello that Thomas Jefferson donated to an Italian winegrower in 1773. The Italian, Philip Mazzei, had early success at making wine on the land, but his efforts were interrupted by the Revolutionary War and his grapes were trampled by the horses of a Hessian general who had rented the property.

For more information about wineries, accommodations, restaurants, night life, shopping, real estate, retirement and cultural life in the Charlottesville area, refer to the specific chapters in this guide. The complimentary *Charlottesville Guide*, available throughout the city, is a good source of current events, including happenings in Orange and Madison counties, Waynesboro and Staunton.

You can also contact the Charlottesville/Albemarle Convention & Visitors Bureau, P.O. Box 161, Charlottesville 22902; (804) 977-1783.

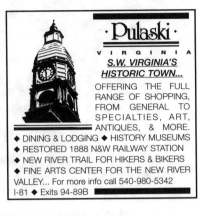
Nelson County

Roughly a quarter of this rural, agricultural county lies in the George Washington National Forest. Wintergreen Resort, a four-season vacation paradise with a year-round residential community, hugs the mountains in the western part of the county. Crabtree Falls, a spectacular series of cascades, is one of the highlights of the forest along Va. 56, the scenic road that crosses the mountains and enters the Shenandoah Valley at Vesuvius.

Apples are the mainstay the local economy, and beef cattle is the second-leading industry.

Earl Hamner Jr., who wrote the hit family television show of the '70s, *The Waltons*, grew up in the tiny town of Schuyler (pronounced SKY-ler). For years, fans have come to Schuyler searching for the old home place and other landmarks of the show. In 1992 the Walton's Mountain Museum opened in the very school attended by Hamner and his siblings. Actual sets from the show are set up in former classrooms, and all sorts of interesting memorabilia is displayed. A video documentary with interviews with

Photo: Lexington Visitors Center

The Lexington Carriage Company provides rides to visitors through historic downtown.

Hamner and the actors and screenwriters is shown regularly.

Well worth a visit is the intriguing Swannanoa Marble Palace and Sculpture Garden, an estate with a romantic history and beautiful grounds. This Afton Mountain wonder is also the site of the University of Science and Philosophy, a fascinating storehouse of New Age thinking (read more about it in our Arts and Culture chapter).

Another attraction in Nelson County is Oak Ridge, a 4,800-acre estate that belonged to Thomas Fortune Ryan, a leading financier at the turn of the century. A restored 50-room mansion, with its formal Italian gardens, greenhouse and 80 out buildings, serves as a backdrop for a variety of festivals and cultural events, including the big Summer Festival in June.

Nelson County has several vineyards offering tours and wine tasting, enjoyable outings any time of year but especially in the autumn.

Accommodations in the county include luxury condominiums and suites at Wintergreen Resort (see our Resorts chapter) and many bed and breakfast inns.

One of the best places to eat — and eat hearty — is the Rodes Farm Inn on Va. 613 near Nellysford. Owned by Wintergreen Resort, Rodes Farm Inn is an unpretentious country-style restaurant housed in a 200-year-old farmhouse.

For more information on Nelson County, contact the Nelson County Department of Tourism at (804) 263-5239 or (800) 282-8223.

Lynchburg and Amherst County

I consider it one of the most interesting spots in the state.

— Thomas Jefferson

Democracy's founding father, who scandalized Lynchburg society by eating a "love apple" (tomatoes were thought to be poisonous), summed up best how Lynchburg's citizens feel about their city and its vast array of cultural, educational and recreational opportunities.

For the past 25 years, the national spotlight has shone on Lynchburg's politically active pastor of the internationally known Thomas Roads Baptist

Church here, the Rev. Jerry Falwell. Known as the City of Churches, Lynchburg (population 70,000) has 129 other houses of worship in addition to the church that launched the Moral Majority. Although the Quakers were the first religious group to settle here and strongly influenced Lynchburg's history, their opposition to slavery caused them to migrate to Ohio and Indiana.

Long before Falwell built his national church from a small Lynchburg congregation, Lynchburg's central location and role in transporting goods by river and railroad had already made it famous.

Lynchburg's founder and namesake, John Lynch, was from hard-working Irish stock. His father, Irish runaway Charles Lynch, decided to learn a trade and, at the age of 15 apprenticed himself to a wealthy Quaker tobacco planter. The relationship worked out so well the Roman Catholic Lynch married the planter's daughter. Their equally enterprising son, reared as a Quaker, started a ferry service across the James River in 1757 — at the tender age of 17. In 1786 the Virginia General Assembly granted John Lynch a charter for a town, 45 acres of his own land. Lynchburg was incorporated as a town in 1805 and a city in 1852. Lynch also built the city's first bridge, replacing his ferry in 1812.

Historically known as the Hill City, Lynchburg attracted industrial magnates who dealt in tobacco and iron, the chief products of early Lynchburg. Their ornate, luxurious homes, bordered by enormous decorative wrought iron fences, are alone worth a visit. Three of them have been made into sumptuous bed and breakfasts: Madison House, The Mansion and Langhorne Manor. Proprietors at all three will pamper you in the manner the original inhabitants were accustomed to.

The inns are in three of Lynchburg's seven original "hill" neighborhoods: College Hill, Daniel's Hill, Diamond Hill, Federal Hill, Franklin Hill, Garland Hill and White Rock Hill. Walking tour maps of the area are available from Lynchburg's dynamic tourism marketing team at its Convention & Visitors Bureau. You can call them at (804) 847-1732 for a rundown on so many attractions it will take you a good week to see them all. There are many fine restaurants and great shopping here as well.

In the decade before the Civil War, Lynchburg was one of the two wealthiest cities per capita in the United States. As you would expect, its moneyed citizenry spawned a rich culture. Sarah Bernhardt and Anna Pavlova appeared at the Academy of Music, which opened in 1905. The old music hall has been purchased by Liberty University, which plans to restore it. Jones Memorial Library was completed in 1908 and is one of America's foremost genealogical research libraries. Lynchburg's Fine Arts Center, the city's cultural nucleus, houses two art galleries, a theater, two dance studios and the oldest continuous theater group in the country. Each year, 100,000 people — more than the city's population — take classes, hear concerts and see plays, ballet and art exhibits at the center.

Scores of famous authors sprang from Lynchburg's culture. Two of its most famous, curiously enough, gained their fame for their books on the opposite sides of democratic and racial issues. The great historian Dr. Douglas Southall Freeman, born in Lynchburg in 1886, received 24 honorary degrees and two Pulitzer Prizes, one in 1936 for his four-volume work, *The Life of Robert E. Lee.* The other, in 1948, was for a series on George Washington.

Anne Spencer, an African-American poet born in 1882, is the only Virginian whose works are included in the *Norton Anthology of Modern American and British Poetry*. She helped establish Lynchburg's first lending library for African-Americans and started Lynchburg's first NAACP chapter. Frequent visitors to Spencer's restored home, garden and studio, Edankraal (open by appointment to visitors at 1313 Pierce Street), included Dr. Martin Luther King, Dr. George Washington Carver, Jackie Robinson and Marion Anderson, the African-American singing star who was denied entrance to perform in Washington's Daughters of the American Revolution concert hall because of her race. Interestingly enough, one of the founders of the DAR, Ellet Cabell, was born at Point of Honor, a beautifully restored Lynchburg mansion, now a museum, in the same area as Spencer's house.

Point of Honor, so named for the gun duels fought there, was built by Dr. George Cabell Sr., whose most famous patient was Patrick Henry. East of Lynchburg, at Brookneal, is Red Hill Shrine, the last home and burial place of Henry, the great patriot and orator. Point of Honor is part of Lynchburg's city museum system, one which other cities would do well to emulate.

Any discussion of Lynchburg's history must also include the influence of Carter Glass, born in Lynchburg in 1858 and Secretary of the Treasury under President Woodrow Wilson. Glass served as a Virginia state senator from 1899 to 1902, in the U.S. House of Representatives from 1902 to 1918 and represented Virginia in the U.S. Senate from 1920 to 1946. He was the first living person to appear alone on a regular U.S. coin.

Lynchburg's quality of life is also greatly enhanced by its bustling community market at Bateau Landing, where shoppers can choose fresh produce and homemade goods. The annual Festival on the James and The Bateau Festival held in June celebrate the historic James River's contributions with entertainment, historic crafts exhibits and the start of the bateau race to Richmond. Kaleidoscope is an annual fall festival celebrating life in Central Virginia with an arts festival, bands, Riverfront Jamboree, craft show, pops picnic (dining on the lawn to some great music) and the Lynchburg Symphony.

Lynchburg has long been a leading industrial city. It has the highest per capita manufacturing employment in Virginia. Today it is also home to 3,000 businesses and led the way in developing one of the state's first small business incubators.

It is extraordinary how many early industries are still in business. The second-oldest funeral home in America, Diuguid's, has been comforting the bereaved since 1817. Lynchburg Gas Co., founded in 1851, was one of the first in the country to shed light on operating a gas utility. Wiley & Wilcox Engineering, started in 1901, is one of the oldest engineering firms in the United States. In 1901 John Craddock tried the first shoe company in the South on for size in Lynchburg, founding Craddock-Terry. It was a perfect fit; today Craddock-Terry's downtown outlet store offers a dazzling array of 300,000 pairs of shoes.

In 1889 the young pharmacist Charles Brown began selling his Chap-Stick lip balm. Since, his C. B. Fleet Company's product line has expanded to other national lines, including the first disposable enema and Summer's Eve douche. Babcock & Wilcox Co. and General Electric are other major employers.

As an major manufacturing center, Lynchburg played an important role in the Civil War. Perhaps none was more urgent than the advance of medicine for Civil War soldiers brought to the Pest House by Dr. John Jay Terrell. At the Pest House, in the historic Lynchburg Confederate Cemetery, you can view displays of Dr. Terrell's pace-setting work in establishing sanitary standards, including his 19th-century medical kit.

Lynchburg is home to nine diverse colleges. Randolph-Macon Woman's College was the first woman's college in the South to be accredited and the first to receive a Phi Beta Kappa chapter. The Maier Museum, an outstanding collection of American art, is also at the college. Sweet Briar is another well-known woman's college and is affiliated with the Virginia Center for the Creative Arts, an internationally recognized Amherst County working retreat for writers, artists and composers. Also here are Jerry Falwell's Liberty University, Lynchburg College, a liberal arts school, a community college, seminary and two business colleges.

Lynchburg's public schools also are outstanding. Both of its high schools and one of its middle schools have been designated as model schools by the Commonwealth of Virginia. The city also has 10 private schools, the most famous of which is The Virginia School of the Arts, a private boarding school for students grades 7 through 12. Talented young people from around the nation compete to enter the school, which encourages them to achieve the highest standards for performance in dance, drama, music or the visual arts.

High school sports also are popular. Lynchburg is home to the Virginia High School Coaches Association All-Star Games, bringing the best in high school sports to the area. Colleges offer spectator sports, and when springtime comes fans head for the diamond to see the area's only Double A professional sports team, the Lynchburg Red Sox.

Golf, tennis and swimming are other popular pastimes. The city operates 10 parks, 24 playgrounds, 34 tennis courts, 26 baseball diamonds and eight community centers. Miller Park is home to an Olympic-size pool. In the heart of Lynchburg is Blackwater Creek Natural Area with the Ruskin Freer Preserve, a 155-acre animal sanctuary.

Lynchburg's two hospitals, Virginia Baptist and Lynchburg General, have gained national attention by sharing staff and services to avoid duplication and keep down expenses.

Lynchburg is served by an $8 million airport terminal, built in 1991. A hub for daytrips, tourists can go north to Schuyler (pronounced SKY-ler), the restored home of Earl "John-Boy" Hamner, author of the book on which *The Waltons* TV series was based. Just west of the city is Poplar Forest, Jefferson's summer retreat, now being restored but nevertheless open to the public. Twenty miles east is Appomattox, the site where our nation reunited after the Civil War. Monument Terrace, in the center of Lynchburg's downtown, honors the heroes of all wars.

Whatever you decide to see and do while in Lynchburg, you'll probably echo the words of Thomas Jefferson in deciding it is one of the most interesting spots in the state. For more information, contact the Greater Lynchburg Chamber of Commerce at P.O. Box 2027, 2015 Memorial Avenue, Lynchburg, Virginia 24501; (804) 845-5966.

North of Lynchburg, Amherst County (population 29,000) was first inhabited by the Monocan Indians. It is named for Sir Jeffrey Amherst, the British commander of all forces in America from 1758 to 1763. Amherst led the British armies that successfully drove France from Canada and was the British hero of the Revolutionary War battle of Ticonderoga against the upstart Colonists.

Amherst County was created in 1761 from a section of Albemarle County. In 1807 it was divided, and the northern part became Nelson County. Tobacco and apples were early cash crops.

Three-fourths of the county's rolling terrain is forests. The Blue Ridge Parkway offers dramatic views while providing the perfect spot for an afternoon picnic. The county is a popular recreation area boasting magnificent mountain views, clean air and thousands of acres of unspoiled forests, rivers and lakes. Numerous leisure and recreational activities can be found in the George Washington National Forest. The Appalachian Trail bisects Amherst County and affords the serious hiker the ultimate challenge.

Winton Country Club, the 18th-century manor that was once the home of Patrick Henry's sister, opens its 18-hole championship golf course to the public here.

Twenty industries also are tucked away in the hills, including a German cuckoo clock-maker, Hermle-Black Forest Clocks.

Sweet Briar College, a private woman's college built on the grounds of an old plantation near the town of Amherst, contributes to the arts experience and educational quality of life. It has hosted anthropologist Jane Goodall, the Glenn Miller Orchestra and Isaac B. Singer, winner of the Nobel Prize in Literature. The most famous Sweet Briar affiliation is The Virginia Center for the Creative Arts, an artists-in-residency program that brings in the world's most talented writers, visual artists and composers and gives them a place of peace and quiet to help foster creativity.

The Amherst County Historical Museum, in the German Revival-style Kearfott-Wood House, built in 1907 by Dr. Kearfott, is being expanded to include four exhibit rooms and a gift shop. The upstairs is used for storing the museum's collection and office space. A reference library here is available to the public.

Amherst County serves as a springboard into many other daytrips. It is close to Charlottesville and Wintergreen Resort.

Smith Mountain Lake

How do you spell relief?

L-A-K-E. Smith Mountain, that is, western Virginia's biggest playground and Virginia's largest lake. Smith Mountain Lake is 20,000 acres of placid waters, 40 miles long and surrounded by 500 miles of shoreline.

It touches Franklin, Bedford and Pittsylvania counties (combined population 142,000). The lake is a colorful place where people love to go and hate to leave. Purple sunsets, stunning blue water and a lot of wildlife, such as glossy green-headed mallard ducks and chubby, gray-striped bass, add to the local color.

Until recently, Smith Mountain Lake was a place for people who owned their own vacation home or knew somebody who owned a boat. Thanks to the state's finally opening a public beach at Smith Mountain Lake State Park, the lake is now for everyone to enjoy.

As lakes go, Smith Mountain is relatively new. Like its older sister, Claytor

Lake, south in Pulaski, Smith Mountain was formed when the Roanoke River was dammed to generate electrical power for Appalachian Power Company. It took six years and a crew of 200 to move 300,000 cubic yards of earth to make way for the 175,000 cubic feet of concrete used to build the Smith Mountain Dam. Full pond is 613 feet above sea level. The river started filling Smith Mountain Lake on September 24, 1963, and reached capacity on March 7, 1966.

Archeologists examining the excavation necessary to build the dam determined the Algonquins fished and hunted here long before anybody else did.

While Smith Mountain was a popular spot from day one, a real breakthrough for the lake was when developer Dave Wilson started Bernard's Landing Resort in the early '80s. Wilson, who later ran into financial problems, is widely credited with being the moving force behind opening the lake to everyone and making it a major western Virginia tourism attraction. Since, Bernard's Landing Resort and its gourmet restaurant, The Landing, have become the most important tourist attractions at the lake, bringing in people from around the country as condominium owners, many of whom offer public rentals. For people who enjoy bed and breakfasts, the historic Manor at Taylor's Store on Va. 122 has been featured in *Southern Living* magazine (see our chapter on Bed and Breakfast and Country Inns).

A second important addition to the lake's culture was the building of Bridgewater Plaza at Hales Ford Bridge on Route 122. The center of Smith Mountain's social and night life, the Plaza has restaurants, a marina, small shops and Harbortown Miniature Golf Course, which is built out over the water. Bands play here weekends during the summer. It's a fun place to take the kids to play arcade games or just pick up an ice-cream cone while listening to the band.

The year-round lake community has only about 5,000 residents. Throughout the area, its significant staid German Baptist population rarely mingles socially with outsiders. They dress similarly to Mennonites and can be identified by the women's mesh bonnets and the men's long beards. Widely known for their agricultural prowess, they live on some of the most beautiful farms you'll ever see and make or grow virtually everything they need.

The anchor of community events is the Smith Mountain Lake Chamber of Commerce/Partnership, whose members support the lake's goals and run a Welcome Center staffed entirely by volunteers. Many of them are retirees from the North. At the Partnership, (800) 676-8203, you can pick up a lot of brochures and material about marinas, Jet Ski and boat rentals, lake homes for rent, campgrounds, fishing guides and anything else you need to have a good time during your stay.

Annual events include the Partnership's Fall Festival, the Wine Festival held at Bernard's Landing, various golf tournaments and dances and the Smith Mountain Tour of Homes to benefit the National Multiple Sclerosis Society. The 1994 event was one of the most successful fund-raisers in the nation as people from all over came to see lake living at its best. The 1995 event will be held in October.

The lake offers plenty of things to do weekdays and weekends. The major attraction is Booker T. Washington National Monument, the former home of the famous African-American statesman,

6 miles south of Hales Ford Bridge on Route 122. Also stop by APCO's Visitor Center at the Dam off Va. 40 on Va. 908. It's full of hands-on exhibits for the kids and interesting audiovisuals about how the lake was formed. Smith Mountain Lake State Park, (540) 297-6066, has a full calendar of summertime activities including swimming, fishing and canoeing (see our Recreation chapter).

Golf is a major attraction for residents. However, unless you're a member of the Waterfront or Water's Edge residential communities, your game will be at Chestnut Creek's 18 beautiful holes or Mariner's Landing. Chestnut Creek's restaurant is also open to the public. As with the other planned communities, it sells villa homesites for those who want to live and play by a golf course.

Other pastimes are balloon flights offered by Blue Ridge Balloons of Vinton, (540) 890-3029; parasailing at Bridgewater Marina, (540) 721-1203; and riding Jet Skis (call the Partnership for a list of rental places).

For the serious boater, of which there are many, there is the Smith Mountain Yacht Club and at least several dozen marinas offering services ranging from restaurants to dry-dock. Again, the Partnership will give you a complete list. A word of caution: If you are interested in a quiet day on the water, Saturday probably is not the day to be out and about. That seems to be when weekenders, intent on an extra good time and sometimes bolstered by too much drink, take to the water. Sundays and weekdays, however, are relatively calm.

Now, let's talk about fishing, the original reason many people came to the lake. Smith Mountain has a well-deserved reputation as an angler's paradise, especially for striped bass. Some coves literally churn with stripers, especially in the autumn. Getting them to bite your bait is another matter (see our Recreation chapter's "Fishing" section).

Now that you've hooked your fish and are also hooked on the lake, let's turn our attention to buying your own vacation home here. Many a millionaire was made from lake real estate. People all over western Virginia are kicking themselves that they didn't buy when land was cheap. There are many tales of people recouping their original investment 10 times over within a decade. Those days, however, are long gone. A prime waterfront lot can easily sell at a starting point of $100,000. Still, lake property remains inexpensive to Northerners used to New Jersey-type real estate prices (see our Real Estate and Retirement chapter).

Regardless of whether you're just visiting or planning to buy real estate and stay, Smith Mountain will win your heart while you're here. There's nothing more spectacular than a Smith Mountain sunset or more beautiful than the early morning mist blanketing the lake. You'll return many times to enjoy the view and have some fun. And that's no fish tale!

Bedford City and County

It's here Thomas Jefferson came to get away from it all at his summer home, Poplar Forest. That alone should tell you something about the quality of life in Bedford County. And some things never change. Even if nobody ever finds the famous Beale Treasure here, you can easily make a case that Bedford County and its charming county seat are a real "find" in themselves (see our sidebar for more about the tantalizing treasure). Let's talk history.

The fastest-growing county outside Virginia's Urban Crescent of Northern Virginia, Bedford County (population 45,349) borders Smith Mountain Lake and is home to Smith Mountain Lake State Park. Bedford also is off the Blue Ridge Parkway, close to one of the Parkway's main attractions, the Peaks of Otter Lodge and Restaurant at Milepost 86, on a spectacular twin-peaked mountain that can be seen for miles.

Bedford is a Main Street Downtown Revitalization City with organizations devoted to its historic past. A wonderful museum and the Bedford County Public Library are downtown.

Bedford County was named for John Russell, fourth Duke of Bedford, who, as Secretary of State for the Southern Department of Great Britain, had supervision of Colonial affairs. The county was formed in 1754 from Lunenburg County and part of Albemarle County. The city was chartered in 1968; in the early '80s it renovated its historic downtown, where interesting shops and restaurants contribute to the ambiance. Bedford has two quaint bed and breakfast inns, Bedford House and Otters Den. If you're into natural organic food, try the Gunstock Creek Cooperative, a quaint 19th-century store on Va. 640 in Wheats Valley at the foot of the Blue Ridge.

Recreation abounds in Bedford County, with the Jefferson National Forest on the north offering the many diversions of the Blue Ridge, including hunting, fishing, camping, picnicking and trails for both horseback riding and biking. Part of the Appalachian Trail passes through the area, with this section especially full of wildflowers and wildlife. The James River flows through in the northeast. City residents enjoy the 59-acre Liberty Lake Park, the heart of recreation. Bedford Lake and Park, 35 acres with a white sand beach off Va. 639, offers swimming, boating, fishing and camping.

The county is largely rural, with half of its land devoted to farming, dairy and beef cattle and orchards. One of the oldest trees on record, definitely the oldest in Virginia, stands at Poplar Park in Bedford County.

Bedford also is a manufacturing base for industries that make everything from pottery, clocks and golf carts to food flavoring and stew.

Bedford citizens have a rich small-town culture. There's The Little Town Players, a community theatre organization. The county's Sedalia Center offers classes in everything from classical music to back-to-the-land survival skills and is a tremendous asset to the community. Every Christmas, an estimated 100,000 visitors come to see the lighting display erected by the 200 retired Benevolent and Protective Order of Elks at that fraternal organization's national home.

Poplar Forest, just outside of Lynchburg, is one of the area's most popular destinations as history-lovers flock to see the ongoing excavation and renovation of Thomas Jefferson's beloved octagonal vacation home (see our Arts and Culture chapter).

The devout Christian with an imagination will enjoy seeing Holy Land USA, a 400-acre nature sanctuary whose aim is to be a replica of the Holy Land in Israel. Its owners invite study groups and individuals for a free walking tour. Primitive camping is allowed.

For more information, contact the Bedford Area Chamber of Commerce at 305 East Main Street, Bedford, Virginia 24523, (540) 586-9401.

Beale Treasure
Is a 100-year-old Mystery

Over the past century, thousands of folks with shovels and backhoes have come searching for the world-famous Beale Treasure, but have gone home empty-handed, but that's not to say you will. But beware — 100 members of the Beale Cypher Association, comprised of the country's most renowned computer experts, are still trying to crack the last two treasure codes.

The legend of the Beale Treasure began in 1885 with the publication of the Beale Papers in Lynchburg. The author told how the Beale Papers came into his possession through Robert Morris, a respected Lynchburg hotel owner. It seems on several occasions Morris gave room and board to Thomas Beale. On his last visit in 1822 he entrusted Morris with a metal box and asked him to keep it for him. A few months later Beale wrote a letter explaining that if he did not return within 10 years, the important papers inside should be read. He explained, however, that without a "key," which a St. Louis friend would be mailing, the three papers would be unintelligible.

Beale never returned and no key ever arrived. After 23 years, Morris finally opened the box and tried to read its incomprehensible contents. One letter he could read, however, stated that Beale and his party of 29 friends had come to Bedford County several times to bury a treasure they found out west. It would be worth $23 million today. The other two documents, written in cryptic ciphers, told where it was.

After 20 years of trying, Morris was only able to break the ciphers, which cryptanalysts call multiple substitution ciphers, on one document. The message revealed the content of the treasure: 2,981 pounds of gold and 5,092 pounds of silver, plus jewels — a pretty package by anyone's standards. The key was based on the Declaration of Independence.

Since 1885, all attempts to break the two remaining ciphers have been unsuccessful. Over the years, many treasure hunters have bypassed the ciphers and just started digging. Both the town's librarian and postmistress say they regularly receive correspondence and inquiries from around the world regarding the treasure. Recently, one woman, her dog and the man whose backhoe she hired were arrested for digging up a corpse in a cemetery. The two humans were jailed and fined, and poor Fido was incarcerated in the county pound.

The most recent hunter was Mel Fisher, the famous searcher who has recovered millions of dollars from wrecked Spanish galleons. After the local newspaper offered a blow-by-blow account of his daily diggings he abandoned his search in 1989 but vowed to return.

So the question remains: Is there really a Beale Treasure, or is the whole incredible story just a ruse? Nobody knows for sure. But most people figure if Thomas Jefferson himself kept returning to beautiful Bedford County, the area must hold treasure enough that is much easier to find.

Franklin County

Franklin County calls itself the Land Between the Lakes, Smith Mountain and Philpott. More miles of shoreline touch Franklin County than either of the other two border counties, Bedford or Pittsylvania. Excluding part-time residents who own lake vacation homes, Franklin County's population is 39,549.

For such a small, rural area, Franklin County has several national claims to fame. It has one of the proudest African-American cultures of any place in the Blue Ridge, evidenced by the Booker T. Washington National Monument. The famous former slave who became one of America's most important scholars and educators lived on a farm that is now the focus of the park near Hales Ford Bridge (see our Arts and Culture chapter).

Franklin County's other national claim to fame is a Blue Ridge researcher's dream, the acclaimed Blue Ridge Institute at Ferrum College, where the annual October Folklife Festival pays tribute to the treasured yet nearly forgotten skills of its Blue Ridge culture (see our Arts and Culture chapter).

The Institute is a national treasure that promotes a culture greatly transcends what many Franklin Countians take for granted as everyday life. The Institute offers a museum, archives and records division and a re-created 1800s German-American farmstead to preserve the best of Blue Ridge culture. One of is finest creations, produced for Franklin County's Bicentennial in 1986, is a pictorial record of Franklin County life and culture.

The Blue Ridge Institute's Fall Festival brings many skilled, working craftspeople in for the delight of visitors. You will see demonstrations of spinning, quilt making, shingle chopping and other homespun crafts. The Festival also offers unique spectator sports, such as Coon Dog Trials.

Another popular festival is the Boones Mill Apple Festival held each fall. Boones Mill is a great place for antiquing on the U.S. 220 corridor to Roanoke. One word of caution when driving through: Slow down. The speed limit changes abruptly when you enter the town, and Boones Mill's town officer has had national write-ups for his official police car, a white Camero, which sits on the curb and catches a lot of out-of-state speeders. It might be an important source of revenue to the town, but you'll probably want to make your donations to the county in another manner!

Ferrum College greatly enriches the quality of life for Franklin Countians. Its fine arts program supports the Jack Tale Players, whose song and drama touring company brings to life the legends of the Upland South. Its Poetic Arts Company demonstrates through performance how poetry plays a vital role in everyday life. Both students and residents enjoy participating in the Blue Ridge Summer Dinner Theatre.

The culture of the lake is vastly different, from the early settlers in the county seat of Rocky Mount to the transplanted Northerners at Smith Mountain Lake. Yet a third culture, the German Baptist population, mostly keeps to itself. One exception is Boone's Country Store in Burnt Chimney. The best sticky buns on earth and other tempting edibles are prepared daily at this German Baptist store. People who live an hour's drive away admit to negotiating the winding road up Windy Gap Mountain just to stock their freezer with their "fix" of the sweet pastry.

Moonshiners

The gentle mountain culture of Franklin County includes a bit of notoriety most residents there would just as soon put behind them: a long history of moonshining (the illegal manufacture of whiskey). 'Shinin' still goes on in the mountainous, rural county. Rarely a month goes by without a story in the local newspaper about someone being arrested for moonshining, often for the second or third time. Some people admit to subscribing to the *Franklin County Post* just to read the excuses given by those who get caught with their hands on the still.

At one recent hearing, a moonshiner solemnly pleaded not guilty. When the judge asked him just what he had intended to do with the trainload of sugar on the track by his backyard, he replied his wife "is fond of putting up preserves."

Some residents hold in awe the folklore of independent, enterprising mountain men doing what it took to survive, while others pretend moonshining never existed and still doesn't. Although the county's underground industry has been to some the source of amusement and the butt of jokes, a new breed of moonshiner — one selling illegal drugs, as well — is causing fewer people to be amused.

Franklin County's history is as rich and varied as its people. Its first residents were German, French, English and Scotch-Irish settlers who moved from Pennsylvania in 1750. The county was formed in 1786 by the General Assembly. Munitions for Revolutionary War patriots were made from locally mined iron ore at an iron works on Furnace Creek, which is the county's oldest landmark.

One of the Civil War's most respected Confederate leaders, Lt. Gen. Jubal Early, second in command only to Gen. Stonewall Jackson, was born here. A foundation to restore his birth home was founded in 1995. Rocky Mount is full of many interesting historical buildings. One, the Claiborne House bed and breakfast inn, is open to the public. The Chamber of Commerce, in the courthouse downtown, can give you other pamphlets on historical tours and antique shopping opportunities.

Franklin County is also an outdoor paradise for hunting and fishing. Smith Mountain and Philpott lakes offer wonderful fishing if you have the patience and the right bait. Philpott, a 3,000-acre lake built by the U.S. Army Corps of Engineers, is more rustic than Smith Mountain and also offers boating, a beach and camping. Smith Mountain Lake has been called the best bass fishing lake in the country. For hunting, wild turkey proves to be the most popular game in the area.

The county's recreation department also offers a host of leisure-time sports and a county recreation program including the largest volleyball league in the state. Ferrum College also gives you a chance to root for championship teams in both men's and women's sports.

Another popular site in Franklin County is Whitey Taylor's Franklin County Speedway, with one of the best payoffs for a short track 75-lap race in the country, a $5,000 fund. A lot of race car fans travel to the Speedway to "go racin'."

Of all the counties surrounding the lake, Franklin's housing costs and taxes are generally the lowest, excluding its lakefront property. Farm land, scarce in so many areas of the Blue Ridge, is plentiful here. You're within easy commuting distance of either the Roanoke Valley or Martinsville, a furniture and knitting mill area with great furniture outlets (Stanleytown and Bassett) and the Tultex (sweatsuit) outlet stores. Franklin County's low taxes attract a lot of manufacturing industry. Cabinet makers, such as the 50-year-old MW Company and Cooper Wood Products, call the county home.

When you're between stops visit the land between the lakes. Whether you play, shop or visit one of its national attractions, you'll find plenty to fill up your time. For more information, contact the Franklin County Chamber of Commerce at 124 E. Court Street, P.O. Box 158, Rocky Mount 24151; (540) 483-9542.

New River Valley Region

The academically stimulating, scenic and mountainous New River Valley of Virginia is one of the most steadily growing areas of the Blue Ridge. It includes Montgomery County and the towns of Blacksburg and Christiansburg, the city of Radford, and Floyd, Giles and Pulaski counties. Although all are in the same area, you couldn't find a more diverse cultural group. The common thread again is the sheer beauty of their environment.

From the '70s to 1990, the New River Valley's population grew by nearly a fourth, to 152,720. People just keep on coming, and few ever leave. That's due to the presence of Virginia Tech, Virginia's largest university with 22,000 students, as well as Radford University's 8,000 students. Every year, scores of mountain-struck students are smitten by the New River Valley Flu, a curious mental illness that causes them to turn down lucrative jobs in the big city and vow to flip hamburgers or do whatever they have to in order to stay.

Blacksburg was named by Rand McNally as one of the top 20 places to live in the United States. A publication for mature adults names it as one of the best retirement spots in the country. The reasons why are diverse but mostly involve the winning combination of a scenic mountain vacation land and extraordinary cultural enrichment from its multinational university population.

An interesting historical fact is the New River is actually old — really old! According to legend it's the second-oldest river in the world; only Egypt's historic Nile is older. The 300 million-year-old river is an anomaly because it flows from south to north and cuts through the Alleghenies from east to west. The New River is 320 miles long from its headwaters near Blowing Rock, North Carolina, to the point in West Virginia where it tumultuously joins the Gauley River to form some of the best whitewater rafting in the East. Outfitters at the Gauley River Gorge regularly host celebrities and nearby Washington politicians, such as Ted Kennedy, who are looking for a refreshing crash of water instead of a staggering crush of paper.

Unlike the populous Nile River area, the New River Valley was a vast, empty land with no permanent inhabitants when the first white explorers saw the area in 1654. Drapers Meadow near Blacksburg is regarded as the first New

River settlement. Germans in Prices Fork and Dunkards in Radford established themselves about the same time. Native Americans ventured in only to hunt.

For the first settlers, the natives were a threat greater than cold or starvation. Bands of Shawnees periodically would sweep in to kill settlers and destroy their homes. One such episode — a 1755 massacre of many Drapers Meadow residents — became the inspiration for a play. In the attack, Mary Draper Ingles and Betty Robinson Draper were taken hostage; Mary escaped and found her way home by following the New River. Her riveting saga, *The Long Way Home*, is re-created each summer on an outdoor stage in Radford. It is acted out at the homestead where Ingles and her husband eventually lived. Until her death in 1988, Ingles' great-great-great-granddaughter, Mary Louise Jeffries, who lived on the homestead, played the part of Ingles' mother, Elenor Draper.

The New River Valley has an exciting textbook history that's matched by its history of research and development. Virginia Tech's IBM 3090 supercomputer was the first in the nation to be fully integrated with a university's computing network and made generally available to faculty and students. It's a fact there are more computers than telephones on campus; *The National Enquirer* once described Blacksburg as a village that had gone computer berserk.

Virginia Tech's Corporate Research Center has 500 employees looking into everything from why illnesses can affect the immune system, very important to AIDS virus research, to robotics and fiber optics, all on the same 120-acre site. All total, $100 million is spent each year by Virginia Tech researchers, many of whom enjoy a national reputation. Business and industry are the largest users of the Center and often bring their problems for analysis by some of the nation's greatest minds.

Here is a brief overview of the New River Valley's communities, with a short history and current attractions, many of which can be found outlined in detail in other chapters.

Blacksburg

The largest town in Virginia, Blacksburg (population 35,000) sits majestically on a mountain plateau between two of nature's masterpieces, the Blue Ridge Mountains of Virginia and the great Alleghenies.

The growing town has a national recognition as an ideal community, charming, but with a constant flow of professors and students who lend to it most of its culture. Rand McNally has rated Blacksburg in the top 20 places for both quality of life and retirement. Newcomers, students and others are easily and quickly assimilated into the town's uniquely wonderful, abundant social life.

Touring Broadway shows, well-known speakers and popular musicians appear regularly on campus. Several university performing arts groups, the Audubon Quartet and Theatre Arts Program, are recognized nationally. Tech's NCAA Division I basketball and football teams often appear in postseason contests, and tailgating is *the* event every autumn. You've never seen anything until you see the enthusiasm (and the traffic!) when the Tech Hokies meet the University of Virginia Cavaliers.

These glowing quality-of-life reports can be attributed to the sprawling presence of Virginia Tech, its students and

5,000 employees and its innumerable cultural offerings, many of which are free to the Blacksburg community. It would be difficult to find another community in Virginia with as many professionals of every type, from educators to seafood industry experts. One of its most famous, Prof. James Robertson (see the Civil War chapter and his New River Valley profile) was named the foremost Civil War historian in America by the United Daughters of the Confederacy.

Tech's outreach into the community through its Extension Service and other programs affects the quality of life across Virginia. While businesses are sending their problems to researchers, local veterinarians, for example, routinely send their toughest cases to Tech's Veterinary School.

However, Tech wasn't always the town's main focal point. Blacksburg's name comes from the William Black family, who contributed acreage after Blacksburg was granted a town charter in 1798. For 75 years the town was known as a quiet and pleasant place to live. Then, in 1872, Dr. Henry Black petitioned the General Assembly to establish a land-grant university in his town. The university opened with one building and 43 students.

Since then the town-gown relationship has created a community that combines a small-town atmosphere with big-city sophistication. Shopping malls and Blacksburg's active downtown offer many things you usually see only in places like Washington, D.C. Yet the pace of life is relaxed. You won't see any smog to speak of, smell many fumes or be bothered by excessive noise. Blacksburg takes its quality of life seriously. Its town council is mostly made up, traditionally, of Tech

educators who put their theories into practice.

Amidst all this heady academia, there's a universal love for recreation. You can immerse yourself in all kinds of outdoor fun within minutes. Floating down the New River with an innertube and cooler is a popular pastime. Swim in Blacksburg's municipal pool, which sits on a ledge overlooking the spectacular mountain range, or hike in the forest and sightsee along the Blue Ridge Parkway.

Transportation is efficient, with a terrific bicycle path reminiscent of big-city parks. The National Association of Public Transit ranks Blacksburg's municipal bus system as the best in the nation for its size. The heavily used Virginia Tech Airport sees many corporate jets.

As one of the fastest-growing, progressive communities in Virginia, many more people come to Blacksburg than leave. And, with all the area has to offer, that's liable to remain the trend for a long, long time. For more information, contact the Blacksburg Chamber of Commerce at 141 Jackson Street, Blacksburg 24060; (540) 552-4061.

Christiansburg

Christiansburg, Montgomery County's seat and the fourth-largest town in Virginia, is a charming, historic town anchoring a county population of 73,913. The county's rural villages of Shawsville and Riner are equally quaint. Va. 8 W. connects the county to the 469-mile-long Blue Ridge Parkway.

A quiet river that flows under Main Street (the Wilderness Trail) marks the continental divide, where flowing groundwater changes its course toward the Ohio-Mississippi river system.

The last legal gun duel in this country, the Lewis-McHenry, was fought in Christiansburg's renovated Cambria historic district. Depot Street, location of the Christiansburg Depot Museum, was the site of the depot burned in 1864 by the Union Army. The Cambria Emporium, built in 1908, is now the site of a fabulous antique mall with its own antique General Store.

The town's skyline is dotted with history including the steeples of Old Methodist Church, built sometime in the early 19th century; Christiansburg Presbyterian, c. 1853; and Schaeffer Memorial Baptist, erected in 1884.

Christiansburg's founder was Col. William Christian, an Irish Colonial settler. It served as an outpost on the Wilderness Trail, opened by Daniel Boone as the gateway to the west for settlers such as Davy Crockett. In 1866 the legendary Booker T. Washington of nearby Franklin County supervised the Christiansburg Industrial School for black children.

The northern portion of Montgomery County contains nearly 20,000 acres of the Jefferson National Forest. The Bikecentennial and Appalachian trails pass through the county. Between Blacksburg and Christiansburg, on U.S. 460, is the 90-acre Montgomery County Park, one of the area's many recreation spots. Facilities here include a swimming pool, bathhouse, fitness trail and picnic area. In all, the county has four 18-hole golf courses, 68 outdoor and five indoor tennis courts, 18 swimming pools, 37 ballfields and numerous playgrounds.

An added plus for the area is that real estate, both land and houses, costs significantly less than it does in Blacksburg. For the same money you can get so much more, with a fantastic quality of life as well.

Floyd County

Follow Route 8 south from Christiansburg and you'll find yourself in Floyd County (population 12,005). Just as movie stars are attracted to Charlottesville, '60s-era holdouts have been migrating to Floyd for the past 30 years. Their tie-dyed counterculture communes nestle quietly along with small farms in a county that promotes an employer of six (Chateau Morrisette Winery) as one of its major industries. Many residents live quietly off the land.

Another employer makes gasohol, touted by some since the '70s gas crisis as the only way to fuel autos. Other promotional county material outlines SIRIUS (Solar Innovative Republic for Independent United Survival) in Earthships, a planned counterculture community in Riner with restricted living. SIRIUS accepts you only after you've been interviewed and analyzed according to what you can offer the community and humanity. Call them at (540) 763-2651 for a video showing the property and discussing the concept, which is based on homes with three-foot-thick rammed earth walls and inspiration, the latter furnished by author Mike Reynolds' books *Earthship, Vol. I and II* and *A Coming of Wizards*.

Just don't go to Floyd actively looking for the counterculture. They have ingratiated themselves to the local farmers with their true sense of community spirit and are safely tucked away, bothering no one and expecting the same treatment, in the hills of Floyd. The followers of this alternative lifestyle are most visible elsewhere, actually, at regional arts and crafts shows, where they sell their wares ranging from twisted grapevine baskets to tie-dyed and batik clothing and pottery.

However, you don't have to leave Floyd to buy their wares.

One of the most prolific and amazing arts and crafts stores in the Blue Ridge, New Mountain Mercantile, 6 miles off the Blue Ridge Parkway on Locust Street, is the central location for area craftspeople to display and sell. You can spend hours investigating the building, art gallery and upstairs Byrd's Walden Pond Products, which offer self-help tapes and herbal body care, among other back-to-the-earth products.

Locals also can be found hanging out at the Blue Ridge Restaurant, in an early-1900s bank building, and Pine Tavern Restaurant and Lodge, a comfortable country inn where the fine food includes vegetarian fare.

The most famous regional landmark for both locals and tourists is the inimitable Cockram's General Store, where every Friday is a hoedown! During the day, the store sells the likes of corn cob jelly and local crafts. There's no admission for the Friday Night Jamboree with pure mountain music and dancing and a fun, friendly family atmosphere. Next door is the largest distributor of bluegrass and old-time music in the world. Other places that endear Floyd County to shoppers seeking the wild and wonderful are Schoolhouse Fabrics, housed in what was once an 1846 school; Brookfield Christmas Tree Plantation, a national shipper of holiday trees; and Chateau Morrisette Winery and Le Chien Noir Restaurant in Meadows of Dan (see the Shopping and Arts and Culture chapters for the whole scoop).

The most famous national landmark here is the picturesque Mabry Mill Blue Ridge Parkway Visitors Center, campground and recreation area. The restaurant here is quite good. The real feast, however, is one for the senses at the old-time, water-powered grist mill and interpretive historical buildings. This is usually the first place western Virginians take internationals for a true taste of American history and beauty.

The history of Floyd is actually rather sketchy, according to its Chamber of Commerce. Early land surveys showed an attempt to settle the area in 1740. The county was officially formed from Montgomery County in 1831. Floyd's original name was Jacksonville, named for Andrew Jackson, our nation's seventh president. Incorporated in 1858, the town changed its name to Floyd in 1896, although there's no official reason why.

When you visit the New River Valley, take a day to check out Floyd County, mingle with the locals, see some terrific arts and crafts and listen to some of the best bluegrass and gospel you'll ever hear. Floyd County truly is a sightseer's delight and photographer's paradise with the Blue Ridge Parkway's misty mountain views and miles of split-log fences. A map is smart when traveling Floyd's miles of rural, obscure back roads. You can receive this map and other information from the Floyd County Chamber of Commerce, P.O. Box 510, Floyd 24091; (540) 745-4407.

Giles County

If you love dramatic mountain scenery, don't miss Giles County, especially the autumn vista from U.S. 460 traveling south from Blacksburg. Giles County (population 16,366) is a mountain haven of forests, cliffs, cascading waterfalls, fast-flowing creeks and streams and, of course, the scenic New River. Its county seat, Pearisburg, is one of only two towns on the Maine-to-Georgia Appalachian Trail. Of the four covered bridges left in the Blue Ridge, two are in Giles County at Sinking Creek (see the Other Attractions chapter).

Giles County is a paradise for the lover of the outdoors. Whether your preference is for golfing a challenging emerald-green course, fly casting in an ice-cold mountain stream for trout, canoeing the New River's white water or hiking, Giles has it.

Giles' most scenic attraction and one of the most-photographed in the Blue Ridge is the Cascades waterfall, which awaits you at the end of a rigorous, 3-mile hiking trail in Pembroke (see our Recreation chapter); the trek is not recommended for small children. After your uphill pull, which seems to last forever, your excellent reward for this adventure is bathing at the foot of the tumbling, 60-foot-high waterfall.

A tamer destination, and just as much fun for kids, is Castle Rock Recreation Area, for golf, tennis and swimming. Or rent a canoe and kayak (see our Recreation chapter).

Giles County's most famous attraction is the fabulous Mountain Lake Hotel and Resort, set atop the second-highest mountain in Virginia and overlooking the town of Blacksburg, miles away (see our Resorts and Restaurants chapters). For years, it has been known for the beauty of its stone lodge and its gourmet cuisine. Of late, it is best known for the movie *Dirty Dancing*, filmed here as the epitome of early '60s-era great resorts

Another popular scenic destination is the attractive village of Newport, with its country store and steepled church. The quaint hamlet nestles at the foot of Gap Mountain at Sinking Creek.

Formed in 1806, the county was named for Gov. William Giles. In addition to tourism, Giles County's biggest employer is the Hoechst-Celanese Plant in Narrows. A bedroom community to many professionals, the county has a school system with one of Virginia's lowest student-to-teacher ratios — 16-to-1 — emphasizing a personal approach to instruction.

In addition to far-flung outdoor recreation Giles also offers the culture of its historic Andrew Johnston House, Giles Little Theatre and great antique shopping. A lot of Virginia Tech educators and professionals have discovered Giles, so you may have trouble finding available farmland. However, many gorgeous mountaintop chalets and homes are on the market at any given time. Contact the New River Board of Realtors. For more information on Giles County, contact the Chamber of Commerce at P.O. Box 666, Pearisburg, Virginia 24134, (540) 921-5000.

Radford

For quality of life, Radford (population 15,940) has the whole country beat — that is, if you want to stake it on longevity. The late Margaret Skeete, who died there in 1993 at the age of 114, was considered the oldest person in the United States and was listed in *The Guinness Book of Records*. Maybe living beside one of the oldest rivers in the world, the New River, had something to do with Skeete's remarkably long life. The river, which flows through this university city, adds something special to its quality of life.

Radford, the region's only independent city, was incorporated in 1892 and grew to be an important rail division point. It also became the home of Radford University, enrollment 8,000, and is the site of Virginia's only outdoor historical drama, *The Long Way Home*, depicting the famous story of Mary Draper Ingles' escape from the Shawnees.

Another of Radford's major attractions is 58-acre Bisset Park, with a walking trail beside nearly a mile of the tree-lined New River. This perfect park is capped off with a gazebo, swimming pool, several playgrounds and a tennis court. Colorful hot-air balloons also take off from the park. If you were to design the recreational area of your dreams, this would probably be it!

Radford's energetic downtown is a Main Street community and has seen numerous unique small businesses start up, many serving the student population. To encourage small business development, Radford even publishes its own brochure, "New Business Start-up Guide."

The impact of Radford University on the city is comparable to that of neighboring Virginia Tech's on the town of Blacksburg. The Dedmon Center, a $13 million athletic facility, is an unbelievable community gem featuring an air-supported fabric roof atop a gymnasium and natorium. The adjacent grounds have several softball, soccer, field hockey and flag football fields. Radford is also fanatic about its high school Bobcats' sports teams.

Other noted Radford facilities include 2,000-square-foot Flossie Martin Art Gallery, one of the Blue Ridge region's finest. A guest professor program has brought in entertainer Steve Allen, civil rights activist Jesse Jackson, Nobel Prize winner Elie Wiesel, Egypt's widowed Jihan Sadat (who displayed her own personal Egyptian art collection) and columnist Jack Anderson.

The city also has an outstanding academic tradition with its primary and secondary schools. Its school system, heavily influenced by college educated parents, has been nominated by the Commonwealth of Virginia as one of the nation's best.

Radford's environment beside the sometimes placid, sometimes raging New River is symbolic of Radford's dynamic quality of life. For more information, contact the Radford Chamber of Commerce at 1126 Norwood Street, Radford 24141; (540) 639-2202.

Pulaski

The town of Pulaski and Pulaski County (population 34,496), named for Count Pulaski of Poland, a Revolutionary War hero, has attractions ranging from the historic sites to vast water recreation and sports, including a speedway and farm baseball team.

Old Newbern, Pulaski's first county seat and the only Virginia town totally encompassed in a historic district, is recognized by both the National Historic Register and the Virginia Landmarks Commission. You can tour the Wilderness Road Museum, treat yourself to ice cream at the old-time soda fountain at PJ's Carousel gift shop and village, where the kids can ride the 1923 carousel from the Cincinnati Zoo, and then stop by the local historic restaurant, Valley Pike Inn, for a family meal (see our Shopping and Restaurants chapters).

Pulaski's newly renovated historic Main Street is also a fun stroll past 20 charming shops and quaint restaurants, mostly examples of Victorian architecture. Pulaski's downtown also is blessed with the New River Valley's cultural gem, its Fine Arts Center, which is housed in an 1898 Victorian commercial building (see our Arts and Culture chapter).

Outdoor enthusiasts will feel right at home at Claytor Lake. Like its younger counterpart, Smith Mountain Lake, Claytor was formed in 1939 to generate electricity for Appalachian Power Company. It is now the centerpiece of a 472-acre state park that's a haven for boaters, anglers, horseback riders, campers and swimmers (its white sand beach will make you think you're at the ocean). Nearby is a spectacular condominium development, Mallard Point. The county has another nice outdoor area, Gatewood Reservoir Park (see our Recreation chapter).

Sports fans will appreciate the Pulaski County Speedway, on U.S. 11. Open early April through late September, it is a NASCAR-Winston racing series track seating 10,000.

Pulaski County also is home to the highly respected New River Community College in Dublin. The New River Valley Fair also is held in Dublin each summer and offers such charming events as a children's pet show.

Pulaski County workers also have an impressive mix of job opportunities. The Volvo White Truck Corp. is one of the largest employers; others are Burlington Industries, Western Electric and the Pulaski Furniture Company.

For more information, contact the Pulaski County Chamber of Commerce at P.O. Box 169, Pulaski 24301-0169; (540) 480-1991.

Alleghany Highlands Region

Alleghany County

Lovers of the outdoors, sports, antiques, railroads, history and good food can find their favorite things in Alleghany County (population 27,820). The county, situated on the Allegheny mountain range and half-covered by the George Washington National Forest, is the western gateway to Virginia. This vacation playground filled with gorgeous scenery is next door to wild, wonderful West Virginia's Greenbrier County, home of the world-famous Greenbrier Resort.

Before the formation of Alleghany County, property records were provided from Fincastle in Botetourt County, a two-day trip. So, in 1822, the County of Alleghany was formed, named after the mountains in which they lie, although the mountains are spelled differently than the county name.

Its county seat, Covington, was named in honor of Gen. Leonard Covington, hero of the War of 1812 and confidante to James Madison and Thomas Jefferson. Clifton Forge, the county's other populous area, was named for its iron production; it contributed cannons and cannonballs to the Civil War effort. During the Civil War, Alleghany County furnished more soldiers to the Confederacy than it had voters and suffered greatly in the war, since it was located next to West Virginia, which joined the Union.

After the war Clifton Forge was selected by the Chesapeake and Ohio Railway as the site of its new depot. The coming of the railroad triggered economic growth here, and in 1906 Clifton Forge received its city charter. Natural resources have always been Alleghany County's main industry; hemp, used in rope production, was an early product. But the biggest boost to industrial progress here came in 1899, when the West Virginia Pulp and Paper Co. decided to put a mill in Covington. Both the railroad and Westvaco Paper Mill continue to play important roles in the county's culture and economy.

As expected, many of its attractions are tied to its history. In the charming historic city of Clifton Forge, the C&O Historical Society Archives preserves the railroad's artifacts and equipment. Also worth a visit is the Alleghany Highlands Arts and Crafts Center, displaying fine regional arts and crafts (see our Arts and Culture chapter).

Lucy Selina Furnace stacks, more than 100 feet tall, are reminders of the area's 19th-century iron industry. A stunning Victorian mansion built by the owner of the rich iron mines has been turned into the charming Longdale Bed & Breakfast. Local lore says a staff of eight was required just to maintain its gardens.

Nearby is the Longdale Recreation Area, which features miles of mountain trails, camping and sand-beach swimming. All are located off I-64's Exit 10 on Va. 269 in Longdale. Roaring Run Recreation Area, the site of the ruins of an 1838 iron furnace, is another wonderful place to hike and picnic. It's off U.S. 220 S.

Other historic points of interest are Fort Young, a reconstruction of the original French and Indian War fort off I-64, Exit 4, near Covington. Lovers of architecture will enjoy seeing Oakland Grove Presbyterian Church, which served as a hospital during the Civil War. It can be seen in Selma off I-64, Exit 7.

Water has also played a role in the history and life of the county. The unassuming, unmarked source of Quibell water, which rivals Perrier nationally, is next to a cattle grate crossing near to Sweet Chalybeate Springs. The water is trucked away daily for bottling in Roanoke.

Sweet Chalybeate (pronounced Ka-LEE-bee) Pools and gazebo off Va. 311 near the West Virginia border dates back 150 years as a great pre-Civil War resort. It was renovated after lying in waste following the demise of the Civil War aristocracy. The pools now offer bathers the most highly carbonated mineral water in the world. Locals swear by the water's healing powers and many either take a dip or drink its water daily. For more information, write to them at Va. 3, Sweet Chalybeate, Covington 24426.

Outdoorsy fun awaits at several other Alleghany County sites. Twelve miles of water entice visitors to Lake Moomaw, a relatively new lake formed for power generation 19 miles from Covington. Signs point the way. Residents and visitors have taken advantage of water skiing, boating, fishing and swimming. Douthat State Park's 50-acre lake also offers a beach, bathhouse, boating and excellent trout fishing. Other facilities include a visitors center, restaurant and lodge as well as cabins, campgrounds and miles of hiking trails. And the world's largest pump storage facility in the world, Virginia Power's Back Creek Pump Storage Station, Call (540) 279-2389, is also worth seeing.

For obvious reasons, anglers find Paint Bank State Trout Hatchery on Route 311 an interesting place to visit. It is open daily from 7:30 AM until 4 PM. Rock lovers will want to visit Rainbow Gap or Iron Gate Gorge, which create a geologist's paradise a mile south of Clifton Forge on U.S. 220. For 12 million years, the Jackson River has been working on this masterpiece.

Across the border in West Virginia, the attractions are overwhelming. The big one, of course, is the world-famous Greenbrier Resort (see our Resorts chapter). The grounds alone are magnificent;

Photo: Nelson County Division of Tourism

Crabtree Falls in Nelson County is a series of cascades.

the resort welcomes visitors, even if you don't spend the night.

Also close to the West Virginia border, but still in Virginia, is a great dining experience in a place called Crows. If you blink, you'll miss it, so keep a look out for the rustic sign with the eagle, indicating Eagle's Nest Restaurant (see our Restaurants chapter). Built beside a rolling waterfall, the restaurant has gourmet food so good that corporate officials flying into the area from around the world are some of its most loyal customers.

Several other West Virginia attractions within an hour's drive are north up W.Va. 92. Blue Bend swimming hole in Alvon, one of the best in the Blue Ridge, is one of them. Lake Sherwood, farther up Route 92, is nice too and rents paddleboats. The Cass Scenic Railroad is close to Marlinton, as is Snowshoe Ski Resort. The town of Lewisburg, cultured and sophisticated, is also worth a visit for its charming downtown shops and Carnegie Hall, built by the same industrialist tycoon as its more famous counterpart.

The people are friendly and downright glad to see you in Alleghany County. Brochures of all the area's attractions can be picked up at the Jerry's Run Virginia Visitor's Center at I-64's Exit 1. Better yet, contact the Alleghany Highlands Chamber of Commerce at 403 E. Ridgeway Street, Clifton Forge 24422; (540) 962-2178.

Bath County

Nestled between Alleghany and Highland counties and bordering West Virginia, Bath County (population 4,799) doesn't even have a stoplight. What it does have are pleasures of every kind for its visitors, whether they're on a budget or staying at the world-famous Homestead resort.

The bubbly mineral springs, or baths, that gave the county its name are a source of pleasure for visitors. Bath County was founded in 1745 by pioneers of mostly Scotch-Irish descent, most notably John Lewis, who settled at Fort Lewis. One son, Charles, died in the historic Battle of Point Pleasant in 1774. The other son, John, built the first hotel on the site of the present Homestead resort in 1766. His structure was destroyed by fire in 1901. In the meantime, M. E. Ingalls, president of the Chesapeake and Ohio Railroad, bought the site and the modern era of the resort was launched.

Some historic sites in the county are the Warwickton Mansion Bed and Breakfast at Hidden Valley, site of the movie *Sommersby*; the Anderson Cottage in Warm Springs; and Windy Cove Presbyterian Church at Millboro.

The real history of the county, however, lies in its springs, which have been drawing people for more than 200 years. Wrote one visitor in 1750, "The spring water is very clear and warmer than new milk." Thermal springs are found at Warm Springs, Hot Springs and Bolar Springs, at temperatures ranging from 77 degrees F to 106 degrees F. They flow at rates ranging from 2,500 to 5,000 gallons a minute. The water has a soft fizz of tickling bubbles, and taking of the baths is like lowering yourself into a warm vat of Quibell, whose source springs are in Alleghany County.

Public pools have been open at Warm Springs since 1761 and look today much as they did then. The covered pools were the cultural center of the rich and famous. Thomas Jefferson "took the waters" here for his health, as did the frail Mrs. Robert

E. Lee (she had crippling arthritis), whose chair, used to lower her into the pool, is still on display at the ladies' pool.

Thus, the stage was set for the aristocracy to visit this scenic land, which is nearly 90 percent forest. That's how the internationally known Homestead resort, detailed in our Resorts chapter, came into being. As Bath County celebrated its Bicentennial in 1991, the Ingalls family celebrated its 100th year of running the famous Homestead resort. It was purchased in 1993 by Resorts International of Dallas, Texas, and is undergoing extensive renovation. The Homestead offers the superlatives of everything — recreation, dining, shopping, recreation — in a setting of style and grandeur equalled only by its neighbor, The Greenbrier, in nearby White Sulphur Springs, West Virginia.

The same crowd that goes to The Homestead are regulars at an absolutely serendipitous place, Garth Newel Music Center. The sound of critically acclaimed chamber music wafts through the mountains throughout the year, attracting cultured people from around the world. You never know which celebrity you'll see there taking in a concert while staying at The Homestead or with friends at a country estate. Locals leave them alone, though.

You don't need to be rich, however, to really enjoy your stay in Bath County. The county has many nice bed and breakfast inns and two outstanding ones, Meadow Lane Lodge and Fort Lewis Lodge. At Fort Lewis, hunting is the autumn and winter mainstay, and spring and summer offer lazy tubing down the placid Cowpasture River, hiking and camping and Caryn Cowden's wonderful cooking. It's a wholesome, airy retreat the whole family will enjoy (see our Bed and Breakfast and County Inns chapter).

Dining is a pleasure here, as well. The Inn at Gristmill Square, restored by the Hirsh family, is the center of Warm Springs, with its dining, shops and lodging. More great shopping awaits at the Bacova Outlet (see our Shopping chapter).

Spelunkers will find adventures in Burnsville's large caverns and sunken caves, while the forests and mountains beckon those who hike, hunt, fish or ride. The George Washington National Forest, Gathright Game Management Area and Douthat State Park are in the county.

The Bath County Chamber of Commerce has visitors guide that will tell you everything you need to know about this natural, genteel land. Contact them at P.O. Box 718, Hot Springs 24445; (800) 628-8092.

Highland County

Nicknamed the Switzerland of Virginia, scenic Highland County (population 2,800) has more sheep than people, on land with a higher mean elevation than any county east of the Mississippi River.

Few places have preserved their surroundings and privacy so well. Even Highland County's official brochure invites businesses to locate here providing their "environment won't be endangered." One of the most influential conservation groups in America, the Ruffled Grouse Society, was founded here in 1961.

Highland County was established in 1847 from the counties of Bath and Pendleton, in what is now West Virginia. Its county seat, Monterey, sits 3,000 feet above sea level, while its western border in the Allegheny Mountains reaches elevations of 4,500.

Once the hunting grounds for the Shawnee, Highland was first entered by

European settlers in the 1700s, when it was still a part of Augusta County, which it remained until 1787. In the 10-year-long Indian War of 1754, the county was on the frontier. Highland men also made up the company that fought the Battle of Point Pleasant under the command of Col. Andrew Lewis.

An interesting note: German Gen. Erwin Rommel, the Desert Fox, visited Highland County prior to World War I so he could study Stonewall Jackson's military tactics at McDowell. Talk about biting the hand that feeds you! Later, Rommel used the same tactics against the United States and its allies.

To the visitor, Highland County is both beautiful and severe. Every March, this small population rallies to put on one of the top-20 festivals in America, the Highland County Maple Festival, which draws 70,000 over a two-weekend span. The festival takes you back to the time when tree sugar and tree 'lasses were found on every table, and when "opening" the trees and boiling down the sugar water were highland spring rituals. The tours and exhibits are both educational and enjoyable. Pancake (with maple syrup, of course) and trout suppers centered around the county seat of Monterey are unforgettable.

A Sugar Tour winds through some of the loveliest spots in Virginia, Va. routes 637 and 640. Maple sugar camps throughout the county welcome visitors to view the actual process of syrup-making, from tapping the trees to collecting the colorless, almost tasteless sugar water. Gathered in plastic buckets or by plastic tubing, the water is then boiled in kettles, pans or evaporators until a barrel is finally reduced to a gallon of pure maple syrup. The camp sites are Rexrode's Sugar Orchard, Puffenbarger's Sugar Orchard,

Sugar Tree Country Store & Sugar House and Eagle's Sugar Camp. Tour maps are provided at the festival. One of the best things about the festival is tasting and shopping for all the pure maple syrup goodies — sugar candy, donuts glazed with maple syrup and funnel cakes — available at a cost vastly below retail. Highland's downtown antique stores also open for the occasion. Most are clustered around the classic Victorian Highland Inn, a downtown landmark, c. 1904, that has been restored and is now on the National Register of Historic Places. Its 20 rooms are furnished with antiques.

The Maple Museum on U.S. 220, a mile south of Monterey, is another fun stop depicting the traditional skills in sugaring (see our Arts and Culture chapter).

Summers are as cool here as any in the East. One word of warning: If you're driving in from another part of the Blue Ridge, expect to find snow on the ground as late as April, since Highland County gets about 65 inches of the white stuff a year. Bring a jacket for the kids; the temperature will probably be at least 10 degrees colder than where you came from.

Outside of the maple culture, there are other interesting places to visit. If you want to see where many of those mouth-watering trout come from — and part of the reason behind this area's distinction as Trout Capital of the Eastern United States — visit the Virginia Trout Company, on U.S. 220 north of Monterey. In business for 35 years, the facility hatches rainbow trout from eggs and raises them to adulthood. You can fish for your own, buy them frozen or just watch them swim in the cold mountain water. The hatchery is open seven days a week, weekdays from 8 AM to 4 PM and weekends from 9 AM to 4 PM.

Shenandoah Valley Profile:
Rupert Cutler

Dr. Rupert Cutler may very well be the most interesting man in the Shenandoah Valley. He is definitely its most notable raconteur. If you've never before met a man who can talk to anybody, anywhere, about anything — meet Rupert Cutler.

Mostly, he talks about Virginia's Explore Park. Now in its second year, Explore has attracted the number of visitors projected for its first year and, 1995's hot and rainy weather not withstanding, probably will surpass that goal through extensive outreach to schools and the community. Even with layoffs

Dr. Rupert Cutler

caused by cost over-runs for its first year, an excellent, dedicated interpretive staff is on hand.

At first, Explore was going to be a zoo. Then it was going to be the Colonial Williamsburg of the Western frontier, with advice from an all-star cast of historians. The Explore Park that opened in 1994 bears little resemblance to any of the much-hyped and much-changed plans touted by its founders nine years and $30 million dollars ago.

The fact that Virginia's Explore Park, western Virginia's newest attraction, opened at all is a tribute to Cutler, a tall, physically fit 61-year-old whose low-key personality belies his determination and power of persuasion. After being drafted into the job of park director, Cutler seized the vision of the impossible task before him and shot every arrow from his political quiver to change the political boondoggle that was Explore into a viable attraction the public could identify with and buy into.

How Cutler, with a long pedigree of heading environmental causes, ended up in that position, as well as executive director of the Virginia Recreational Facilities Authority, was something even Cutler himself didn't expect. After being told of the project in the early '90s by its brilliant but controversial founder, Bern Ewert, Cutler asked to come aboard and offered to raise his own salary. Ewert was happy to oblige.

Cutler had something Ewert lacked: a diplomatic personality and experience raising funds for environmental causes within Washington, D.C.'s, inner sanctum. His most visible position was assistant secretary for Conservation, Research and Education under the Carter Administration.

From 1988 to 1990, Cutler was CEO of the 80,000-member Defenders of Wildlife. From 1984 to 1988, he was executive director of Population-Environment Balance, educating the public about the effects of population changes on the quality of life. Prior to that, he was senior vice president for programs and chapter relations for the National Audubon Society. The rest of his biography reads like a who's who of environmental causes.

Apart from his political finesse, Cutler's greatest gift is probably his ability to impart passion for Explore to everyone he meets, from the hunter in the woods to the wealthy matrons of Hunt Country. Cutler can talk the talk and walk the walk.

He talks about Explore in an educational image. So far, it consists of a reassembled 1830s farmstead with interpreters, garbed in native dress, acting out lives from that period of time. As funds are raised, more buildings will be reconstructed.

Cutler calls it "a living-history museum in a wilderness-like setting."

It seems everybody thought of a million reasons why Explore would never open. That was before they met Rupert Cutler and he told them a million reasons why it should. Every chance he got.

He's expecting 100,000 visitors a year, depending on the weather, of course.

While you're in Highland County, you also can see the Confederate Breastworks (breast-high trenches) built in 1862 by 4,000 Confederate troops as a defense against Union soldiers. They are at the top of Shenandoah Mountain on U.S. 250 at the Highland-Augusta County line.

Also on U.S. 250 east of McDowell is the McDowell Battlefield, where 4,500 Confederate troops under Gen. Stonewall Jackson defeated 2,268 Union soldiers in a bloody conflict in 1862. This engagement was the first victory in Jackson's famous Valley Campaign. Nearby McDowell Presbyterian Church was used as a hospital and soldiers are buried there.

People enjoy Highland as much for what is missing — traffic, pollution, noise and crowds — as for what is there. The pace is slow and the scenery, beautiful. It's considered the best place in Virginia to bird watch, and fans say species that have flown the coop from other parts of the state can still be found here.

If you feel like flying the coop yourself, come to Highland and slow down like the maple sugar in January. Contact the Highland County Chamber of Commerce at P.O. Box 250, Monterey 24465; (540) 468-2550.

Photo: Virginia Division of Tourism

A section of the Confederate line masses for attack during the re-enactment of the 1864 Battle of New Market.

Inside
The Civil War

It was, as the poet Walt Whitman described, "A strange, sad war." More Americans lost their lives in the Civil War (1861 to 1865) than in both world wars combined. No other state has suffered the trauma that Virginia endured in the Civil War, say some historians. Beginning with the war's first major battle at Bull Run (First Manassas) and ending with the surrender in the tiny, peaceful village of Appomattox Court House, 60 percent of the Civil War's battles were fought in Virginia.

Interest in the Civil War has never been keener. So many inquiries have been made that The Insiders Guides® Inc. and *Richmond Times Dispatch* have published a separate book, *The Insiders' Guide® to the Civil War in the Eastern Theater*, available for $12.95 in most bookstores.

The Old Dominion was one of the last states to leave the Union, but because it was the most exposed geographically of the seceding states, Virginia became the major battleground of the Civil War. One borderline Shenandoah Valley city, Winchester, changed hands from Confederate to Yankee no fewer than 72 times. Thousands of men, out of a strong sense of duty and honor, heeded the call to arms and never returned. Is it any wonder that, nearly 130 years later, the War Between the States is not forgotten? Certainly, it is not forgotten in the Blue Ridge, where generations of family farms and history

were laid waste, sometimes out of spite rather than necessity.

It is not unusual to find senior citizens who fondly remember former slaves called "Auntie" and "Uncle," revered as family and given plots of land on the family farm after they refused to leave their masters when they were freed. On the flip side, you can see some of the earliest tintype photos ever taken showing slaves whose backs bore ribbons of scars from the beatings they endured at the hands of their taskmasters. Who was in the right, and just what was the Civil War all about? Slavery alone?

The answer to those questions can be found in the Blue Ridge, the site not only of some of the bloodiest battles in the Civil War, but also home to one of the country's most noted Civil War scholars and authors. History professor James I. Robertson of Virginia Tech is past executive director of the U.S. Civil War Centennial Commission. His most recent book, *Civil War! America Becomes One Nation*, an illustrated history for young readers, probably best answers those questions in a way that young and old can clearly understand. Robertson, whose books have been nominated for the Pulitzer Prize, teaches a Civil War class that is one of the hottest tickets on campus. His enthusiasm for Civil War history comes as no surprise, since his great-grandfather was the great Confederate general Robert E. Lee's cook. Robertson's latest book takes into account the political and socio-economic mood of the 1860s and the events that set off a movement that the South anticipated would be over within weeks, but which, in fact, lasted four years and destroyed a way of life.

The fact that the Confederacy even survived for the duration of the war was in large measure due to the excellent military leadership of Virginia's Blue Ridge generals, Robert E. Lee and Thomas J. "Stonewall" Jackson. Jackson's nickname came, so the story goes, out of the battle of First Manassas. Gen. Barnard Bee of South Carolina pointed to Jackson's troops and shouted, "There stands Jackson like a stone wall." In addition to his legendary nickname, Jackson's Rebel yell became his battle signature. To this day, the U.S. Army regularly conducts "staff rides" into the Shenandoah Valley for its officers, following the course of Jackson's famed Foot Cavalry.

Tragically, according to Robertson, Northerners and Southerners were both fighting for the same thing: America, as each side interpreted what America should be. On the other hand, within time, the Civil War contributed to a stronger union of the United States of America, allowing it to withstand foreign leaders bent on conquering the world just 50 years later during World War I, followed by World War II. If the South had won the war, would the history of the 20th century have been drastically rewritten? Would we be speaking German today instead of English?

When discussing the role the Blue Ridge played in the Civil War, Robertson emphasizes the Shenandoah Valley's geographical position as a spear pointing into the North and as the "Breadbasket of the Confederacy." The number of major battles in the region attests to the constant wrenching for control of the Valley, which prompted Jackson, the "pious blue-eyed killer," to push his men so hard in the spring of 1862 that their shoes fell apart in the fields.

And who can ever forget the heartbreaking Battle of New Market, when the fateful day, May 15, 1864, is retraced and its startling events reenacted? On that rainy Sunday afternoon, 247 Virginia Military Institute cadets advanced side by side with veteran Civil War infantrymen into a hellish cannon and rifle fire. The soldiers forged onward with parade-ground precision, using each step to free the other from the furrows of mud caused by the heavy rainstorm.

The Confederate commander of Western Virginia, Major Gen. John C. Breckinridge, had enlisted the cadets to join his ragtag force of 4,500. The cadets marched forward, their muzzle-loading muskets slung over shoulders that were destined to bear a far heavier load, their VMI flag leading the way. Looming ahead was a battle that would go down in American history as one of the most valorous and one of the last Confederate victories in the Shenandoah Valley. As the smoke of the battle cleared, 10 cadets lay dead, including Cadet Thomas G. Jefferson, 17, descendant of our nation's third president. Another 47 cadets were wounded.

Visitors can relive this segment in American history by touring the New Market Battlefield Park and its museum, the Hall of Valor. Together, they honor these 247 brave young cadets. In the Hall of Valor are displays of Civil War muskets, uniforms, tintype photos, day-to-day accessories and a replica of the type cannon captured by the cadets. It is one of the most stirring of all the Blue Ridge Civil War

Photo: R. J. Reber

The Exchange Hotel, a restored railroad hotel that served as a Civil War hospital, is now an excellent Civil War Museum.

sites. Young and old alike are fascinated by its sense of history and urgency.

Beyond the Shenandoah Valley, Southwest Virginia was also a region of vital importance to the Confederacy, points out Robertson. Through it ran the Virginia and Tennessee Railroad, the only lifeline between Richmond and the West. The lead mines at Austinville, the salt works at Saltville and the coal mines throughout the region provided the embattled South with essential natural resources. The May 1864 Battle of Cloyd's Mountain near Dublin in Pulaski County remains the largest engagement ever fought in Southwest Virginia. A future president, Col. Rutherford B. Hayes, was a hero of the battle. Today only a marker commemorates the site.

Roanoker Gary C. Walker, author of *The War in Southwest Virginia and Hunter's Fiery Raid Through Virginia's Valleys*, outlines in great detail the way the war was fought in this region of Virginia. He captures the mood of the area, geographically a third of Virginia, which broke away to join the Yankees and form its own state, West Virginia. Walker's book on Maj. Gen. David Hunter, known for his unquenchable hatred of slavery, shows how Hunter wreaked his vengeance upon Southwest Virginia before its secession. States Walker, "Civilian property became an official military target. Both men and women were arrested without charge. Routinely, Southern ladies and their crying babies were forced from their homes with nothing but the clothes on their bodies. Their manor houses were plundered and burned before their horrified eyes." In Hunter's books, one can almost smell the smoke, feel the perspiration drip from the brow and hear the heart pound as the lines clashed and the men fell with hideous and gaping wounds.

Walker also is a consultant to the growing number of hobbyists of Civil War battle re-enactments, held all along the East Coast. The most recent Blue Ridge addition is Roanoke County's re-enactment of Hunter's Raid at Green Hill Park, which was held in the summer of 1995. Also during 1995 Civil War buffs can see a re-enactment at Cedar Creek in Middletown (see the listing under "Middletown.")

The Battle of Cedar Creek in 1864 marked the end of Confederate dominion over the Shenandoah Valley and its essential food supplies. It also marked the end of famed Gen. Jubal Early's career and of the war-weariness that had plagued the North. This battle also put to rest any hopes the Confederacy may have had for a negotiated peace with the Union. The victory freed Gen. Philip Sheridan and his men, including Gen. George Custer (who had the misfortune of tangling with Chief Sitting Bull at the Battle of Little Big Horn) to play crucial roles in the final battles of the Civil War the following spring.

The Cedar Creek Battlefield Foundation is fighting to save the battlefield's 158 acres from development. So far $375,000 of the $450,000 needed has been raised. If the rest is not forthcoming, the land will be developed. In the meantime,

the history preservationists are hoping their visitors center, book shop and annual battle re-enactments will help stave off the bulldozers. Their October event includes open camps, drills, dress parades, demonstrations of military and civilian life and a special education symposium.

For schedules of battle re-enactments throughout the country, write the Camp Chase Gazette, P.O. Box 707, Marietta, Ohio 45750. If you've never seen one of these events, you're in for a real experience. The men who do this take it very seriously, as does Vinton attorney Bruce Mayer. Since taking up his hobby eight years ago, Mayer has appeared in the movies, *Glory* and *Lincoln*, in a National Geographic TV special and in the TV film, *North South*. His 15-man unit performed at a birthday party for actor and Civil War buff Richard Dreyfuss at Smith Mountain Lake during the filming of *What About Bob?* Mayer is also in *Killer Angels*, based on the Battle of Gettysburg.

Mayer says authenticity is a must. Sack cloth, shell jackets and frock coats are re-

Photo: New Market Battlefield Historical Park

This life-size centerpiece in the Hall of Valor represents the Union and Confederate artillery men who fought in the Battle of New Market.

quired of all participants on the field. Eyeglasses must be of period construction. Only period footwear is allowed, preferably mule hide with square toes and wooden pegs. Uniforms must be woolen. Many of the soldiers carry their own original binoculars, pistols and bayonet rifles. No, they don't use real bullets, but they do use real gunpowder.

Regardless of whose side, if any, you believe was right in the War Between the States, hundreds of monuments, museums and battle re-enactments await you in the Blue Ridge of Virginia. The region also has more than 250 historic markers that are on-the-spot history lessons. In the pages that follow, we list only actual sites where you can see or do something. For a complete list of Virginia Civil War battlefields and markers, write the state of Virginia at 1021 East Cary Street, Richmond, Virginia 23219 or call (804) 786-2051. A great guide is Robertson's book, *Civil War Sites in Virginia, a Tour Guide,* published by the University Press of Virginia. And our sister publication, *The Insiders' Guide® to the Civil War in the Eastern Theater,* provides 15 tours that anyone interested in the Civil War — including kids — will enjoy.

Unless otherwise noted, admission is free of charge.

Shenandoah Valley Region

Winchester

GEN. STONEWALL JACKSON'S HEADQUARTERS
515 N. Braddock St.   (540) 667-3242
Open April-Oct. 10 AM to 4 PM Mon.-Sat.,
12-4 PM Sun; weekends in Nov. and Dec.
Adults $3.50, children $1.75

From this brick house, Jackson commanded his forces in defense of the strategic Shenandoah Valley. The French-style house contains artifacts of Jackson, his cavalry chief Gen. Turner Ashby and others.

STONEWALL AND NATIONAL CEMETERIES
Several blocks east of business district

Buried in these two cemeteries are 3,000 Confederate and 4,500 Union soldiers killed in nearby battles. National is one of the largest national cemeteries in Virginia.

Middletown

BELLE GROVE PLANTATION
Cedar Creek Battlefield   (540) 869-2028
Open daily March-Nov. 10 AM-4 PM
Mon.-Sat., 1-5 PM Sun.
Adults $5, ages 13-17 $2.50, ages 6-12 $2

Spared during the Civil War even though it served as Gen. Philip Sheridan's headquarters during the decisive 1864 Battle of Cedar Creek, Belle Grove was built between 1794 and 1797 with the design assistance of Thomas Jefferson. James and Dolley Madison honeymooned there. Today, the house and grounds exemplify the home and working farm of a wealthy Federalist planter.

CEDAR CREEK BATTLEFIELD FOUNDATION RE-ENACTMENT
Cedar Creek Battlefield   (540) 869-2064
Adults $8, children 12 and younger free

On October 21 and 22, 1995, the Cedar Creek Battlefield Foundation, which is striving to save the 154-acre historic battlefield from development, will stage a Civil War Living History Weekend. Re-enactments of the battle will take place at 3 PM Saturday and 1:30 PM Sunday. Various drills, dress parades and military and civilian demonstrations will be presented throughout the weekend. Sutlers (vendors) Row, presented by the Frederick Ladies Relief Society, will be a living history in Belle Grove. All proceeds go to the preservation of the battlefield. For more information write: P.O. Box 229, Middletown,Virginia 22645.

CEDAR CREEK RELIC SHOP
7841 Main St.   (540) 869-5207
Open Fri.-Sat. 10 AM-5 PM, Sun. 11 AM-5 PM

Cedar Creek Relics has the largest collection of authentic Civil War relics for sale in the Shenandoah Valley. This includes swords, bayonets, carbines, muskets, buttons, plates, artillery shells, tintypes, documents and other relics. The store also sells tapes and books. Civil War and antique weapons are bought and sold.

Strasburg

HUPP'S HILL BATTLEFIELD PARK & STUDY CENTER
U.S. 11 S.   (540) 465-5884
Open 10 AM-5 PM daily summers; other seasons 10 AM-4 PM Mon., Wed., Thur., Fri.; 11 AM-5 PM Sat. and Sun.
Adults $3.50, ages 7 to 16 $2

A living history learning experience, Hupp's Hill features the third-largest collection of Confederate currency in the world, as well as a 100-foot, hand-painted mural depicting the history of the Civil War and the world's largest map on the Battle of Cedar Creek. The museum is dedicated to teaching visitors, especially children. They can try on costumes and uniforms, among other hands-on experiences.

STRASBURG MUSEUM
East King St.   (540) 465-3175
Open 10 AM-4 PM, May-Oct.
Adults $2, children $1

There are many quality Civil War and railroad relics to see here. You'll enjoy the blacksmith, cooper and potter's shop collections.

Front Royal

BELLE BOYD COTTAGE
101 Chester St.   (540) 636-1446
Open 10 AM-4 PM Mon.-Fri., Nov.-April; 10 AM-4 PM Mon.-Fri. and noon-4 PM Sat.-Sun., May-Oct.
Adults $2, students $1

This cottage museum, dedicated to the famed Confederate spy, teenager Belle Boyd, depicts life in Warren County and Front Royal during the Civil War. Belle was famous for the information she gathered that helped Jackson win the Battle of Front Royal on May 23, 1862.

WARREN RIFLES CONFEDERATE MUSEUM
95 Chester St.   (540) 636-6982
Open 9 AM-5 PM weekdays, noon-5 PM weekends, April 15-Nov. 1

Included in this museum is memorabilia from generals Lee, Jackson, Early and Ashby and spy Belle Boyd. Other artifacts of the war are abundant.

PROSPECT HILL CEMETERY
Within the cemetery, you will find a memorial, Soldier's Circle Monument, over the graves of 276 Confederate dead. Also there is Mosby Monument, flanked by two Parrott rifled cannon. The marker is a memorial to seven members of a Confederate group named Mosby's Rangers, illegally executed as spies in 1864.

Edinburg

EDINBURG MILL
U.S. 11

In 1864 Union soldiers began a systematic destruction of the Shenandoah, known as "The Burning." Now a restaurant and noted for its child ghost, "Frankie," Edinburg Mill was miraculously saved when two young women tearfully begged Gen. Sheridan to spare it, since it was Edinburg's only livelihood. Sheridan ordered his soldiers to extinguish the flames. There are several stories about just who the child ghost is, but the most noted is that Frankie was a slave who was caught in the mill wheel. Waitresses over the years have claimed he plaintively appears and reappears at unusual times.

New Market

NEW MARKET
BATTLEFIELD HISTORICAL PARK
I-81, Exit 264   (540) 740-3101
Open daily 9 AM-5 PM except holidays
Adults $5, ages 7 to 15 $2

New Market Battlefield Historical Park, owned and operated by Virginia Military Institute, offers a family adventure into one of America's most dramatic eras and is one of the finest Civil War museums in Virginia. Children can climb on cannons where in 1864 6,000 Federals clashed with 4,500 Confederates, including the famous VMI cadets desperately recruited from college to help the South's cause. It was the first and only time in American history that an entire student body was recruited to fight a war.

The Hall of Valor, focal point of the 260-acre battlefield park, presents a concise, graphic survey of the entire war. Exhibits highlight the war chronologically. There are two films, including a stirring account of the cadets' baptism by fire and one about Stonewall Jackson, a former VMI professor. You will see a life-size artillery unit, a model railroad, exquisitely sculptured soldiers and four battle

scenes among the three-dimensional exhibits in the Virginia Room.

The c. 1825 Bushong farmhouse, around which part of the battle, still stands, with its reconstructed blacksmith shop, meat and loom house, wheelwright shop, oven, hen house and other artifacts of life in the 1860s. It served as a hospital after the battle. Scenic pathways lead to the "Field of Lost Shoes," where the mud was so thick that soldiers' mulehide shoes were often irretrievable. The celebrated Shenandoah River flows nearby.

NEW MARKET
BATTLEFIELD MILITARY MUSEUM
Collins Dr.   (540) 740-8065
Open 9 AM-5 PM daily, March 15-Dec.
and by appointment
Adults $6, ages 6-14 $3

Modeled after Gen. Robert E. Lee's Arlington House, the museum stands where the battle of New Market began in the spring of 1864. The museum houses a fine collection of more than 2,500 artifacts focusing on the Civil War and other American wars from 1775 to the present. A film shown regularly gives patrons an overview of the Civil War in the museum's 54-seat theater.

Harrisonburg

WARREN-SIPE MUSEUM
Harrisonburg-Rockingham
Historical Society
301 S. Main St.   (540) 879-2681
Open 10 AM-4 PM, April-Oct. Call ahead since
hours fluctuate due to volunteers.

The highlight of this museum is its huge electrified relief map with accompanying audio cassette outlining Stonewall Jackson's Valley Campaign of 1862 for control of the Shenandoah Valley. There are many interesting artifacts, photos and paintings that help illustrate what happened in Rockingham County. Don't miss it for a blow-by-blow scenario of the great Jackson.

FORT HARRISON

Off U.S. 42 S., Dayton (540) 879-2280
Open 1 PM-5 PM weekends May 31-Oct. 31

Guided tours are available for the home of Daniel Harrison, brother of Harrisonburg founder Thomas Harrison. The stone house was a natural fort used by local citizens when tribes of Indians terrorized the area during the 18th century and later during the Civil War.

Lexington

STONEWALL JACKSON MEMORIAL CEMETERY

300 block of S. Main St.

Marked by Edward Valentine's bronze statue of the general, which faces South, Stonewall Jackson Memorial Cemetery contains the remains of the 39-year-old leader of battle, who died May 10, 1863, from wounds received at the Battle of Chancellorsville. The statue is probably the only time Jackson ever turned his back on his enemy. Some 400 other Confederate soldiers also are buried there. John Mercer Brooke, the inventor of the ironclad ship, the *Merrimac*, is at final rest here. So is William Washington (1834-1870), well-known artist of the Civil War period. He is especially known for his painting of the Battle of Lantane.

STONEWALL JACKSON HOUSE

8 E. Washington St. (540) 463-2552
Open Mon.-Sat., 9 AM-5 PM, Sun. 1-5 PM; until 6 PM June, July and Aug.; closed holidays.
Adults $4, Ages 6 to 12 $2

Built in 1801, the only home Jackson ever owned is furnished with his personal possessions. A brief slide show and guided tours interpret Jackson's life as a citizen,

soldier, VMI professor of natural philosophy, church leader and family man. Guided tours of the home and restored garden are given every half-hour. You may also visit the museum shop, which specializes in books, prints and Victoriana.

WASHINGTON AND LEE UNIVERSITY

Main St. (540) 463-8400

W&L's beautiful front campus includes Lee Chapel, the focal point of the campus. Robert E. Lee served as the school's president in the five years after the Civil War. The remains of Lee and most of his family are entombed here. Edward Valentine, who also did the statue of Stonewall Jackson in the cemetery, sculpted the famous pose of the recumbent Lee. In the basement is a museum emphasizing Lee. His office is preserved as he left it.

VIRGINIA MILITARY INSTITUTE AND MUSEUM

VMI Parade Grounds
N. Main St. (540) 464-7000
Open 9 AM-5 PM Mon.-Sat., 2-5 PM Sun. Closed holidays.

Since its establishment in 1839, VMI has been known for the officers and men it contributed to the Confederacy. In the center of campus is a statue of Jackson standing in the wind. Nearby are cannons from the Rockbridge Artillery. The famous statue, "Virginia Mourning Her Dead," a monument to the VMI cadets who fell at New Market, stands on the Parade Grounds. In Jackson Memorial Hall is a mural of the historic cadet charge during the battle. The VMI Museum includes Jackson's beloved war horse, Little Sorrel (yes, the real hide, stretched over a plastic form . . . considered state-of-the-art taxidermy in those times), among many other Civil War exhibits.

East of the Blue Ridge Region

Charlottesville

JACKSON STATUE
Fourth St.

Charles Keck created a bareheaded Jackson galloping forward on his favorite mount, Little Sorrel.

LEE STATUE
Park between First and Second Sts.

The work of sculptors H.M. Shrady and Leo Lentelli, this is an equestrian statue of Lee.

UNIVERSITY CEMETERY
Alderman and McCormick Rds.
North of UVA Football Stadium

Even during the Civil War, Charlottesville was known for its healthcare facilities. The remains of 1,200 Confederate soldiers lie in University Cemetery, most the victims of disease. A bronze statue of a bareheaded Confederate soldier is at the center.

Lynchburg

APPOMATTOX COURT HOUSE NATIONAL HISTORICAL PARK
Appomattox, 20 minutes east
of Lynchburg   (804) 352-2621

This site is not to be missed! If you're going to Lynchburg to see Civil War his-

tory, just 20 minutes farther will put you at Appomattox, where our nation reunited on April 9, 1865. Living history exhibits are held during the summer, and the park is open daily except holidays November through February. In the park, you will find a totally restored village as it was during the day when generals Grant and Lee ended the war on a handshake. There are Meeks Store, Woodson Law Office, Clover Hill Tavern and Surrender Triangle, to name a few. You will find the Appomattox County Museum located in Court House Square. Every autumn, Appomattox is the site of its famous Railroad Festival.

DANIEL MONUMENT
Intersection of Park Ave., Ninth
and Floyd Sts.

John Warwick Daniel was a member of Gen. Jubal Early's staff who went on to become a distinguished orator and U.S. senator. This monument to the "Lame Lion of Lynchburg," so named for Daniel's wound at the Battle of the Wilderness, was created by Sir Moses Ezekiel, a famous postwar sculptor.

LYNCHBURG MUSEUM AT OLD COURT HOUSE
Fifth St.   (804) 847-1459
Open daily 1-4 PM, closed holidays
Admission $1

The tragedy of the Civil War is one of many facts gleaned from the exhibits seen in this historical representation of

Because of growing interest in the Civil War, some Blue Ridge colleges and universities sponsor special seminars on campus. Many of them are adjacent to important battlefields. A popular one is the Civil War Institute at Shenandoah University in Winchester.

Insiders' Tips

Lynchburg's history. The city was at the center of Confederate supply lines, making it a frequent target. Housed in Lynchburg's Old Court House, built in 1855, it is one of Virginia's outstanding Greek Revival civil buildings.

PEST HOUSE MEDICAL MUSEUM
AND CONFEDERATE CEMETERY
Old City Cemetery
Fourth and Taylor Sts.   (804) 847-1811
Open sunrise to sunset, self-guided tours
or by appointment

Founded in 1806, Old City Cemetery contains graves of 2,701 Confederate soldiers from 14 states. The Pest House Medical Museum is a restored white frame building that was built in the 1840s and served as the medical office of Dr. John Jay Terrell. By 1861 Lynchburg was a major Civil War hospital center, and the Pest House was used as the quarantine hospital for Confederate soldiers. The dead were buried a few yards away. Dr. Terrell discovered the wretched conditions of the Pest House and assumed responsibility for the soldiers. The reforms enacted by Dr. Terrell reduced the Pest House mortality rate from 50 percent to 5 percent. On display are medical instruments from the 1860s, including a surgical amputation kit used on many soldiers. Dr. Terrell died at age 93, leaving a heroic medical legacy to Lynchburg.

SPRING HILL CEMETERY
Fort Ave.

Buried here is Gen. Jubal Early, who saved the city of Lynchburg from destruction during 1864 when he ran empty railroad cars up and down the tracks to convince the Yankees that Confederate reinforcements were arriving for a major battle. The Union forces retreated, and Lynchburg was saved from the destruction of Gen. David Hunter.

SOUTHERN SOLDIER STATUE
Monument Terrace, center of downtown

Honoring heroes of all wars, a statue of a Southern infantryman stands at the top of Monument Terrace. It was designed by James O. Scott and erected in 1898.

RIVERSIDE PARK
2240 Rivermont Ave.

Here you will find a fragment of the hull of the canalboat Marshall, which transported the body of Jackson from Lynchburg to Lexington for burial in 1863.

Bedford

BEDFORD CITY/COUNTY MUSEUM
201 E. Main St.   (540) 586-4520
Open 10 AM-5 PM Mon.-Sat.
Adults $1, children 50¢

This interesting local collection includes a number of artifacts from the Civil War, including weapons, flags, photos and personal effects.

LONGWOOD CEMETERY
Bridge St.

A Civil War monument of valor marks the final resting place of soldiers who died at one of five Confederate hospitals located in and around Bedford. A tall obelisk stands over the single grave of 192 soldiers and a nurse.

New River Valley Region

Pulaski County

THE WILDERNESS ROAD MUSEUM
Newbern   (540) 674-4835
Open 10:30 AM-4:30 PM Tues.-Sat.
1-4 PM Sun.

Operated by the New River Historical Society, the museum consists of three historic structures on a six-acre tract.

There are various Civil War displays, including a drum, since the area is close to Cloyd's Mountain, the major Civil War battle (May 9, 1864) site for Southwest Virginia. Each year, the museum has a Civil War Weekend in mid-June.

Alleghany Highlands Region

Bath County

WARM SPRINGS SPA
Warm Springs
In the Ladies Bath House of the spa is a chair made especially for the arthritically crippled Mrs. Robert E. Lee, who came often while her husband undertook his duties as a professor at Washington and Lee University after the Civil War.

Highland County

McDOWELL PRESBYTERIAN CHURCH
U.S. 250 W.
McDowell is the site of the second major battle of Jackson's valley campaign; a roadside marker commemorates the event. Inside the village is McDowell Presbyterian Church, used as a hospital during and after the fighting.

New River Valley Profile:
Professor James Robertson

Interest in the Civil War has grown enormously in recent years. Fueling the fires is Virginia Tech's James I. "Bud" Robertson, Alumni Distinguished Professor and noted Civil War historian. He teaches what is believed to be the largest Civil War history class in the nation at Tech's auditorium and has received the Virginia Tech Certificate of Teaching Excellence award eight times since 1967.

Robertson's academic career has lapsed only once, from 1961 to 1965, when he served at the White House, appointed by President John F. Kennedy to head the Civil War Centennial observation. Now, It's standing-room-only for Robertson's classes. Students vying to compete in the campus Civil War Weekend he presents with the alumni association have even been known to offer bribes to others to get in the program.

"I don't think I've ever seen an audience when he was talking that wasn't spellbound," says a former student who now owns a Civil War memorabilia shop.

Credit: Lin Chaff

James I. Robertson

Robertson asserts that the very face of America was shaped by the war and that no other era has ever produced the famous leaders of those war-torn years, when fully half of the men in the South were either disabled or killed.

"It starts with Lincoln and Lee and Grant and Sherman and Stuart and on down the line," says Robertson. "We don't have those great men today. I'm beginning to think one of the reasons for the popularity of the Civil War today may be that we're looking at the past out of — I won't say a sense of desperation — a sense of longing, so to speak. The Civil War has to be one of the greatest moments, if not the greatest moment, in history, for out of it came the United States."

Robertson adds that the Civil War was, in many respects, the "last war between gentlemen . . . the last war in which niceties were observed, the last war of personal leadership and inspiration." It also qualifies as the bloodiest war in American history, with more American soldiers dying in it than in all other wars combined, because all who died in the Civil War — nearly 700,000 — were Americans.

A Danville, Virginia, native, Robertson began his illustrious career as a Civil War historian after studying at Emory University under Bell Wiley, who had written copiously about Johnny Reb and Billy Yank. His interest in the Civil War came naturally. His great-grandfather, John Compton, survived Pickett's Charge and lived to pass on the glory to his awed family. Robertson family legend has it that Compton also served as Gen. Robert E. Lee's cook.

Robertson has written nearly a half-dozen books and edited 20 more about the Civil War. His books have been nominated for a Pulitzer Prize, named a main section in the History Book Club and chosen the Best Book for Young Readers by the American Library Association. Robertson's next book is a biography of Gen. Stonewall Jackson, a man with a stern reputation which Robertson attributes to an unhappy childhood. He is often asked to provide commentary for Civil War TV specials and films such as the Discovery Channel's *Three Days at Gettysburg*. However, he's not a big fan of Hollywood's attempts to glamorize what he calls a "filthy war full of suffering," although he admits it was a war also filled with endless acts of gallantry, drama and excitement.

A self-described workaholic, Robertson was an ACC college football official for 28 years. He quit when he found he couldn't accomplish much else during autumns. For relaxation, he plays the drums of his youth (he was a Big Band drummer in college). Robertson has less and less leisure time, however, as his reputation continues to soar nationally, putting Virginia Tech on the map and creating thousands of converts to Civil War history. It gets hectic, he admits, but there's nothing else he'd rather do. Thousands of Virginia Tech alumni and students are glad he feels that way.

Inside
The Blue Ridge Parkway and Skyline Drive

It's seems like a miracle that in the late 20th century you can drive almost the entire length of an East Coast state without seeing fast-food restaurants, trucks or glaring billboards.

This miracle in Virginia is made possible by a scenic stretch of highway that begins in Front Royal as the Skyline Drive, runs the length of Shenandoah National Park and becomes the Blue Ridge Parkway at Waynesboro. From Waynesboro, the Blue Ridge Parkway meanders 469 miles, all the way to the Great Smoky Mountains in North Carolina, offering magnificent views of valleys, forests and mountain ranges along the way.

Construction of the Skyline Drive began in 1931, spurred on by President Herbert Hoover, who spent many a weekend at his fishing camp in the area. Hoover, so the story goes, was riding his horse along the crest of the Blue Ridge Mountains one day in 1930 when he turned to a companion and said: "These mountains are made for a road, and everybody ought to have a chance to get the views from here. I think they're the greatest in the world."

The road was built by local farmers who were paid from drought relief funds; the Civilian Conservation Corps pitched in to build rock walls, picnic areas and

Photo: Roanoke Convention and Visitors Bureau

Bikers ride through an underpass of the Blue Ridge Parkway near Roanoke.

scenic overlooks. The 105-mile-long Skyline Drive was finished on August 29, 1939, during the administration of Franklin D. Roosevelt.

Today it costs $5 per vehicle to enter the Skyline Drive at any point. That fee and the 35 mph speed limit help keep the road free of commuters and speedsters.

Most visitors traveling the Skyline Drive expect to see clear views of the Shenandoah Valley and distant mountain ranges. Unfortunately, this is not always possible. Visibility in Shenandoah National Park has dropped 50 percent over the past 40 years and is at its worst during summer months. At least 75 percent of the haze seen on hot summer days is pollution, much of it caused by coal-burning power plants in the Ohio Valley and from as far away as northern Indiana. And unless the trend is reversed, the problem is likely to worsen.

Park officials do a visibility check every day at 1 PM and post the results around the park by 2 PM. If you want to know what the visibility is like before you go, contact the dispatch office at (540) 999-3644 or (540) 999-3500.

Just like Shenandoah National Park, the Blue Ridge Parkway is governed by the National Park Service but is a separate and distinct facility. The legislated purpose of the parkway was to link Shenandoah National Park with Great Smoky Mountains National Park in North Carolina and Tennessee by means of a scenic highway. That goal was accomplished in 1936 and was recognized world-wide as a significant engineering achievement. The designers often took the long route, which would have been avoided by conventional highway builders, to provide access to scenic, historic and natural features of the region. The route follows the mountaintops at an average elevation of 3,000 feet.

Along both the Skyline Drive and the Blue Ridge Parkway you'll find lodges, cabins and campsites where you can spot deer and raccoons from your doorstep. Waysides (rest areas) offer souvenirs, fudge, ice cream and Southern specialties such as Virginia ham, blackberry cobbler and buckwheat pancakes.

Of course, there are hundreds of restaurants, motels, hotels and bed and breakfast inns near the Skyline Drive and the Blue Ridge Parkway, but this chapter includes only places on these scenic highways. The facilities in Shenandoah National Park are operated by ARAMARK, a concessionaire for the National Park Service. Some of the restaurants and accommodations along the Blue Ridge Parkway are privately owned and operated, which we have noted. This is because the parkway's boundaries are quite narrow in places, bordering private property where people live or make a living.

Accommodations, restaurants and snack bars described in this section are organized from north to south. Locations are identified by mileposts, beginning with 0.6 at the Front Royal Entrance Station. The numbering system starts over when the Skyline Drive meets the Blue Ridge Parkway at Rockfish Gap.

For more information about accommodations, restaurants and attractions on or near the scenic highways, contact one of the following.

• **ARAMARK Shenandoah National Park Lodges**, P.O. Box 727, Luray 22835; (800) 999-4714 or (540) 743-7883

• **Blue Ridge Parkway Association**, P.O. Box 453, Asheville, North Carolina 28802; (704) 298-0398

Both associations will send you directories and strip maps of the drives.

Photo: Virginia Division of Tourism

Mabry Mill is one of the most recognized landmarks of the Blue Ridge.

Skyline Drive

Lodges

SKYLAND LODGE

Mile 41.7   (800) 999-4714, (540) 999-2211

This is the first lodging facility you reach when driving south on Skyline Drive from the Front Royal entrance. George Freeman Pollock, one of the people instrumental in establishing the Shenandoah National Park, built a private resort, Stoneyman Camp, with cabins and a dining hall on this site in 1894.

The Skyland facilities sit at 3,680 feet — the highest point on Skyline Drive — and several of its 177 guest rooms overlook the Shenandoah Valley. Skyland offers a variety of lodging, from rustic cabins and motel-style lodge rooms to suites. Some are equipped for those with disabilities. Amenities include a glass-walled dining room and the Tap Room with live entertainment nightly during the summer. Guest rooms do not have phones, Guest rooms do not have phones, but some have televisions. Service shelters have pay phones and ice and soda machines.

Skyland is a lively place for a family vacation. Adults can take guided horseback trips, and children may ride ponies. The playground has swings, bars, seesaws and plenty of grass and dirt. An amphitheater serves as an outdoor classroom where the National Park Service conducts educational programs. Naturalists lead hikes along numerous trails near the lodge in spring and summer and offer evening programs on such topics as bird watching, wildflowers and acid rain. You can also gaze through a telescope at the brilliant stars. Skyland's gift shop is stocked with mountain crafts, photo supplies, daily papers and magazines. The lodge has meeting rooms and audiovisual equipment to accommodate conferences.

Rates range from $74 to $80 per night for a single lodge unit on weekdays to $140 per night for a one-bedroom suite on weekends. Rustic cabin rooms are $45 to $77 per night on weekdays and $47 to

$79 per night on weekends. The lodge is usually open from late March to the end of November.

The most popular month is October, that magical time of brilliant color in the Blue Ridge. Room rates are slightly higher this month. Reservations are often made a year in advance for these autumn nights. It's not a bad idea to make reservations well in advance for summer nights too.

BIG MEADOWS LODGE

Mile 51.3   (800) 999-4714, (540) 999-2221

Nine miles south of Skyland Lodge you'll come to a clearing, the only large treeless area in the Shenandoah National Park. The Byrd Visitor Center and the Big Meadows Wayside overlook the meadow, which was probably created by fire set either by lightning or by Native Americans to encourage the growth of wild berries. The Park Service keeps the area clear to this day, and it's an excellent place for visitors to see a diversity of wildlife, including berries and wildflowers.

The resort is a short drive from the meadow. The main lodge was built in 1939 by mountain labor using stone from the Massanutten Mountains across the Shenandoah Valley. Paneling throughout the building came from native chestnut trees that grew in the Big Meadows area. This tree is nearly extinct today because of the chestnut blight in the early 1930s.

The resort includes 11 rustic cabins and 70 motel-style rooms. The main lodge's 21 rooms offer the warm, rustic atmosphere of the historic lodge, while the cabins with fireplaces sit among the trees. The most modern units feature king-size beds, fireplaces and sitting areas with televisions.

The main lodge has an outdoor deck where guests can lounge by day and stargaze by night. For a quarter you can look more closely at the stars through a telescope.

The lofty central room of the main lodge is a casual place where you can relax and enjoy the valley view. Several board games are available, and a lot of comfortable sofas and chairs and a fireplace create a relaxed ambiance.

The dining room offers a tremendous view of the Shenandoah Valley. On a clear day you can enjoy the panoramic view 40 miles across the entire Appalachian Range into West Virginia. The Tap Room, made cozy by a fireplace, is open from 4 to 11 PM.

Big Meadows Lodge offers naturalist activities and a children's playground. Also plan to spend some time in the Byrd Visitor Center, where exhibits illustrate the park's history, the folkways of its former inhabitants, and the growing threat of air pollution. Dozens of books for children and adults are for sale, from wildflower coloring books to histories of the region.

The resort is open from early May through October. Rates range from $60 per night in the main lodge on weekdays to $112 per night for a one-bedroom suite on weekends. Rates are slightly higher in October.

Cabins

LEWIS MOUNTAIN CABINS

Mile 57.5   (540) 999-2255

For an even more tranquil experience, you can spend the night in one of the cabins on Lewis Mountain, where no room phones or televisions disturb the peace. The heated cabins have furnished bedrooms and private baths, with towels and linens provided. Cooking is done in connecting outdoor areas equipped with fireplaces, grills and picnic tables.

The cabins are open from mid-May through October. Rates range from $52 per night on weekdays for a single room cabin to $80 per night on weekends for a two-room cabin. Rates are slightly higher in October.

POTOMAC
APPALACHIAN TRAIL CLUB CABINS
(540) 242-0315

If you're game for a bit of backpacking, the Potomac Appalachian Trail Club maintains six cabins and seven trailside huts in the back country of the park. The huts, which provide shelter from the elements, are along hiking trails at intervals of 8 to 14 miles. You must have a valid back-country camping permit for three or more nights.

The cabins provide a bit more comfort, and staying in one can be a gritty or sublime experience, depending upon your perspective. You must hike in, gather your own firewood and draw your own water from a nearby spring. Each cabin has a table and fireplace, bunks for up to 12 people and a pit toilet. There's no electricity, so you must also bring your own source of light.

The cabins are Range View (Mile 22.1), Corbin (Mile 37.9), Rock Spring (Mile 81.1), Pocosin (Mile 59.5), Doyles River (Mile 81.1) and Jones Mountain (accessible from Criglersville, but not from Skyline Drive).

All cabins are locked, so you must get a key from the PATC by mail prior to your visit. For reservations, call the number above or write PATC, 118 Park Street S.E., Vienna 22180. The cabins are popular, so reserve early.

Campgrounds

Shenandoah National Park operates two campgrounds on a first-come, first-served basis: Lewis Mountain (Mile 57.5)

and Loft Mountain (Mile 80). The nightly fee is $12. At Big Meadows Campground, you can make reservations up to eight weeks in advance for sites from late May through October by calling (800) 365-2267. Big Meadow's nightly fee is $14.

All campgrounds have a 14-day limit, allow pets and do not accept credit cards. Tents, tent trailers and recreational vehicles can be accommodated. However, water and electric hookups are not available for RVs. Shower and laundry facilities are near the campgrounds.

For further information, call Park Headquarters at (540) 999-2229 or refer to our Recreation chapter.

Places to Eat

ELKWALLOW WAYSIDE
Mile 24.1   (540) 999-2253

From May to late October, this stop has a small selection of groceries and camper supplies.

PANORAMA RESTAURANT
Mile 31.5 at U.S. 211   (540) 999-2265

This is the place for that hearty breakfast before hitting the trail. Panorama serves three meals a day from April to mid-November. Lunch and dinner menus often include local specialties such as fried catfish and country ham along with staples such as hamburgers, sandwiches, soups and salads.

SKYLAND LODGE
Mile 41.7   (540) 999-2211

One of the best views on the drive is from the window tables in this glass-walled dining room, which offers full meal service every day from late March through November. The Stonyman (corned-beef hash topped with poached eggs) and the four-cheese omelet are

Photo: Richmond Newspapers

Skyline Drive motorists can enjoy the grandeur of mountain vistas and overlooks.

breakfast standouts. Menus change, but dinner selections often include prime rib, trout with pecan butter, eggplant or chicken Parmesan and vegetable-stuffed ravioli. The Tap Room has a limited bar menu to go with the beer, wine and spirits dispensed from 2:30 to 10:30 PM daily.

BIG MEADOWS WAYSIDE
Mile 51   *(540) 999-2221*

The coffee shop has carry-out service and a menu similar to the Panorama Restaurant listed above. It serves three meals daily from mid-April through November.

BIG MEADOWS LODGE
Mile 51.2   *(540) 999-2221*

A four-cheese omelet, Belgian waffles and blueberry pancakes are breakfast features. Lunch offerings include the popular Salmon Burger and "Comin' Thru the Rye," a hearty Reuben. The dinner menu includes fried chicken, baked Virginia trout, catfish and chicken scaloppine. The restaurant is full-service May through October. The Tap Room, open 4 to 11 PM, offers a limited bar menu.

Blue Ridge Parkway

Accommodations

PEAKS OF OTTER LODGE
Mile 86   *(540) 586-1081*
In Virginia   *(800) 542-5927*

Unlike the lodges in Shenandoah National Park, Peaks of Otter is open year round. The lodge setting is idyllic, a valley surrounded by gentle mountains and facing a beautiful lake. Each room has two double beds, a private bath and a private balcony or terrace that overlooks the lake. The rooms have no televisions or phones.

The lodge's restaurant serves hearty Southern fare and has a sumptuous salad bar. The gift shop sells fine Virginia crafts, stationery, books, jellies and more.

You can also camp at Peaks of Otter. Park rangers give talks on nature topics during peak season, and hikers can trek along miles of well-marked trails near the lodge.

Rates are about $71 for two people per room weekdays or weekends, slightly higher on holiday weekends.

ROCKY KNOB CABINS
Mile 174   *(540) 593-3503*

These cabins were built in the 1930s for the Civilian Conservation Corps workers who constructed much of the Blue Ridge Parkway. They have no fireplaces and no other source of heat, so it's understandable that they are only open from late May through Labor Day. The cabins have completely furnished electric kitchens, but no bathrooms. However, private showers and laundry facilities are in a bathhouse within 50 feet of each cabin. Rates are about $41 for two, $5 for each extra person. Children 12 and younger stay for free.

DOE RUN LODGE RESORT AND CONFERENCE CENTER
Off Parkway near Mile 189   *(540) 398-2212*

This family-oriented private resort sits on beautiful Groundhog Mountain and offers tennis, swimming, saunas and golf. Choose from pool-side chalets, townhouse villas, tennis center chalets and single-family residences. Natural stone, wooden beams and floor-to-ceiling windows make this resort a tribute to the environment. All the accommodations are large suites with a fireplace, two bedrooms, two full baths and a living/dining area. Many have complete kitchens. The

High Country Restaurant serves seafood, steak and Southern specialties. Doe Run offers a honeymoon package at its Mill-pond Hideaway, as well as a range of golf packages.

Families can especially benefit from the good deals here, because children younger than 12 stay free. Weekday rates are $109 for two adults; weekend daily rates are $129. Breakfast is included. Rates are somewhat lower after November.

Campgrounds

The Parkway has nine developed campgrounds with tent and recreational vehicle sites (no water or electric hook-ups) and two backcountry camping areas on or near the Drive. Peaks of Otter, a half-mile east of Milepost 86 on Va. 43, is one of the most popular campgrounds because of its beautiful lakeside setting. All campgrounds have restrooms (no showers), sewage dumping stations and telephones. Grills and tables are provided at each site.

Campgrounds are open May through October. The limit is 14 consecutive days June 1 through Labor Day; 30 days for the calendar year. Reservations are not accepted, but you probably won't need them. Do plan to make camp early during the peak summer months or the fall foliage season. Leashed pets are allowed. All campgrounds charge $9 per site for up to two adults, $2 per additional adult. Children younger than 19 stay free. Backcountry campers must apply for a free permit from Parkway headquarters. For more information, call (540) 857-2213.

Places to Eat

WHETSTONE RIDGE
Mile 29   (540) 377-6397

This casual dining spot near Montebello serves hearty fare from early May through October, with breakfast specialties such as buckwheat pancakes. The simple dinner menu lists fried chicken, hamburger steak, flounder or country

Photo: Va. Department of Economic Development

Canoeing is a fun way to see the beauty of the Blue Ridge up close.

East of the Blue Ridge Profile:
Gov. George Allen

He dips Copenhagen, drives a pickup truck, listens to bluegrass music and owns a log cabin in the Blue Ridge Mountains of Albemarle County.

Sounds like your basic Blue Ridge Everyman, right?

Well, not exactly. He's George Allen, the iconoclastic young governor of Virginia.

To put it mildly, he's not your typical governor. And Virginia — a state synonymous with time-honored traditions — hasn't seen the likes of such a chief executive for a long, long time.

That's no knock against Allen. His meteoric rise through Old Dominion politics, capped by an unbelievable come-from-behind gubernatorial victory in 1993, has earned the 43-year-old Republican a healthy dose of respect. From the white-collar power corridors of Richmond and Northern Virginia to the mist-shrouded hollows of Cumberland Gap, the mere mention of the governor's name can launch an hour's worth of policy discussions. But no matter where they side, all Virginians agree that Governor Allen has a mandate for political change.

Gov. George Allen

Allen's professional accomplishments, which have included terms in the Virginia House of Delegates and the U.S. House of Representatives, seem even more extraordinary when you consider his past. Allen grew up in Southern California, the son of the famous football coach of the Los Angeles Rams. When George Allen Sr. took over the helm of the Washington Redskins in 1971, George junior also came East, enrolling at the University of Virginia, where he went on to play football and earn bachelor's and law degrees. During this time, Coach Allen's winning ways in Washington made him as popular a figure in Virginia as any modern-day governor.

The younger Allen, however, soon forged his own strong identity as a Charlottesville lawyer, part-time farmer and outdoor enthusiast. During his tenure in the Virginia House of Delegates, he represented Thomas Jefferson's district, a fitting position because he has always espoused Jefferson's conservative principles. As governor, his goals have been to promote work, not welfare; to stress academics; and to reduce the size and reach of government.

Allen is supported in his endeavors by his active wife Susan, who has a background in tourism, the state's second-leading industry. The couple have two children, Tyler and Forrest.

Though he is not a native, Allen has put down deep roots in Virginia and the Blue Ridge Mountains. He says moving to these hills — and staying — "was one of the best decisions I've made."

ham. Don't miss the warm apple dumpling for dessert.

OTTER CREEK RESTAURANT

Mile 60.8   *(804) 299-5862*

Family favorites make up the menu, which is the same as the menu at Whetstone Ridge, listed above. The restaurant is next to a year-round campground and small gift shop and is open mid-April through mid-November.

PEAKS OF OTTER LODGE

Mile 86   *(800) 542-5927*

Friendly service and hefty portions make this a popular dining spot among locals as well as travelers. Like the lodge, the restaurant is open year round. Breakfast are the stick-to-your-ribs sort, and lunch specials include big salads, burgers and ham steak with buttered apples. The dinner menu offers Southern dishes such as barbecued ribs and country ham, as well as prime rib and tenderloin steak. The coffee shop prepares picnic lunches for guests wanting to eat outdoors.

HIGH COUNTRY
RESTAURANT AT DOE RUN LODGE

Off Parkway near Mile 189   *(540) 398-2212*

Open year round, this restaurant serves breakfast, lunch and dinner seven days a week. The menu is seasonal and offers such gourmet selections as she-crab soup, venison, fresh rainbow trout from Doe Run's stocked pond, lamb, duck, steaks and country ham. The restaurant also prepares picnic lunches.

MABRY MILL COFFEE SHOP

Mile 176   *(800) 542-5927*

This coffee shop at Mabry Mill, a famous pioneer attraction along the parkway, serves a single menu all day. Country ham, barbecue, and corn and buckwheat cakes are specialties. Mabry Mill is open from late April through October. Hours are 8 AM to 7 PM during summer months and 8 AM to 6 PM in May, September and October.

ORCHARD GAP DELI

Off Parkway between
Mile 193 and 194   *(800) 542-5927*

This private establishment is about 50 yards from the Parkway in Fancy Gap and is worth the slight detour for its big deli sandwiches, homemade sourdough and raisin bread, Moravian sugar cake and imported and domestic beer and wine. The deli, which is open seven days a week, carries a full line of groceries, fresh produce and gasoline.

Inside
Recreation

Recreation: It's a concept we learn in kindergarten that stays with us all our lives. The whole world loves to play. Historically, visitors came to the Blue Ridge Mountains to partake of pristine waters and gaze upon lofty peaks, a tonic for body and soul. That's still true today — but mostly they come to play.

There are so many leisure activities in the Blue Ridge that the wise visitor will plan an itinerary well in advance. However, getting sidetracked is also a regional pastime, hazardous only to a tight vacation schedule, certainly not to the spirit or health.

Many visitors come year after year, and some chose to live here permanently.

There's a common bond among residents of the Blue Ridge, a smugness that comes from living every day in a region that others travel hundreds, even thousands, of miles to visit. It is to the Blue Ridge that Virginia owes much of its international recognition in the realm of outdoor recreation.

The big draw, of course, is the scenery. Mother Nature blessed Virginia's Blue Ridge with lush vegetation, sparkling streams and mountain peaks that dress in dazzling colors for fall and pristine white in winter. Between the mountains are valleys patchworked with fields of grain and grassy meadows in which languid dairy cattle graze among wildflow-

Photo: Lance Hill

Whitewater katayaking on the Russell Fork River in Dickenson County.

ers. Many small towns are postcard images, with covered bridges and steepled churches that withstood the Civil War. Among the region's scenic highlights is Natural Bridge, one of the seven wonders of the natural world.

In this spectacular setting are recreational opportunities for every budget from the camper on a shoestring to the golfer luxuriating at The Homestead or The Greenbrier, two of our nation's Mobil four- and five-star resorts.

Among the region's greatest recreational treasures are its parks and forests. Two national forests with acres of precious wilderness have become one — the George Washington and Jefferson National Forest. The Shenandoah National Park, Virginia's mountain playground, is here. State parks, including Claytor, Douthat, Sky Meadows and Smith Mountain Lake, offer recreational opportunities galore, from horseback riding to cross-country skiing.

Two outdoor mega-attractions are here also — the Bikecentennial Trail that spans the country from Williamsburg, Virginia, to the West Coast; and the Appalachian Trail, stretching from Maine to Georgia. Natives in small towns take for granted a continuing stream of blaze orange-clad backpackers and bikers enjoying country byways.

Blue Ridge forest preserves offer some of the finest fishing and hunting in the Southeast. Some hunters and anglers prefer to go it alone, while others engage local guides who know the way of the woods and streams. Licenses can be obtained at a variety of stores.

Most visitors come to see rather than stalk, and they're never disappointed. The hills are home to black bear, deer, turkey, small game and a wide variety of songbirds.

There's bountiful water in the region — fresh mountain streams, rivers and lakes, including Smith Mountain Lake, the state's largest inland body of water. These lakes and waterways offer the popular sports of boating, swimming, rafting, canoeing and tubing — a pastime especially enjoyed by college students who tow a "refreshment" tube stocked with cold drinks and snacks. It's a great way to spend a hot summer afternoon.

The Blue Ridge is also revered for its subterranean world, a maze of commercial and wild caverns that delight spelunkers and rock climbers.

If your idea of a hazard is a sand-filled bunker on the edge of a tiered green, you'll find a plethora of excellent public, semiprivate and resort courses in the Blue Ridge.

As you're probably beginning to suspect, choosing an activity in the Blue Ridge Mountains is like trying to select a meal from a mile-long Virginia buffet. There are far too many recreational opportunities to list completely in these pages. We highly recommend that you send for brochures and guides offered by the Commonwealth of Virginia and tourism and recreation associations. This is especially important for many camping areas that require reservations. Look for information contacts listed within the various recreation categories in the following pages. Then go out there and have fun! You'll be in good company.

Hiking

It almost goes without saying that Virginia is a hiker's paradise. There are thousands of trails over diverse terrain, enough to fill several books. In fact, many good reference books have already been written on the subject. Among them, we recommend: *Hiking the Old Dominion* by Allen de Hart (a Sierra Club Totebook), *Walking the Blue Ridge* by Leonard M. Adkins and *Backpacker Magazine's Guide to the Appalachian Trail* by Jim Chase.

If you're uneasy about planning your own outing in unfamiliar country, Mountain Memory Walks, (540) 253-9622, in The Plains organizes two- to seven-day hiking trips in the Blue Ridge, with lodging in comfortable inns. Other hiking companies include Inn to Inn Hiking, (540) 839-2231, in Warm Springs; and Fort Lewis Lodge, (540) 925-2314, in Millboro.

Here's a sample of hiking opportunities the Blue Ridge has to offer.

FRONT ROYAL CANOE CO.

Canoe, Tube, Kayak & Raft Trips On The Shenandoah River

P.O. Box 473 Front Royal, VA 22630 540-635-5440

Appalachian Trail

This famous trail zigzags along the crest of the Appalachian Mountains from Georgia to Maine. More than 500 miles of the AT — about a quarter of its total distance — wind through Virginia. The portion of the trail that runs through the Shenandoah National Park, starting in Front Royal and ending at Rockfish Gap at I-64, is considered by veteran hikers to be one of the most beautiful sections of the trail.

Continuing south through the George Washington and Jefferson National Forest (the two areas merged in early 1995), the trail then passes through the Mount Rogers National Recreation Area, a spectacular stretch of land in Southwest Virginia that includes the state's two highest peaks.

Shenandoah National Park

The Shenandoah National Park's 194,327 acres contain not just the AT but

421 miles of other hiking paths. These range from rugged climbs up steep, rocky terrain to easy nature trails with interpretive guideposts. Some of the best day hikes in the park include:

• **White Oak Run.** A cascade hike along this portion of the AT offers a view of six falls ranging in height from 35 to 86 feet over a distance of about a mile. This trail can be reached from Skyland Lodge (Mile 41.7 on Skyline Drive) on the White Oak Canyon Trail.

• **The Ridge Trail.** This path leads to Old Rag Mountain, the park's most celebrated peak. On this route the AT travels through narrow rock-walled corridors that are the remains of the dikes through which lava flowed 700 million years ago. This is a challenging hike, but the rewards are great when you reach the top, catch your breath and stretch out on a boulder to enjoy the panoramic mountain view.

• **Big Meadows Trail.** Big Meadows, the only large treeless area in the park, is great for hiking. Depending upon the season, you'll find wildflowers, strawberries and blueberries along the path. This is also an excellent place to see a diversity of wildlife, since many animals depend on this grassy area for sustenance. Big Meadows Trail begins near the lodge of the same name at Mile 51.3 on Skyline Drive.

Excellent hiking maps and trail guides to the Shenandoah National Park are available at both visitor centers, entrance stations and by mail from the Shenandoah Natural History Association, Route 4, Box 348, Luray, Virginia 22835. Or call (540) 999-3581.

The Shenandoah National Park and Skyline Drive end at Rockfish Gap just east of Waynesboro. Here is the gateway to the Blue Ridge Parkway, the 469-mile-long scenic route which passes the Cherokee Indian Reservation in North Carolina.

Blue Ridge Parkway

The National Park Service maintains dozens of trails near the Parkway that are highly accessible, even for the laziest of walkers. But if you have the energy, you can hike through tunnels of rhododendron leading to rushing waterfalls or out to soaring peaks covered with mountain laurel and spruce.

Hiking in these mountains also provides a glimpse of what life was like for its early settlers. It's not uncommon to stumble upon the crumbling rock foundation of an old cabin or a stone wall that used to keep in livestock. The ridges and valleys were inhabited by a few hardy souls when the Park Service began to obtain land for the Parkway decades ago.

Many trails lead to farms and communities that have been reconstructed by the Park Service. For instance, at the Mountain Farm Trail near Humpback Rocks (close to Charlottesville) you might see a ranger posing as a grandma churning butter on the front porch of an old cabin, and brother John plucking on a handmade dulcimer nearby.

Many interpretive programs are offered by the Park Service along Blue Ridge Parkway trails. Rangers conduct guided walks during the heaviest tourist months, talking about everything from endangered plants to old-time farming methods.

Most Blue Ridge Parkway trails are so short and well-marked that you don't need a map to walk them. But it would be helpful to have national forest maps because they can lead you to additional trails, campsites and campgrounds. Also, if you're going to hike any of the other trails in the George Washington and Jefferson National Forest you should have a map. These trails are used less than the Parkway trails and are not as well maintained.

For a map of the George Washington section of the national forest (which covers the Blue Ridge Parkway from Mile 0 to 63.7) write to Forest Supervisor, G.W.

National Forest, P.O. Box 233, Harrisonburg, Virginia 22801, or call (540) 564-8300. For a map of the Jefferson section (which covers the Parkway from Mile 63.9 to 104.3) write to U.S. Forest Service, Jefferson National Forest, 5162 Valleypointe Parkway, Roanoke, Virginia 24109-3050, (540) 265-6054.

Here are some of the best day hikes along the Blue Ridge Parkway.

• **Mountain Farm Trail.** This ¼-mile trail at Mile 5.9 along the Parkway is an easy, self-guiding route that begins at the Humpback Rocks Visitor Center, not too far from Charlottesville. It passes log cabins, chicken houses and a mountaineer's garden, reminders of the everyday life of the Blue Ridge's former inhabitants.

• **Humpback Rocks Trail.** This is a steep and rocky section of the Appalachian Trail that can be reached from the Mountain Farm Trail described above. Then it's a strenuous 4-mile hike to the summit of Humpback Mountain, from which you can see Rockfish Gap and the Shenandoah National Park to the north, the Shenandoah Valley to the west and the Rockfish River Valley to the east. In late spring, mountain laurel and azaleas make this a colorful, fragrant hike.

• **Crabtree Falls Trail.** This 3-mile hike in Nelson County leads to the highest cascading falls in Virginia. Its trailhead is a parking lot on Va. 56, a few miles east of Montebello. Five major waterfalls tumble down the mountain, and well-worn trails make it possible to enjoy it all without getting dangerously close to the falls. Hikers are advised to stay on the trails and off the slippery rocks.

• **Rock Castle Gorge Trail.** This 10-mile loop in northern Patrick County is noted for its high meadows, sweeping views, waterfalls and historical sites enroute to the 3,572-foot summit of Rocky Knob. Until the 1920s a mountain community thrived in this rugged area, where the rushing waters of Rock Castle Creek fueled sawmills and grist mills. This hike is one of hundreds in the 4,500-acre Rocky Knob Recreation Area, which has a Park Service visitors center, campground, picnic grounds and rustic rental cabins.

And here are several other trails near the Parkway.

• **Mount Rogers National Recreation Area.** Farther west of the Blue Ridge Parkway lies a vast sliver of land measuring 55 miles long and nearly 10 miles wide. This spectacular area, part of the Jefferson National Forest, is often said to resemble the Swiss Alps because of its high plateau and Alpine-like meadows.

The area has 300 miles of trails, many of which climb to the crest zone — where three mountains reach to nearly 6,000 feet. Mount Rogers is dazzling with its purple rhododendron, dense red spruce and Fraser fir, wild horses and panoramic views. For more information, contact the area's headquarters at Route 1, Box 303, Marion, Virginia 24354, (540) 783-5196.

• **The Virginia Creeper Trail.** A former railroad grade between Damascus (at the southernmost tip of the Mount Rogers area) and Abingdon, this trail is 34 miles long, but with many starting and stopping points. The easy grade provides a great way to enjoy fall foliage without working up too much of a sweat.

• **Little Stoney Creek Trail.** In Giles County west of Blacksburg there are wonderful hikes on the Appalachian Trail and in other recreation areas. One excellent 2-mile day hike follows Little Stoney Creek, which takes you to the 60-foot Cascades waterfall. The Civilian Conservation Corps constructed this beautiful trail in the 1930s. It's well-maintained, with benches along the creek and pretty wooden bridges. During the summer the pathway is lush and heavily shaded, a perfect place to cool off. You can also take a dip in the clear mountain pool at the base of the falls. To get there, go to Pembroke then take the road marked Cascades Recreation Area just east of the Dairy Queen on U.S. 460.

State Parks and Recreation Areas

The Blue Ridge's state parks and city and county recreation areas offer great hiking opportunities. Some of our favorites are described below.

• **Sky Meadows Trails.** Just outside of Paris, in Fauquier County, is the easily accessible Sky Meadows State Park, (540) 592-3556. Once a working Piedmont plantation, Sky Meadows' 1,100 acres along the eastern slope of the Blue Ridge entice weekend warriors with its maze of hiking trails, including a stretch of the Appalachian Trail.

• **Wildlife Management Area Trails.** Between Lexington and Staunton the state operates a 34,000-acre wildlife management area. Here, alluring trails offer solitude and scenic views of the Maury River, the gorge at Goshen Pass and a variety of flora and fauna.

• **Laurel Run Trail.** This moderate path starts near the wayside picnic area at Goshen Pass on Va. 39 and travels 2 miles uphill beside a creek coursing down to the Maury River. Rosebay rhododendron, oaks, maples and hemlock decorate the trail.

• **Old Chessie Trail.** Linking historic Lexington with Buena Vista, this 7 miles of old Chesapeake and Ohio railroad grade is now owned and maintained by the Virginia Military Institute Foundation. The flat, easy path offers glimpses of the Maury River and is bordered by wildflowers in the spring. In Lexington you can get to the trail from N. Main Street at VMI by taking a side street down to Woods Creek and a parking area on VMI Island. Follow trail signs, cross a pedestrian bridge over the Maury River and pass under the U.S. 11 bridge.

• **Buck Lick Trail.** Don't miss this easy hike in Douthat State Park, which spans Bath and Alleghany counties with 4,493 acres of scenic high ridges and more miles of hiking trails than almost any other state park. Buck Lick Trail was constructed by the Civilian Conservation Corps in the '30s and has 17 interpretive signs about geological features, trees, wild animals, lichens and forest succession. The park's trails are color-coded and generally in good condition. A hiking map from the visitors center is recommended for long hikes.

• **Sounding Knob Trail.** In Highland County, best known for its annual Maple Festival, there are also endless possibilities for hiking in a 13,978-acre wilderness area operated by the state. One option is a strenuous 5-mile hike up an old fire road to 4,400-foot Sounding Knob, the best-known landmark in the county. The mountaintop has a grazed open area and splendid views. The trail begins at the junction of Va. 615 and the Fire Trail Road, established by the Civilian Conservation Corps.

• **Ivy Creek Natural Area.** This is one of the many nature trails in municipal parks throughout the region. In Charlottesville the 215-acre Ivy Creek Natural Area is an unspoiled stretch of forest, streams and fields traversed only by footpaths. A network of 6 miles of trails includes self-guided ones. Ivy Creek is on Hydraulic Road, 2 miles north of the city.

Photo: Heidi Crandall

A skilled fly fisherman casts into the Rapidan River in the Blue Ridge.

• **Ash Lawn Historical Trail.** Several miles from Charlottesville at Ash Lawn, a 535-acre estate that was once home to President James Monroe, a historical trail leads through pastures and woods to the top of Carter's Mountain. Ecology markers are posted along the 3-mile-long path, which begins at the museum shop. Ash Lawn is just off I-64, 2½ miles beyond Thomas Jefferson's Monticello (see the Arts and Culture chapter for more information about Ash Lawn and other historical sites).

• **Smith Mountain Lake State Park and Visitors Center.** This park is not just for water enthusiasts, although it's a great place for swimming at the beach area, paddleboating (rentals available) and boating. The park also offers miles of hiking trails, camping, picnicking, a visitors center and interpretive programs. It's on Va. 626, Huddleston; call (540) 297-6066.

• **Grayson Highlands State Park.** The Appalachian Trail and more than 9 miles of other trails pass through this scenic 4,754-acre park on the eastern edge of Mount Rogers National Recreation Area. The park, which has ample camping and picnic facilities, hosts the Pig Pickin' on the Mountain festival in June and the Grayson Highlands Fall Festival in September.

• **New River Trail State Park.** Following the course of the historic New River, this linear park is a 57-mile trail running from Galax to Pulaski. The trail, which is frequented by hikers, bikers and horseback riders, has several convenient parking areas and access points along its entirety. The southern termiinus is on E. Stuart Drive (Va. 58) in Galax.

Mountain Biking

Virginia's Blue Ridge and neighboring Allegheny Mountains are a mountain biker's mecca. From technically and physically demanding single-track to gravel roads and rider-friendly rail-trail conversions, bikers have a wide range of terrain to suit their abilities.

The majority of public land open to mountain biking is in the George Washington and Jefferson National Forest, which encompasses more than 1½ million acres of mountain lands. Each is divided into a number of ranger districts with individual maps available showing most of the trails, forest roads and other significant features for two-wheel travel. The Washington and Jefferson Forest contains several thousand miles of trails and gravel roads, all of which are open to mountain bikers, with the exception of the Appalachian Trail and those trails within designated wilderness areas.

If you are a beginning mountain bike rider, you should probably stick to forest development roads until you get the hang of using all the gears on sometimes long climbs and steep descents. While single-track riding — also called narrow trail riding — is often touted as the epitome of the mountain bike experience, ascents and descents on rough, rocky and sometimes minimally maintained surfaces can be pretty tricky.

Regardless of experience, anyone riding in the national forest should heed the following Forest Service advice.

• Since none of the back country trails are maintained for continuous riding, you can expect to carry your bicycle across obstacles. Outside of designated wildernesses, you may ride behind the gated and mounded earth tank traps of closed roads. These roads are closed to motorized vehicles but are open to pedal-powered bicycles, horses, and hikers.

• While riding the trails, anticipate meeting horse riders and hikers. Hold your riding speed down on narrow trails and when approaching blind curves. You should be able to stop in half the distance you can see in front of you. Just as hikers should yield to horse riders, mountain bikers should yield to both horse riders and hikers by stopping and allowing them to pass when meeting head on, or by dis-

mounting and asking to pass when meeting from behind. As the newest user group in the back country, mountain bicyclists have to earn the respect of hikers and horse riders while those more established user groups learn to share the trails with you. Mutual cooperation and courtesy will go a long way toward keeping back country trails open to all users.

The Big Levels area near Sherando Lake in the Pedlar Ranger District of the Washington and Jefferson Forest is a favorite for many mountain bikers. The Big Levels, along the Coal Road (FDR 42), is a great place for pedaling along the relatively flat Reservoir Trail and Orebank Creek Road or any of the myriad unmarked former logging roads that meander through these 32,000 wooded acres.

Hardier and more skillful riders will continue along the Mills Creek Trail as it ascends Bald Mountain via a number of tortuous switchbacks before arriving at the Bald Mountain Primitive Road just off the Blue Ridge Parkway.

Beginning mountain bikers may find comfort in some of the George Washington section's flatter trails such as the North River Gorge Trail in the Dry River District and the Hidden Valley Trail in the Warm Springs District. An added bonus to riding on either of these routes is the accessibility of a cool trout stream that runs adjacent to each, great for fishing or just cooling off.

Heading into Southwest Virginia, you'll find two splendid rail-trail conversions that offer fantastic mountain biking opportunities. The 57-mile New River Trail is actually a state park that runs from Pulaski to Fries and Galax, 29 miles of it adjacent to the New River, thought to be the second-oldest river in the world. There are numerous access points along the way, but your ride will be made easier by purchasing a $4 *Map and User's Guide* and arranging a shuttle through Lanny Sparks at New River Bicycles, (540) 980-1741. His shop is in Draper, the 6-mile point along the trail.

Although you'll no longer hear the whistle from the old Virginia Creeper, you'll most certainly enjoy making tracks downhill from Whitetop Station through Damascus and on to the end of the line at Abingdon along the Virginia Creeper Trail. Maintained jointly by the Town of Abingdon and the Mount Rogers National Recreation Area of the Jefferson National Forest, you're sure to enjoy the ease of riding and spectacular scenery along this 33-mile former rail bed. Like the New River Trail, there are numerous access points from which to enter the trail, but many cyclists enjoy arranging a ride through Blue Blaze Shuttle Service, (540) 475-5095, in Damascus and careening downhill from Whitetop Station.

Lori Finley's *Mountain Biking the Appalachians: Northwest North Carolina/ Southwest Virginia*, published by John F. Blair, provides a lot of good information about traveling along the Virginia Creeper and New River Trails as well as the Mount Rogers National Recreation Area, (540) 783-5196. According to forest service literature, "Whoever invented mountain bicycles surely had the Mount Rogers National Recreation Area in mind!" Finley has gone the distance to share Mount Rogers' best mountain biking spots.

In addition, the Clinch Ranger District, (540) 328-2931, of the Jefferson section of the national forest has a brochure available detailing four loop rides. The headquarters for the consolidated forest is in Roanoke, (540) 265-6054, and a service center for the George Washington section is in Harrisonburg, (540) 564-8300.

Advice on additional places to ride in either section of the national forest is as close as any bike shop or district ranger office. In addition, both Douthat State Park, (540) 862-7200, just north of Clifton Forge, and Grayson Highlands State Park, (540) 579-7092, adjoining the southern edge of the Mount Rogers Recreation Area, allow mountain biking on their trails. Assistant park manager Sandie Purick and the staff at Grayson Highlands have developed what may be the first two mountain bike trail guides in the Virginia State Park System to help two-wheel travelers find their way around the park. Due out in spring 1996 is Randy Porter's book, *A Mountain Biker's Guide to Western Virginia*, which will provide specific descriptions for mountain biking destinations including woods roads, trails and rough roads west of the Blue Ridge, primarily in the George Washington and Jefferson National Forest.

The following companies offer cycling touring trips in Virginia.

• **VCC Four Seasons Cycling**, (540) 672-4850, 119 Madison Road, Orange, Virginia 22960.

• **Vermont Bicycle Touring**, (800) 245-3868, Travent International, P.O. Box 711, Bristol, Vermont 05445.

• **Backroads**, (800) 462-2848, 1516 5th Street, Suite L101, Berkeley, California 94710-1740.

• **Pineapple Pedalers**, (540) 249-3156, P.O. Box 6, Port Republic, Virginia 24471. (This is a bed and breakfast inn in the Shenandoah Valley with hiking, canoeing and cycling trips offered to guests.)

• **All Adventure Travel**, (800) 537-4025, 5589 Arapahoe, Suite 208, Boulder, Colorado 80303.

• **Classic Adventures**, (800) 777-8090, P.O. Box 153, Hamlin, New York 14464-0153.

For more information on Virginia bicycle clubs, maps and rides, contact the Virginia Department of Transportation, State Bicycle Coordinator, (804) 786-2964, 1401 E. Broad Street, Richmond, Virginia 23219

Boating

Canoe Outfitters

There are many reputable canoe outfitters in the Blue Ridge region. Several are along the South Fork of the Shenandoah River, which meanders between the Massanutten and Blue Ridge mountain ranges before joining the Potomac River at Harpers Ferry, West Virginia. These outfitters also rent rubber rafts, kayaks and tubes, the local's craft

of choice for a lazy afternoon of drifting with the current.

Other outfitters are near the James River, the longest and largest river in Virginia. Only Lexington's James River Basin Canoe Livery leads canoe trips down both the Maury and the James rivers.

Farther southwest, in Giles County, the New River Canoe Livery in Pembroke runs trips down the magnificent New River, reputed to be the second-oldest river on earth.

Most canoe outfitters will only allow you to travel down familiar waters, unless you're an expert and willing to assume the risks (financial and otherwise) of canoeing a less-traveled tributary. Generally speaking, a single fee includes the canoe rental, paddles, life jackets, maps, shuttle service and an orientation. The shortest trips cost anywhere from $22 to $28 per canoe, while longer all-day trips range from $40 to $50. Tubing costs much less.

Here are some good places to rent boats and equipment in the Blue Ridge region, from north to south.

FRONT ROYAL CANOE CO.
Front Royal   *(540) 635-5440*
March 15-Nov. 15

This outfit, 3 miles south of the entrance to Skyline Drive, rents canoes, kayaks, rafts, tubes and flatbottom boats. It offers trips on the Shenandoah River that range from leisurely fishing to mild whitewater adventures. Multiple-day canoe trips can also be arranged. Reserva-

---

Insiders' Tips

If you love to photograph white-tailed deer in their natural habitat, you don't have to stray too far off the beaten path. Loudoun County, in suburban Washington, D.C., has the highest density of deer in the state.

Photo: Wintergreen Resort

An afternoon ride through the mountains.

tions are recommended. This company will also provide a shuttle service for people with private canoes.

DOWNRIVER CANOE COMPANY

Bentonville   (540) 635-5526
April 1-Oct. 31

This company rents canoes for exploring the South Fork of the Shenandoah River, a good waterway for novices and moderately experienced canoeists. Detailed maps describing the river course and the best way to negotiate it are provided. The maps also point out the best camping areas, picnic sites, swimming holes and fishing spots.

Multiple-day trips can also be arranged. Reservations are recommended, but last-minute canoe trips are often possible. This company also has a shuttle service for people with their own canoes.

RIVER RENTAL OUTFITTERS

Bentonville   (540) 635-5050
March 22-Nov. 1; Also open weekends
in Nov. by reservation

"Bring us your weekend . . . and we'll do the rest!" is this business' motto. It offers canoe and tube rentals on the Shenandoah River and organizes fishing, camping, hiking and biking trips. The outfitter will custom-design a weekend vacation for the entire family, including packages with the nearby Skyline Bend Farm, Warren County's oldest licensed bed and breakfast inn.

Reservations are strongly recommended for weekends and holidays. The business also rents kayaks, 10-speed bicycles, fishing equipment and camping gear and sells fishing tackle and all kinds of supplies.

SHENANDOAH
RIVER OUTFITTERS INC.

Luray   (540) 743-4159
Open April 1-Nov. 15

This outfit offers canoe and tube rentals and canoe sales. It also organizes overnight trips complete with tents and sleeping bags. It's situated on the Shenandoah River between the Massanutten Mountain Trails and the Appalachian Trail in the George Washington section of the national forest. All-you-can-eat steak dinners and even music can be arranged in advance. Reservations are recommended.

JAMES RIVER RUNNERS INC.

Scottsville   (804) 286-2338
Open March-Oct.

This outfitter, 35 minutes south of Charlottesville, specializes in family canoe and rafting trips on the James River. Owners Christie and Jeff Schmick will arrange a variety of outings suitable for children older than six.

They also arrange day and overnight trips for larger groups — even conventions. A special two-day package features canoeing for 9 miles the first day, camping overnight by the river and tubing the next day.

Tubing trips for up to 600 people can be arranged, and groups of 25 or more get a discount. Reservations are necessary for groups and recommended for small parties.

JAMES RIVER REELING AND RAFTING

Scottsville   (804) 286-4FUN
March 1-Oct. 31

This business offers canoe, rafting and tubing trips for people at all levels of experience. It specializes in customizing overnight trips to suit the customer's fancy. "Describe what you want and let us design a trip for you," reads its brochure. Trips can be organized for convention groups, which get a 10 percent discount when 11 or more boats are rented. The company maintains a permanent campground on the river and offers two-day canoeing/rafting packages.

The headquarters is on the corner of Main and Ferry streets in downtown Scottsville at the James River Trading Post. Here you'll find fishing and camping supplies and anything else you may have left behind.

JAMES RIVER BASIN
CANOE LIVERY LTD.

Lexington   (540) 261-7334
Open year round

This outfit arranges day and overnight trips down both the Maury and James rivers. You can take an adventurous run down Balcony Falls, the mighty rapids where the James breaks through the Blue

Ridge Mountains. Or you can spend a couple of hours paddling down a slow stretch of the beautiful Maury.

The staff gives a solid orientation, with instructions on safety and basic canoeing strokes. A video program also familiarizes canoeists with the stretch of river about to be boated.

NEW RIVER CANOE LIVERY

Pembroke   **(540) 626-7189**
April-Oct.

Owner Dave Vicenzi rents canoes for trips along the New River in Giles County. The easiest trip is on the 7 miles of river between Eggleston to Pembroke, but the most popular outing is an 11-mile run from Pembroke to Pearisburg, which has several Class II (intermediate) whitewater rapids.

When the water is high in the spring, Vicenzi allows customers to canoe down Walker and Wolf creeks, tributaries of the New River. Multiple-day trips can also be arranged, but customers must supply their own camping gear.

WILDNERNESS CANOE COMPANY

Off I-81, Natural Bridge   **(800) 4CANOE4**

This company specializes in river trips from two hours to two days' duration. The James River headwaters provides quiet recreation for paddlers of all ages, and the staff here can make this outdoor adventure safe and fun. The retail store has Wilderness Canoes, kayaks, fishing boats, bait and tackle, T-shirts, snacks and drinks. Class I and II rapids are available on request. The store is at the intersection of Va. 130 and U.S. 11.

Other Boating Possibilities

Let's not forget boating on Virginia's beautiful lakes. There are three state parks in the heart of the mountains where boats can be rented.

At Douthat State Park near Clifton Forge, you can rent rowboats and paddleboats on a 50-acre lake. Rowboats and paddle boats are also available on a 108-acre lake at Hungry Mother State Park, in the far reaches of Southwest Virginia, near Marion. In Pulaski County, about an hour south of Roanoke, the 4,500-acre Claytor Lake in Pulaski County also rents rowboats.

Generally boats are available on weekends beginning in mid-May and daily from Memorial Day through Labor Day weekend. Smith Mountain Lake's 500 miles of winding shoreline and 20,600 acres of sparkling waters also offer countless possibilities for boating. There are about a dozen places where various types of boats can be rented, from yachts and pontoons to motor boats, sailboats and house boats. For information and brochures, contact the Smith Mountain Lake Visitors Center at (800) 676-8203.

Swimming

Swimmers who enjoy the outdoors can count on the Blue Ridge of Virginia's cool mountain streams, lakes and even waterfalls for the most refreshing dip they'll ever take.

Municipal pools, such as the Town of Blacksburg's, perched atop a mountain vista, or the City of Radford's, beside the ancient New River, are a panacea to the eye and spirit by virtue of their environmentally beautiful settings.

Some of the best swimming can be found in the area's state parks and national forests. Picture yourself swimming at the bottom of a sparkling waterfall after a 2-mile hike at the Cascades in Pembroke in Giles County. Or how about lying on Claytor Lake's white sand beach in Pulaski County while horseback riders amble by! For the strong in spirit, there's icy cold Cave Mountain Lake near Glasgow. All have sparse, but clean and accommodating, changing and shower facilities.

Primitive swimming fans will find the 10-mile venture across the West Virginia border to Blue Bend near Covington worthwhile to delight in the coldest water in the Blue Ridge.

Families with small children will be interested in an abundance of private campgrounds with lovely swimming areas overseen by lifeguards. One of the best-known is Shenandoah Acres Resort at Stuart's Draft, near the Waynesboro intersection of Skyline Drive and the Blue Ridge Parkway.

Following is an Insiders' list of swimming lovers' sites definitely worth the drive from anywhere.

Municipal Pools

CITY OF WAYNESBORO
(540) 949-7665

War Memorial Pool is in the center of lovely Ridgeview Park. Surrounded by a playground, tennis courts, a baseball diamond and an open field, the managers of this Olympic-size pool pride themselves on its cleanliness and pleasing view. Open from Memorial Day to Labor Day, the pool's general admission hours are from noon to 6 PM Monday through Saturday and 1 to 6 PM on Sunday. Family Swim,

when parents only must pay, is offered from 10 AM to noon Monday through Saturday. Fees are $1 for ages 15 and younger and $2 for ages 16 and older.

CITY OF STAUNTON
(540) 886-7946

Gypsy Hill Park Pool is a fairly new L-shaped pool, having opened several years ago. The pool is Olympic-size and has a wading pool. The facility opens for the season around Memorial Day and closes Labor Day. It's open from 11 AM to 6 PM Monday through Saturday and from 1 to 6 PM on Sunday. The fee is $3 for all day, all ages.

CITY OF CHARLOTTESVILLE

Washington Park Pool, 14th St. and Preston Ave.	*(804) 977-2607*
Onesty Pool, Meade Ave.	*(804) 295-7532*
Crow Pool, Rosehill Dr.	*(804) 977-1362*
Smith Pool, Cherry Ave.	*(804) 977-1960*
McIntire Pool, U.S. 250 By.	*(804) 295-9072*
Forest Hills (Ave.) Pool	*(804) 296-1444*

The city of Charlottesville boasts six municipal pools: two outdoor (Washington Park Pool and Onesty Pool); two indoor (Crow and Smith pools); and two wading pools (McIntire and Forest Hills). The outdoor and indoor pools are all 75 feet long and the facilities feature showers, hair dryers and lockers. The indoor pools are heated. The wading pools are small and shallow, designed for children 12 and younger. The outdoor and wading pools are open from Memorial Day to Labor Day. The hours for the outdoor pools are noon to 6 PM Monday through

Friday and noon to 5 PM Saturday and Sunday. The wading pools are open 10:30 AM to 4:30 PM Monday through Friday and noon to 5 PM Saturday and Sunday. The indoor pools are open year round, but hours are widely varied, so call ahead of time. Admission for nonresidents for the outdoor and indoor facilities is $1.25 for children and $2.75 for adults. There is no charge for the wading pools.

CITY OF LYNCHBURG
(804) 528-9794

Two play areas and a place for picnics surround this pool in Miller Park. The Olympic-size pool features a high dive and a kiddie area. Lessons are offered each morning. Miller Park Pool is open from Memorial Day through Labor Day. On Monday, Wednesday, Friday and Saturday, the hours are noon to 6 PM; Tuesday and Thursday, noon to 5:30 PM and 6:30 to 9 PM; Sunday from 1 to 7 PM. Admission is $1.50 for ages 2 and older. The charge for the evening swims is $1. Pass books of 10 tickets can be purchased for $10. These can be used for afternoon or evening swim sessions.

TOWN OF BLACKSBURG
(540) 961-1103

Mountain scenery lovers will gasp at the view from this mountaintop panorama. You'll bathe in mountain beauty as you swim.

The facility is open June through August 15, 1 to 5:30 PM, seven days a week. The fee is 75¢ for ages 3 to 14 and $1 for ages 15 and up. The pool is on Graves Avenue, off South Main Street, past Blacksburg Middle School. And better still, Blacksburg's new 25-yard indoor swimming facility sports six lanes, sauna, spa and diving area. It is on Patrick Henry Drive across from Blacksburg High.

CITY OF RADFORD
(540) 731-3633

Radford's city pool is an Olympic-size swimming pool in Bisset Park, just off Norwood Street in Radford, bordering nearly a mile of the scenic New River. Its setting in a 58-acre municipal park makes this pool unique. It is surrounded by six lighted tennis courts, lighted picnic shelters, playgrounds, a gazebo and fitness station. The facility is open May 23 through Labor Day. Hours are Monday through Thursday 1 to 5 PM and 7 to 8:30 PM; Friday, 1 to 5 PM; and weekends 1 to 8:30 PM. Admission is 50¢ for ages 7 to 15 and 75¢ for ages 16 and older. Children younger than 6 are admitted free with a paying adult.

State Parks

CLAYTOR LAKE
Off I-81 at Exit 33   (540) 674-5492

This beautiful park is near Dublin in Pulaski County. You'll think you're on an ocean beach, with the ample white sand surrounded by a full-service boat marina beside the sparkling water. Camping, horseback riding rentals and sports fishing are also popular at this 4,500-acre lake. Its historic Howe House (c. 1879) features exhibits about the life of early settlers in the region. June kicks off with a family fishing tournament and Labor Day weekend brings the annual Appalachian Arts and Crafts Festival.

SMITH MOUNTAIN LAKE
(540) 297-4062

Directions: From U.S. 460, take Va. 43 to Va. 626 S.

This lakefront beach nestled in the tall blue mountains of Bedford County offers a never-ending show of gliding sailboats in the distance. It's a paradise for water enthusiasts and has a visitor center with especially good nature programs for the whole family during the summer. Special events include the Ruritans Bass Fishing Tournament in March, an Arts in the Park in June and Ruritan Supper and Festival in September.

National Forests

CASCADES
(540) 265-6054

Directions: From Pembroke in Giles County, return to U.S. 460, head north and west about a mile, then turn right onto Va. 623 to Cascades Recreation Area.

Cascades Recreation Area features a 3-mile hike to a 60-foot waterfall. Picture yourself hiking and then jumping into a cool, placid pool of water right under a thundering waterfall. This is one of the most photogenic sites in the New River Valley. Warning: Don't try jumping into the water from the cliffs of the waterfall. There have been at least three deaths in recent memory from careless youths who did. This swimming area is not recommended for small children. For more information write George Washington and Jefferson National Forests, 5162 Valleypointe Parkway, Roanoke, Virginia 24019.

SHERANDO LAKE
(540) 564-8300

Off I-64, near Waynesboro, Sherando Lake, in the George Washington section of the national forest, offers a pristine beach within a natural paradise of camping, boating and fishing. The daily swimming fee is $4 per vehicle or $1 per person.

CAVE MOUNTAIN LAKE
(540) 265-6054

Directions: Off of I-81, take Natural Bridge Exit 49 or 50 and turn onto Va. 130 at Natural Bridge. Follow this road 3.2 miles, then turn onto Va. 759, which you'll follow for 3.2 miles and then turn right onto Va. 781. Drive 1.6 miles to the recreation area's paved entrance road.

The long trip to isolation is worth it. Cave Mountain Lake Campground, in the Jefferson section of the national forest, is nearby with its unusual picnic tables and sites often surrounded by stone, set amidst large pines and hardwoods. There is a large open field with plenty of sunshine, and the lake is cool and refreshing. It's a real getaway.

MONONGAHELA NATIONAL FOREST (WEST VIRGINIA)
Blue Bend Recreation Area   *(304) 536-1440*

Directions: From I-64, take the White Sulphur Springs, West Virginia, Exit to W.Va. 92; go north 10 miles to Alvon. Turn left at the Blue Bend sign and proceed several miles to the Blue Bend Recreation Area.

A true "swimming hole," Blue Bend is known for its chilling mountain stream waters surrounded by huge, flat rocks for sunbathers. Built by the CCC camp workers during the Great Depression, the rock craftsmanship makes this place unusual.

Insiders' Tips

The American dogwood is the state tree. Visit in the spring and you'll see mountains dotted with its snowy blooms.

There is no other more invigorating feeling in the world than baptism by Blue Bend's waters. Swimming is within view of an authentic swinging foot bridge. Primitive camping and picnic tables are nearby in this deeply wooded, out-of-the-way area populated mostly by locals. Don't miss this place but be prepared for a chilly experience. Blue Bend is said to earn its name from the color of the swimmers' lips when they emerge!

Private Swimming Areas

SHENANDOAH ACRES RESORT
(540) 337-1911

Directions: From Skyline Drive and Blue Ridge Parkway, follow the signs from the Waynesboro Exit.

Often called "America's Finest Inland Beach," this site is reminiscent of the 1930s, with its boardwalk-enclosed pavilion. Swimming is superb with a sand-bottomed lake of pure, soft, water — 500,000 gallons a day.

Children are giggly and ecstatic playing with the bubbling water as it emerges from pipes. There are slides, merry-go-rounds, a drop cable and even water volleyball. Life guards are on duty at all times, May through September. The recreational area includes camping, cottages, picnic tables and fireplaces. This is a wonderful family retreat. For more information, write: Shenandoah Acres Resort, P.O. Box 300, Stuarts Draft, Virginia 24477.

Fishing

Naturalist Henry David Thoreau of Walden Pond fame once commented, "In the night, I dream of trout-fishing." In Virginia's Blue Ridge, anglers see their dreams become reality in clear, cold mountain streams, rivers and lakes. Visitors can rest easy at night knowing that, at any given moment, millions of fish are surging upstream or lying tantalizingly in wait in stone river recesses.

An aggressive conservation effort by the state is partly responsible for the plentiful fishing in the Blue Ridge. For example, the mountain streams found in Shenandoah National Park are one of the last completely protected strongholds of the native Eastern brook trout. Savvy Virginia tourism experts report that since Robert Redford's naturalistic film on fly fishing, based on the book, *A River Runs Through It*, hit the screens, the numbers of fly fishing anglers in Virginia were thicker than the black flies they're trying to imitate. But don't worry. The out-of-the-way waters far outnumber those that aren't.

Outstanding waters by species include: brown trout — Lake Moomaw, Mossy Creek and Smith River; largemouth bass — James River; smallmouth bass — James River, Smith Mountain Lake, Claytor Lake and Lake Philpott; striped bass — Claytor Lake and Smith Mountain Lake; and walleye — Smith Mountain Lake, Philpott Lake, Claytor Lake, Carvins Cove and the Roanoke River.

And now for bragging rights! To name a few records: smallmouth bass, 7 lbs., 7 oz., New River; Roanoke bass, 2 lbs., 6 oz., Smith Mountain Lake; striped bass, 45 lbs., 10 oz., Smith Mountain Lake; walleye, 14 lbs., 20 oz., New River; and northern pike, 31 lbs., 4 oz., Motts Run. By the time you read this, some of these records probably already will be broken.

Figures for fish citations are equally impressive. For 1993, the James River set the record with 584 citations of 17 species, followed by Smith Mountain Lake with 259 citations of 12 species; the New

River with 93 of 10; Lake Moomaw with 108 of 11; Claytor Lake with 97 of 14; and Philpott Reservoir with 27 of 6 species.

The primary objective of this chapter is to give directions to some of the Blue Ridge's classic streams, rivers and lakes — the ones where anglers aren't falling over each other. After you get to your spot, you may want to rough it on your own. Or, you can hire your own guide.

Otherwise, there are literally hundreds of fishing places recommended by the Virginia Department of Game and Inland Fisheries. You can find out about real gem daytrips. An especially fun one for lovers of both fishing and horseback riding is the package offered by Virginia Mountain Outfitters in Buena Vista, near Lexington. Trips range from one day to five and include a clinic. Call Deborah Sensabaugh at (540) 261-1910 at Outfitters to find out more.

Farther north, at the charming tin-roofed town of Edinburg, Murray's Fly Shop is the place to find out where you can fish in the Shenandoah Valley for the really big ones. Harry Murray is the author of several books, including *Trout Fishing in the Shenandoah National Park*, and promises to help you catch Valley fish. Murray offers numerous clinics and can be reached at (540) 984-4212 for a complete list.

Wintergreen Resort in Wintergreen offers Fly Fisher's Symposiums. Call Chuck Furimsky at (800) 325-2200 for more information on fishing and lodging at a first-class resort that also offers great golfing and skiing. Also for fly fishing supreme, go westward in Bath County to Meadow Lane Lodge, site of a former Orvis Fishing School on the Jackson River. Call (540) 839-5959.

For details and the widest array of locations, the Department of Game and Inland Fisheries' *Virginia Fishing Guide* is a must. Traditionally, topographic maps published by the U.S. Geological Survey have been the most useful sources of information for anglers. These maps can tell you whether streams flow through open or forested land, how steep the land is and where tributaries enter. Directions on how to get both guides are listed at the end of this fishing section.

So, now you're excited about all the fishing possibilities, we hope. But, don't forget your license, which can be obtained from some county circuit court clerks, city corporation court clerks and a variety of other authorized agents. The first Saturday and Sunday in June have been designated as Free Fishing Days in Virginia. No fishing license of any kind will be required for rod and reel fishing except in designated stocked trout waters. A detailed booklet describing licensing requirements, game fish size and catch limits, special regulations (specific to certain areas) and other regulations can be obtained from the Virginia Department of Game and Inland Fisheries (see address at the end of this section).

License requirements and fees for both residents and nonresidents follow.

RESIDENT

County or city resident to fish in county or city of residence — $5

State resident to fish only: $12

Resident to fish statewide for five consecutive days in private waters or public waters not stocked with trout: $5

State and county resident to trout fish in designated waters stocked with trout, in addition to regular fishing license: $12

Age 65 and older state resident license to fish: $1

Virginia resident special lifetime to fish: $250

Photo: Va Dept. of Economic Development

The New River in Southwest Virginia is a popular place for boating, tubing and canoeing.

NONRESIDENT

To fish only: $30

To fish for five consecutive days statewide in private waters or public waters not stocked with trout: $6

To fish in designated waters stocked with trout in addition to regular fishing license: $30

Virginia nonresident special lifetime to fish: $500

Licenses can be obtained from some county circuit court clerks, city corporation court clerks and a variety of other authorized agents. The first Saturday and Sunday in June have been designated as Free Fishing Days in Virginia. No fishing license of any kind will be required for rod and reel fishing except in designated stocked trout waters. A detailed booklet describing licensing requirements, game fish size and catch limits, special regulations (specific to certain areas) and other regulations can be obtained from the Virginia Department of Game

and Inland Fisheries (see the address at the end of this section).

Regardless of whether you're testing the waters of the Blue Ridge as an experienced angler or a novice, it doesn't hurt to remember safety at all times, especially cold weather hazards. Although getting away from it all is most of the fun, don't forget to let somebody know where you are. Despite the best of precautions, you'll probably fall in at some point. In hot weather, it's an inconvenience. In cold weather, which is most of the year, it can be fatal. Many anglers do not realize that hypothermia can strike when the temperature is in the 40s. Prevention is always best, including wearing waders with rough soles in our streams and life preservers in our rivers and lakes. And don't forget snakes (timber rattlers and copperheads are the two poisonous species) and ticks, the latter of which are "fishing" for you!

Lakes

Listed below are some favorite fishing areas of the Blue Ridge. Source material for complete listings is at the end of this fishing section.

RIVIANNA RESERVOIR

Just outside Charlottesville, this is often called the best bet for fishing in the area surrounding this historic city. It supports good populations of bass, crappie, bream and channel cats, with occasional walleye and muskie. There is a public boat ramp near the filtration plant of the Charlottesville water supply reservoir, which may be reached from U.S. 29 north of Charlottesville by taking Va. 631 (Rio Road) or 743 to Va. 659 or 676. The ramp is at the end of Route 659.

LAKE MOOMAW
(540) 962 -2214

This flood control reservoir was completed in 1981 with the closing of the Gathright Dam on the Jackson River. Ever since, its 43-mile shoreline has proven to be a popular playground for residents of Alleghany, Bath and Highland counties. Much of the shoreline is adjacent to the Gathright Wildlife Management Area. Crappie fishing is outstanding, with 1.5-pounders common. There is an equal complement of large- and smallmouth bass. Thirty-seven citation rainbows have also been pulled from the lake. For more information, call the James River Ranger District in Covington at the number above.

SMITH MOUNTAIN LAKE
(540) 297-4062

Directions: From U.S. 460 take Va. 43 to Va. 626 S.

The striper population is the most noticed at Smith Mountain, bordering Bedford, Pittsylvania and Franklin counties. It's been the source of numerous citation fish. More anglers appear to be converting to fishing live bait over artificial. A real pro, who has been fishing the lake since its beginnings with Appalachian Power Company in the '60s, says the secret for big stripers is live shad, which can be caught at dockside in casting nets.

The state's largest striper, 45 pounds 10 ounces, was caught here in 1995. At the rate these whoppers are growing, that record will probably soon be surpassed. If you're serious about getting one of the big ones, a professional guide is a great idea. Some good ones are R. M. King, (540) 721-4444; Dave Sines, (540) 721-5007; or Spike Franceschini, (540) 297-5611. They'll try to ensure you don't go home with only tales about the one that got away.

The lake provides a lot of camping and recreational opportunities, including a swimming beach, through Smith Mountain Lake State Park.

Insiders' Tips

Roadside stands are great places to pick up seasonal items such as apples, pumpkins, squash, tomatoes, corn and other fresh vegetables. If the vendor has time to chat, you're likely to pick up some interesting local knowledge too.

CLAYTOR LAKE
(540) 961-1103

This lake, also impounded by Appalachian Power, on the New River near Dublin, is known as a fantastic white bass fishery, producing many citations annually. Claytor has traditionally been a good flathead catfish lake too, with fish going up to 25 pounds or more. Crappie also have shown good growth rates. Claytor Lake State Park provides fine marinas, camping, cottages and a swimming beach.

HUNGRY MOTHER LAKE
(540) 783-3422

In the rustic highlands of its namesake state park near Marion, this lake provides good fishing for largemouth bass, bluegill and crappie (up to 13 inches). Camping is available and boats can be rented.

References

STATE PUBLICATIONS

For the total scoop on fishing, the following titles are available from the Virginia Department of Games and Inland Fisheries, (804) 367-1000, 4010 Broad Street, P.O. Box 11104, Richmond, Virginia 23230-1104.

Sportsman Calendar
Virginia Fishing Regulations
Virginia Fishing Guide
Fishing with Nets
National Forest Maps
Virginia Freshwater Fish Identification Booklet
Fishing the Water James
Trout Fishing Guide
References for Fresh Water Fishing Guides

U.S. GEOLOGICAL SURVEY MAPS

Contact the Distribution Branch, U.S. Geological Survey, Box 25286, Federal Center, Denver, Colorado 80225 for individual maps.

VIRGINIA TOPOGRAPHIC MAPS

An outstanding collection of Virginia topographic maps is the *Virginia Atlas & Gazetteer*, published by the DeLorme Mapping Company, P.O. Box 298, Freeport, Maine 04032.

LAKE AND RIVER MAPS

Contact the Alexandria Drafting Company, 6440 General Green Way, Alexandria, Virginia 22312.

BOOKS ON TROUT STREAMS

We recommend two great trout stream books: *Virginia Trout Streams*, by Harry Slone, published by Backcountry Publications; and *A Fly Fisherman's Blue Ridge*, by Christopher Camuto, published by Henry Holt & Company.

Golf

Virginia has more than 130 golf courses, many of which are in the mountains and valleys of the Blue Ridge, including three of the country's top golf resorts. The diverse topography of the region means that the courses vary widely, providing a never-ending challenge which draws visitors back year after year. The fact that Blue Ridge links are generally greener and 10 to 15 degrees cooler in the summer is another draw. The quality of golf here, like the quality of life, has always been nothing short of outstanding.

The nation's oldest first tee is still in use at The Homestead, a highly rated resort in Hot Springs, near golf legend Sam Snead's estate. After generations of ownership by the Ingalls family, the resort is now run by Club Resorts Inc., the same

Photo: Virginia Division of Tourism

A family relaxes on tubes as they leisurely travel down the New River.

folks who resurrected North Carolina's Pinehurst. They plan to make The Homestead a prime golf destination too. Of the resort's three courses, The Cascades is acknowledged as one of the best mountain layouts in the country. It has been the venue for two U.S. Women's Amateur Championships, one Men's Amateur, a Curtis Cup match, a U.S. Senior Men's Amateur and countless state championships. The course has three of the prettiest finishing holes to be found anywhere, with a stream, two ponds and a small waterfall adding challenge as well as beauty.

Thirty miles south of The Homestead is yet another ultimate golf destination, The Greenbrier, a top-rated resort in White Sulphur Springs, West Virginia. It has three historic courses, including a classic by designer Jack Nicklaus.

Wintergreen Four Seasons Resort near Charlottesville is consistently ranked among the nation's top golf destinations. In 1990 designer Rees Jones cut the ribbon on the Stoney Creek course, a valley layout to complement the resort's mountaintop Devil's Knob. Because of Stoney Creek's lowland location, the resort can offer guests skiing and golf on the same day. Massanutten, near Harrisonburg, and Bryce, near Basye, are two other ski resorts with notable golf courses.

Farther north in the Shenandoah Valley, between Winchester and Front Royal, is the Shenandoah Valley Country Club, a 27-hole layout with stunning flowerbeds throughout. The course keeps a full-time flower gardener, and it shows. Next door is Bowling Green Golf Club, with its two challenging 18-hole courses.

In 1993 nursery magnate Bill Meadows opened the Meadows Farm Golf Course in Orange County, a challenging, beautifully landscaped layout with the country's longest golf hole, at 841-yard par 6.

Just off the Blue Ridge Parkway at Groundhog Mountain is the Olde Mill Golf Resort, a scenic, challenging, and relatively unknown gem designed by Ellis Maples in the 1970s. And visitors to Smith Mountain Lake can test their skills on Chestnut Creek, at Bernard's Landing, a popular course in that area or the new course at Mariner's Landing .

So much golf, so little space! With far too many courses to name, much less describe, we recommend three sources for information on public, semiprivate and military courses: *Virginia Fairways Annual Golf Guide*; Virginia Golf Association, (804) 378-2300; Golf Promotions in Virginia, (800) GOLF-NVA; and Golf Virginia Resorts Association, (800) 93-BACK9.

Camping

From primitive campsites to modern RV campgrounds with all the amenities, camping in the Blue Ridge Mountains is a four-season activity.

Forests cover two-thirds of Virginia, with most of it in the Blue Ridge Mountains. Camping here is a huge industry, offering an inexpensive, family-oriented recreational pastime whether you like KOA Kamping Kabins with all the comforts of home or a remote spot in the woods flat enough for your tent. At Blue Ridge of Virginia campgrounds, you'll usually find swimming in cool mountain streams or lakes and copious hiking trails. Some even have boat rentals and horseback riding.

National Forest Campgrounds

In the George Washington and Jefferson National Forest, family camping is on a first-come, first-served basis. The only exception is group camping, for which reservations can be made up to 120 days in advance — and must be made at least 10 days in advance. No rental cabins or other lodging is available in national forest campgrounds. However, if you want to bring along your pets for company, you can, but dogs must leashed.

Virginia State Park Campgrounds

Six state parks in the Blue Ridge have campgrounds, and many also have cabins. Reservations for campsites and cabins must be made by calling the Virginia State Parks Reservation Center at (800) 933-PARK. You can pay by credit card over the phone, or make your reservation two weeks in advance and then mail in a check. We recommend making your reservation as much as 364 days ahead for the most popular sites. The maximum camping period is 14 days in any 30-day period. Leashed pets are permitted.

Developed Campsites

Developed campsites can accommodate one piece of camping equipment and/or one motor vehicle and a maximum of six people. Expect a grill, picnic table and access to bathhouses.

Electrical and Water Hookups

Electrical/water hookup sites which can accommodate recreational vehicles and campers are available only at Claytor Lake and Fairy Stone.

Cabins

Housekeeping cabins ranging from one room to two bedrooms are available in Claytor, Douthat, Fairy Stone, and Hungry Mother state parks. Any cabins not reserved become available on a first-come, first-served basis for a minimum of two nights.

Group Camping

Group camping is available at several parks, with a minimum of three sites.

CAMPING FEES (NIGHTLY RATES)
Primitive sites, $7
Developed sites, $10.50
Group sites, $10.50 per site, minimum three sites
Electricity/water sites, $15
Pet fee, $3 per night
Cancellation fee, $5

CABIN FEES (WEEKLY AND NIGHTLY)
One Room, $265, $55
One Bedroom, $293, $62
Two Bedroom, $405, $77
Lodge (Douthat only), $682.25, $140.50 ($83.25 third through seventh nights)
Extra Bed, $3 per night
Pet fee, $3 per night

Organizations and Information Sources

For camping and visitor information and maps, we suggest the following sources.

• **Virginia Campground Association** (private campgrounds), 2101 Libby Avenue, Richmond, Virginia 23230, (804) 288-3065.

• **George Washington and Jefferson National Forests**, 5162 Valleypointe Parkway, Roanoke, 24019-3050, (540) 265-6054.

• **National Forest group camping reservations**, (800) 280-2267.

• **Shenandoah National Park**, Route 4, Box 348, Luray, Virginia 22835, (540) 999-2266.

• **Virginia State Parks**, Department of Conservation & Recreation, Division of State Parks, 203 Governor Street, Suite 306, Richmond, Virginia 23219.

General Information, (804) 786-1712

Brochures and Reservations, (800) 933-PARK or (804) 225-3867

TDD number, (804) 786-2121

Blue Ridge Parkway Camping, 2551 Mountain View Road, Vinton, Virginia 24179, (540) 857-2213

U.S. Army Corps of Engineers (Philpott Lake, Bassett only), Wilmington District, Philpott Lake, Route 6, Box 140, Bassett, Virginia 24055, (540) 629-2703

• **Virginia Division of Tourism**, Bell Tower on Capitol Square, Richmond, Virginia 23219, (804) 786-4484

• **Shenandoah Valley Travel Association**, P.O. Box 1040, New Market, Virginia 22844, (540) 740-3132

Horseback Riding

If you're unable — or unwilling — to explore these mountains on foot, by all means get on a horse, even if it's your very first time. You'll find that your mount is an amiable companion as well as a comfortable means to get to places you'd otherwise miss. If you squint your eyes just right, you can imagine you're an early frontiersman scouting the uncharted Blue Ridge wilderness. Experienced equestrians do it all the time — trailering their horses to state parks or national forests for a day or weekend of riding.

There are a number of horseback riding outfitters (particularly in the Shenandoah Valley) who offer one- or two-hour rides for beginners, half- or full-day treks for the more experienced and a variety of overnight trips.

You can rough it and camp beside a trout stream with Deborah Sensabaugh's Virginia Mountain Outfitters, grilling

fresh trout over a campfire and listening to the whippoorwills at sunset. Or you can say goodnight to your horse at day's end and retire to a cozy country inn. Several inns specialize in guided trail riding, and most horse outfitters offer packages with nearby inns so that you can soak in a hot tub after a long day's ride.

In this section, we list places that offer guided horseback trips to the public. There are also many private liveries and horse clubs and a plethora of trails, both public and private.

MAINTREE FARM
Leesburg   **(540) 777-3279**

This boarding and training operation offers guests a rare opportunity to enjoy prime hunt country. The stable, across from the Loudoun Hunt kennels, takes out a mock hunt every Sunday morning, a delightful two-hour ride. During foxhunting season, the owners can arrange riding to the hounds with the Loudoun Hunt. If partner Beth Newman rides out with you, ask her how she became one of the country's leading female steeplechase riders. Group lessons and trail rides are $15 per hour; the mock hunt is $25. Though the stable caters to all levels, only experienced equestrians should expect to ride over fences. Reservations are required.

MASSANUTTEN TRAIL RIDES INC.
Front Royal   **(540) 636-6061**

For a taste of the Old West, take a trail ride with Skyline Ranch Resort along the mountain ridges of the George Washington section of the national forest. Western-style rides lasting 90 minutes are $20 per person. Children must be nine or older. The ranch also offers riding lessons at $15 per hour. Skyline Ranch is a members only campground, but nonmembers can reserve campsites within a week of their visit on a space available basis.

MARRIOTT RANCH
Hume   *(540) 364-2627*

This 4,200-acre beef cattle ranch, owned and operated by Marriott Corporation, is home to one of the largest Western trail ride operations in the northern Virginia piedmont. Rides are usually 1½ hours long and are available every day of the week except Monday. Rides go out weekdays at 10 AM and noon; Saturday at 10 AM, noon, 2 and 4 PM; and Sunday at 10 AM, noon and 2 PM. Rates are $22.50 per person on weekdays and $27.50 on weekends; group rates are available. The minimum riding age is 10. The trails run through winding streams, open valleys and wooded hills on the ranch. Horse-drawn buggy, stage coach and haywagon rides are also offered. Reservations are required for all types of rides.

Marriott Ranch also specializes in corporate Western special events like barbecues and country and western dances, as well as business meetings and formal affairs such as wedding receptions and garden parties.

Saturday nights in September and October are lively ones at the ranch. They have parties called "Steak Bake and Boot Scoot" that include haywagon rides, Western-style steak cookouts, country and western dance instructions and Western comedy entertainment. Reservations are required; call for current prices.

MOUNTAIN SPRINGS STABLES
Sperryville   *(540) 987-9545*

Owner/operator Heather Marsh welcomes riders of all ability levels, but her English-style-only operation is geared toward more experienced equestrians. The stable is within an hour's drive of nine of Virginia's esteemed foxhunts, and Marsh can make arrangements for guests to hunt. She'll provide quality field hunters or stabling for your own horse — even accommodations for your groom.

Marsh offers one- to two-hour trail rides "over beautiful but rugged mountain terrain, which demands some skill," she says. The facilities include indoor and outdoor riding arenas in which she gives private riding lessons.

Reservations are necessary for trail rides, but don't hesitate to contact her on short notice in case there's an opening. Trail rides are $40 per person. Call for prices on other services.

FORT VALLEY RIDING STABLE
Kingscrossing   *(540) 933-6633*

In the middle of the Massanutten Mountains, 1.5 miles from the nearest general store, is scenic Fort Valley and the Twin Lakes Campgrounds, where fat trout seem to just jump into your creel. Horseback riding is $15 per hour, $60 for a half-day guided trip, which includes lunch on the trail. A two-day wilderness ride to some of the mountains' most scenic spots is $225 per person, which includes two trail lunches, a country breakfast, a campfire dinner, sleeping bags and tents.

SHENANDOAH NATIONAL PARK
Luray   *(540) 999-2210*

Guided trail rides leave from the National Park's Skyland Lodge several times daily. The route follows the scenic White Oak Canyon trail, which passes several waterfalls. The hour-long ride costs $18 per person and must be booked a day ahead. There's also a more advanced, 2½-hour trek leaving early in the morning on weekdays in the summer. That ride is $36.

GRAVES MOUNTAIN LODGE
Syria   *(540) 923-4231*

This family-owned and operated retreat has a heritage of hospitaly dating back 130 years. Practice does make perfect, for the rustic mountain lodge has the right mix of life's simple pleasures (see our Bed and Breakfast and Country Inns chapter). Porch-sitting ranks right up there with hiking, fishing and swimming, especially after you've spent the day wildlife-watching from horseback.

Working closely with the lodge is Tom Seay of Overnight Wilderness Outfitters, (540) 923-5071, who offers full-day rides in the Blue Ridge Mountains for $90, including lunch. Or take off for one to three days on an excursion to a log cabin in the wilderness. Half day rides are $50 per person, and there are shorter rides on the lodge's 50 miles of trails. Stabling and services are available for horse owners, and groups are welcome.

Special times at the Lodge are the April Spring Fling Festival, the June Festival of Music and the October Apple Harvest Festival.

JORDAN HOLLOW FARM INN
Stanley   *(540) 778-2285*

This is a wonderful vacation spot for horse lovers. The 145-acre farm is nestled in a secluded hollow between the Massanutten and Blue Ridge mountain ranges, 6 miles south of Luray.

You can spend the night at the 200-year-old restored country inn, dine on "country cosmopolitan" cuisine and ride horses through lovely meadows or woods. The facilities also include a pub, recreation room with a pool table and fully equipped meeting rooms.

The inn offers three beginner trail rides a day, Western style, for $25 per person per hour. A more advanced, one-hour

ride is also offered daily, on either English or Western saddles. Pony rides are available for children younger than 8.

All-day rides for experienced riders must be arranged in advance; they cost $10 per person for a minimum of six hours, with a minimum of two riders in the party. There's also a flat fee of $80 for the guide and horse transportation, to be divided among the participants. The all-day riders travel scenic trails in the Blue Ridge and Massanutten mountains.

Horse owners can arrange to ride from Graves Mountain Lodge, on the other side of the Blue Ridge, to Jordon Hollow (or vice versa), a five- or six-hour ride. Jordan Hollow is also the only country inn in Virginia with a full program of competitive carriage driving.

MOUNTAINTOP RANCH
Elkton   *(540) 298-9542*

The folks at this mountaintop ranch between Shenandoah and Elkton are surrounded on three sides by the Shenandoah National Park. Trails lace more than 3,000 acres of unspoiled meadows and forestland. Rides last anywhere from one hour to two days and cost $20 per person for the shortest trip. Fees are $55 for half-day and $90 for full-day rides, including lunch. Two-day overnight trips cost $200 per person. Groups of 10 or more receive a discount.

The ranch also has a fully furnished cabin for eight that can be rented for $90 a night on weekdays and $100 on Friday or Saturday nights.

WOODSTONE MEADOWS STABLE
McGaheysville   *(540) 289-6152*

In the Shenandoah Valley across from Massanutten Resort, this outfit offers leisurely trail rides in the Massanutten Mountains. They match horse and rider according to the rider's ability and give everyone basic instructions before taking off. Hour-long trail rides cost $18 per person if you make a reservation at least an hour in advance. Otherwise, the cost is $25. Riders must be at least 12 years old and four feet tall. The maximum weight is 225 pounds.

OAK MANOR FARMS

Burketown   *(540) 234-8101*

On U.S. 11 halfway between Harrisonburg and Staunton at Burketown, this company leads English-style guided trail rides up and down a small, beautiful mountain in the Blue Ridge. Trips last about an hour and cost $20 per person. Appointments are necessary.

MONTFAIR STABLES

Crozet   *(804) 823-6961*

This outfit offers half-hour, one-hour, half-day and all-day rides for the beginner or expert, on Western or English saddles. Montfair is 15 miles west of Charlottesville at the foot of Pasture Fence Mountain and stays open year round, weather permitting.

Owners Julie and Sam Strong also lead overnight trail rides once a month from May through September. On the overnighter, an afternoon ride up Pasture Fence Mountain is followed by dinner around the campfire. Riders sleep in tents and have breakfast the next morning before heading back down the mountain. These overnight trips are for experienced riders and cost $125 per person.

Fees range from $12 for a half-hour ride and $20 for one hour to $60 for a half-day ride. Groups of six or more can receive a discount. The one-hour rides and overnights are very popular, so make your reservations early.

WINTERGREEN RESORT — RODES FARM STABLES

Wintergreen   *(804) 325-8260*

Guided trail rides in the mountains and Rockfish Valley are offered daily except Wednesdays mid-March through November. The activities include pony rides for kids, sunset trail rides through Rockfish Valley, riding lessons, horsemanship classes and private rides for advanced riders. Wintergreen is the only resort in America to offer the sport of vaulting, or gymnastics on horseback.

Trail rides (English tack only) last one hour and 15 minutes. The cost is $25 for resort guests and $30 for the public during the week, $5 more on weekends. Pony rides are $10 for guests and $12 for other children. Riding lessons are $26. Reservations are required. For more information on Wintergreen, see our Resorts chapter.

RIVER RIDGE RANCH

Millboro   *(540) 996-4148*

This 377-acre ranch about 10 miles from The Homestead in Bath County offers English or Western guided trail rides through unspoiled forests and fields. There's a spectacular view of the Cowpasture River Valley from one of the trails, and riders can count on seeing a lot of wildife during any of the rides. Fees are $25 for an hour's ride or $70 for a half-day ride, plus $5 for lunch. Guests at the ranch receive a 10 percent discount.

Highly popular are the Saturday night haywagon rides and cookouts atop River Ridge Mountain. We're not talking hotdogs on a clothes hanger, but New York strip steaks, barbecued chicken or fresh mountain trout grilled over a campfire. Prices are $27.50 for adults, $12 for children.

River Ridge Ranch has two honeymoon cabins, a lodge and another family unit for overnight accommodations. The ranch can accommodate 12 guests, who have access to fishing and swimming in the Cowpasture River and hiking. Cabins rent for $120 per night, double occupancy; the family unit can accommodate four to six for $150 per night; and lodge rooms are $100 per night, double occupancy. All rates include a full country breakfast. River Ridge is open from April 1 to Thanksgiving.

THE HOMESTEAD

Hot Springs   *(540) 839-5500*

Guided trail rides are among the many activities offered at this five-star resort in Bath County. There are more than 100 miles of trails through beautiful mountain terrain and alongside the resort's golf courses. The riding master can accommodate either English or Western-style iders. Rides lasting from 45 minutes to an hour are $50 per person, including a mandatory helmet. Rides depart the historic stables across from the hotel on the hour from 9 AM to 3 PM. Reservations are necessary. Children who are at least four feet tall are welcome.

VIRGINIA MOUNTAIN OUTFITTERS

Buena Vista   *(540) 261-1910*

Outfitter Deborah Sensabaugh and her horses stay busy year round on a variety of trips in the Blue Ridge and Alleghany mountains. Half-day trail rides covering about 10 miles of mountain trails are $50 per person, including a hearty picnic lunch.

Full-day rides follow any one of the 100 miles of trails Sensabaugh knows. Tell her what you'd like to see — scenic overlooks, deep woods, mountain streams — and she'll oblige. The price is $85 per person for the seven-hour trip. Sensabaugh also organizes overnight rides and furnishes everything except sleeping bags and personal items. Camping ranges from primitive national forest sites to privately owned campgrouds with full services. In either case, there's always access to water for swimming and fishing, so bring your suits and fishing gear. Overnighters are $150 per person, which includes all meals from lunch on the arrival day to lunch and an afternoon snack the following day.

For a three- to five-night getaway, sign up for a pack trip covering 75 to 100 miles. "We ride in all kinds of weather, all kinds of terrain, with a generous dose of history and trail lore along the way," Sensabaugh says. These outings cost $90 per person per day — a price that includes all meals, tents and camping gear other than sleeping bags.

Sensabaugh's most popular package, called "Horse Lovers Holiday," combines two all-day horseback trips with overnight stays at a nearby bed and breakfast inn, Lavender Hill Farm. You can work up quite an appetite riding in these mountains, a hunger that Lavender Hill's hearty European cuisine will more than satisfy. The cost is $255 per person, which includes two nights at Lavender Hill, all meals and the ride.

Sensabaugh also offers packages with a half-dozen other inns, and can tailor a ride to your abilities and desires.

MT. ROGERS
HIGH COUNTRY OUTDOOR CENTER

Troutdale   *(540) 677-3900*

This family-owned business has many years' experience in providing wilderness adventures in the Mt. Rogers National Recreation area south of Roanoke. Day rides, covered wagon trips and pack trips all originate at the Livery Base Camp on Va. 603 in Troutdale. All-day rides in the high country, including lunch, are $75 per person for a group of one to three people, $60 per person for four or more. A most unusual trip is the covered wagon excursion into the mountains where wild horses still run free. You can ride a horse alongside the wagons, if you like, for $20 over the usual fare ($45 for one to three people, $40 for four or more). Overnight covered wagon treks are $200 per person, including all meals and equipment except sleeping bags. Overnight horse trips with pack mules are $125 per day per person, including meals and equipment other than sleeping bags. Groups of 10 or more receive special rates.

HUNGRY MOTHER STATE PARK
Marion (540) 783-3422

A few miles north of Marion is a state park known for its beautiful woodlands and placid 108-acre lake in the heart of the mountains. It's also home to Hemlock Haven, an attractive conference center.

At Hungry Mother, hour-long guided trail rides cost $8 per person. If you have small children, let 'em sit right behind you on the park's gentle horses. The stables are open from Memorial Day to Labor Day. Accommodations at the park include campsites and housekeeping cabins (see Camping in this chapter for rates).

Hunting

A fellow once commented that he hunted to feed his body and his soul. In the Blue Ridge of Virginia, no hunter goes hungry.

As expected, wildlife is concentrated around farmland or other areas where there is food. With much of the Blue Ridge lying in the 1.5 million acres of the George Washington and Jefferson National Forest and state lands, food for wildlife is abundant.

An annual $3 stamp is required to hunt in the national forest and can be purchased at most outlets that sell hunting licenses. Maps of the forests are available for purchase through their regional offices listed at the end of this chapter. Also ask about hunting regulations, license outlets and seasons and bag limits for the particular county you plan to visit.

Hunting is allowed in designated areas of five Virginia state parks, including Fairy Stone in nearby Patrick County, Cumberland State Forest and Grayson Highlands State Park in Grayson County. A $5 hunting fee applies. Also in Patrick County, Primland Hunting Reserve in Claudville, a half-hour south of the Blue Ridge Parkway, is a well-known hunting preserve of 10,000 acres specializing in birds, deer and even sporting clays. Call Rick Hill at (540) 251-8012. Guides and dogs are available.

Westvaco Corporation, a huge paper and bleached board milling concern, also offers hunting and fishing permits on vast holdings of company land in Virginia and West Virginia. Westvaco's office is listed at the end of this chapter.

The most popular game are squirrel, grouse, bear, deer, bobcat, fox, duck, rabbit, pheasant and quail. For truly adventurous pioneers, muzzle-loading rifles, bow and arrow and other primitive weapons are allowed at various times.

The Blue Ridge is home to most of the record-setting areas for hunting in Virginia. Latest statistics single out Bedford County for having the highest turkey harvest of 498 birds. Bedford also came in second highest for deer, with 5,753. In 1993 Virginia's five north central mountain counties (Alleghany, Augusta, Bath, Highland and Rockbridge)

Photo: Nathan Beck

Riders with Mountain Outfitters of Buena Vista cross their horses over Irish Creek on the Blue Ridge Mountains.

harvested a whopping 15,640 whitetail deer.

Whether you're going on your own or signing up with a hunting lodge, you're going to need a valid license, which can be obtained by clerks of circuit courts and other authorized agents (see listings in this section). Licenses and permits are good from July 1 through June 30. Hunting seasons and bag limits are set by the Virginia Department of Game and Inland Fisheries and vary according to county. Some counties are off-limits to hunters of certain species, while others have liberalized hunting rules.

Take note that one outstanding hunting lodge is Fort Lewis Lodge in Millboro, Bath County. It's a mountain paradise; call John Cowden there at (540) 925-2314.

The best suggestion to assure you are hunting within the bounds of the rules and regulations is to send for the latest pamphlet from the Department of Game and Inland Fisheries, "Hunting in Virginia Regulations." The brochure lists everything you need to know about how and where to hunt in the Blue Ridge, or where to find specific game information. To obtain the brochure, write or call the Department of Games and Inland Fisheries, (804) 367-1000, P.O. Box 11104, Richmond, Virginia 23230-1104.

For other information about where to hunt in the Blue Ridge, call or write the following.

• **Virginia State Parks,** (804) 786-1712, 203 Governor Street, Suite 306, Richmond, Virginia 23219.

• **George Washington and Jefferson National Forests,** 5162 Valleypointe Parkway, Ronaoke Va. 24019.

• **Westvaco Corporation,** Appalachian Woodlands, P.O. Box 577, Rupert, West Virginia 25984.

Photo: Wintergreen

Blue Ridge skiing can challenge any skier, from beginner to expert.

Inside
Skiing

It takes two things for skiing: mountains and snow.

Throughout this book we've shown you that Virginia's Blue Ridge has more mountains than a redhead has freckles. Wintergreen and Massanutten, two of the region's four ski resorts, have vertical drops of 1,000 feet or better; they don't come any higher south of New York.

Those mountains attract the white stuff — and keep it — with temperatures ranging 10 to 20 degrees colder than the flatlands. Natural snowfall will vary from year to year, but the snow on the slopes stays consistent because of aggressive snowmaking and the use of Snomax, which makes better snow at higher temperatures. Just because you're not driving in a blizzard doesn't mean they're not skiing up a storm at Wintergreen, Massanutten, Bryce and The Homestead.

There is a catch — but you're going to like it. It's usually warmer skiing in the Blue Ridge than in New England or out West. If you want to dress like Mukluk the Eskimo, you're out of luck. If you're keen on sleek, trim ski outfits with all those nifty colors, come to the Blue Ridge. At Wintergreen, you can even ski and play golf the same day. There's a 15-degree temperature variable between the slopes atop the mountain and the valley links.

Warm temperatures also account for the popularity of night skiing in the area.

All four resorts have lighted slopes, which means more schuss for your buck on a ski trip.

You have to sleep sometime, but while you do, fleets of snowcats — highly sophisticated mechanical behemoths — are stalking the slopes, bulldozing moguls, pulverizing icy spots and smoothing trails so that you're greeted with a brand-new and wonderfully skiable surface come morning.

All that high-tech equipment is fueled with money, but area ski resorts are finding they can afford it. In recent years, the Southeast has shown more growth in skier visits and ski lessons than any other part of the country. Getting all those skiers to the top of the mountain has led to more lifts and faster lifts, including Virginia's first quad chair, at Massanutten.

Blue Ridge resorts are in step with the "shredders," providing snowboard parks, rental boards and lessons for the snowboarding crowd. At Wintergreen, you receive a 1½-hour lesson when you rent a board.

Since skiers have to rest and eat and party too, off-the-slope facilities at our four ski areas have kept pace with spas, après ski activities and good restaurants. They're year-round resorts (see our Resorts chapter), so they're good at everything, even keeping non-skiers happy.

"More and more people are discovering that Virginia offers a terrific ski resort experience, with great skiing and activities for the whole family," says Mark Glickman, president of the Virginia Ski Association.

We haven't attempted to give you rates because there are so many factors variables — whether you ski during the day or at night, rent or bring your own equipment, stay at the ski area or elsewhere or take a private or group lesson. But all the resorts have cost-saving packages.

Of the four resorts, only The Homestead rents cross-country skis and provides trails. But if you own your own equipment, you can make tracks alongside the Blue Ridge Parkway, Skyline Drive, in Mount Rogers National Recreation Area in southwest Virginia — and almost any place with hiking trails or fire roads. Just go with friends and go prepared for emergencies.

For more information, order free brochures from Ski Virginia Association, P.O. Box 454, Nellysford, Virginia 22958, (800) THE-SNOW. For news and comments on local skiing, get a copy of the *Ski Tripper*, a newsletter for Mid-Atlantic skiers, at P.O. Box 20305, Roanoke 24018; (703) 772-7644.

Shenandoah Valley Region

BRYCE RESORT

Va. 263, Basye   (540) 856-2121
Hours: 9 AM to 10 PM

This intimate, family-oriented ski resort is a little over an hour from the Washington Beltway and less than three hours from Richmond. A few miles off I-81, Bryce is tucked into the folds of the Shenandoah Mountains. It's owned by the 400-odd families who own homes there. Many skiers drive to Bryce from

the Washington, D.C., area, but the resort is also popular with the locals, particularly on weekday evenings, when they can ski under the lights and then warm up with a hot-buttered rum in the glass-walled Copper Kettle Lounge.

Manfred Locher manages the resort, and his brother, Horst, directs the ski school, the ski area and an extensive racing program. Both have been at Bryce since the resort opened in 1965.

One of Bryce's notable features is its racing program. For more than 20 years, Bryce has sponsored NASTAR races, starting a trend among Southern ski resorts. Every Saturday, Sunday and holiday at 3:30 PM, the NASTAR races begin, offering skiers the chance to test their abilities against the pros. The races are handicapped according to age and gender. Bryce also has a weekend ski program to train skiers for sanctioned United States Ski Association races.

Bryce's seven slopes cover 20 acres and are serviced by two double-chair lifts and two rope tows. The resort averages 40 inches of natural snow annually but produces enough to blanket all trails.

The broad beginners area is visible from the deck and two lodges at the base. One lodge houses the Copper Kettle Lounge and a restaurant serving hearty breakfasts, lunches and dinner. The second lodge houses a cafeteria, ski rental and repair facility and a ski shop.

The Horst Locher Ski School offers private and group lessons, including a SKIwee program for children aged 4 to 7.

In the summer, grass skiing is a popular sport at Bryce. Invented in Europe as a summer training method for skiers, grass skiing mimics snow skiing but substitutes short, tread-like skates for skis. Rentals and lessons in grass skiing are offered in the summer and fall.

Photo: Wintergreen

A youngster prepares to hit the slopes at Wintergreen Resort.

Condos, chalets and townhouses near the slopes are available for weekend rentals or longer-term stays. For lodging information and reservations, call (800) 296-2121.

Directions: Bryce is 11 miles from I-81. Take exit 273 at Mt. Jackson, follow Va. 263 W. to Bayse and Bryce Resort.

MASSANUTTEN RESORT

Harrisonburg   (540) 289-9441
Hours: 9 AM to 10 PM   (800) 207-MASS

This ski resort is an easy two-hour drive from Richmond, Washington, D.C., or Roanoke. In the heart of the Shenandoah Valley, it sits atop Massanutten Mountain, once a haven for moonshiners.

The resort's 14 trails and 68 acres of skiing tower above an attractive, spacious lodge at the base. Inside are a cafeteria, convenience store and glass-walled night-club with a big dance floor. This place gets real lively on Saturday nights. Another nice feature of the lodge is a large windowed room with tables and chairs

where guests can bring their own food, "camp out" during the day and watch the skiing without spending a dime.

The resort gets only about 34 inches of natural snowfall a year but has greatly expanded its snowmaking. It's been the first to open and the last to close the past two seasons.

Diamond Jim, a 3,400-foot run with a vertical drop of 1,110 feet, is the resort's most challenging run, starting at the resort's highest point (2,880 feet) alongside Paradice, the other expert trail. Both are lighted for night skiing and are served by Virginia's first quad chairlift.

Children 5 and younger receive free lift tickets. For children 5 and older, the Ski Wee program provides lessons, rentals, lift tickets and lunch. On Saturdays and Sundays, one trail is devoted to NASTAR racing. MASS (Massanutten Adaptive Ski School), an extensive program for the disabled, is a special feature at Massanutten.

Overnight lodging and ski packages are offered at Massanutten's chalets, villas and hotel rooms and at hotels in nearby Harrisonburg. The resort's supply of overnight accommodations is limited, so reserve early. For those who are lucky enough to stay "on mountain," a sports complex called Le Club offers indoor swimming, sauna, outdoor hot tubs, an exercise room, children's movies, table tennis and more.

Directions: To get to Massanutten, take Va. 33 east off I-81 in Harrisonburg. Go 10 miles to Va. 644, where you'll see signs to the resort.

East of the Blue Ridge Region

WINTERGREEN

Va. 664, Wintergreen   (800) 325-2200
Hours: 9 AM to 4:30 PM daily, 5 PM
to 10 PM nightly Sunday through Friday,
6 PM to 11 PM Saturdays

Skiing magazine has called Wintergreen "the South's single best ski resort," and it continues to live up to its reputation in accommodations, restaurants, shops and other amenities. The mountain has 17 slopes, ranging from a vast beginners area to the Highlands, a three-slope complex with more than a 1,000-foot drop and runs up to 4,450 feet in length for advanced skiers.

Safety on the slopes is a primary concern at Wintergreen. Its ski patrol is consistently ranked among the best in the nation by the National Ski Patrol Association.

All skiers who rent equipment from Wintergreen are entitled to a free lesson at any level. Children 5 and younger ski free when accompanied by an adult.

You can ski in the morning and golf at the Stoney Creek course in the afternoon for the price of a ski ticket.

A summit ski area, the resort's accommodations and facilities are at the top of the slopes. The restaurant and condominium complexes offer extraordinary views up the spine of the Blue Ridge and off to each side. To the west is the Shenandoah Valley and to the east, the Piedmont.

The resort's headquarters is the Mountain Inn, which recently underwent a spectacular $5 million renovation. Guests can have a sandwich or hot cappuccino by the fire in the Gristmill lobby or browse an array of shops selling everything from exquisite hand-knit sweaters to Blue Ridge Mountain quilts.

The Wintergarden Spa complex has an indoor pool, a Jacuzzi, hot tubs, saunas, an exercise room and the Garden Terrace Restaurant.

Dining at Wintergreen is exceptional in quality and variety. The Copper Mine features gourmet dining in an elegant atmosphere, the Garden Terrace is the place for casual family dining (kids younger than 12 eat free from 5:30 PM to 6:30 PM, and Cooper's Vantage serves salads, burgers and cocktails for lunch and dinner. Wintergreen has seven eateries in all and a grocery store where you can stock the condo kitchen. The 4,000-square-foot Blue Ridge Terrace offers outdoor barbecue and music on the slopes weekends.

Wintergreen's children's programs are rated tops in the country by *Family Circle* and *Better Homes and Gardens* magazines. The Treehouse, at the top of the beginner slope, houses the resort's innovative Camp Wintergreen children's programs for kids ages 2 to 12.

Directions: From areas north or east of Wintergreen, follow I-64 W. to Exit 107 (Crozet, U.S. 250). Take U.S. 250 W. to Va. 151 S. and turn left. Follow Va. 151 S. to Va. 664, 14.2 miles. Turn right and Wintergreen is 4.5 miles ahead on Va. 664.

You can also get to Wintergreen from the Blue Ridge Parkway Reeds Gap exit, between Mileposts 13 and 14. Look for the signs.

Alleghany Highlands Region

THE HOMESTEAD

U.S. 220, Hot Springs

Hotel reservations	*(800) 838-1766*
Ski information	*(540) 839-1766*

Hours: 9 AM to 5 PM weekdays, 8 AM to 5 PM weekends and holidays; 6 to 10 PM Wednesday through Saturday.

This elegant hotel became the South's first true ski resort when it opened its slopes in 1959. In the 1950s northern ski resorts were experimenting with snowmaking. Under the direction of Sepp Kober, a native of Igls, Austria, known as the "Father of Southern Skiing," nearly $1 million was invested to develop a 3,000-foot slope on Warm Springs Mountain, along with side trails, a skimobile and a glass-walled lodge with a circular fire pit, ski equipment shops and a rental service. Since then the slopes have grown 200 feet steeper and the runs more chal-lenging and diverse, and the four-wheeled skimobile has been replaced with modern ski lifts. A snowboard park and 260-foot-long halfpipe were added for the 1994-95 season. At the base of the slopes is an Olympic-size ice-skating rink, with instructors close at hand.

Today, the Homestead is renowned for its ski school and family atmosphere. On the resort's ski staff are several young Austrian ski instructors who can accommo-date group, private and children's lessons.

Nine runs are open for day and night skiing, and half-day rates are available. The resort offers packages with special rates for families that include accommo-dations, breakfast and dinner daily, lift tickets and lessons. Skiers will want to take advantage of its historic spa (with aroma and massage therapy), other sport-ing facilities and exquisite dining.

Directions: The Homestead is about 200 miles from Washington, D.C. Take Exit 61 Va. 257) off I-81, go south on Va. 42, then west on Va. 39 and follow U.S. 220 into Hot Springs. For a lengthier but highly scenic route, take I-64 W. off I-81 near Lexington, then Va. 39 W. to U.S. 220 into Hot Springs.

Mill Mountain Zoo in Roanoke.

Inside
Kidstuff

If your kids are looking for big metropolitan areas full of amusement parks, video games and Disney-type make believe, don't aim for the Blue Ridge. However, if you and your family are looking for a break from the artificial and searching for the real and true, you're heading in the right direction. Even the most jaded city children have been spotted making an amazing transformation from being bored to having some hidden chord struck by history, beauty, the great outdoors or all of the above.

The Blue Ridge offers adults and children alike many opportunities to experience and explore kinds of places that don't exist anywhere else. We have natural wonders such Shenandoah National Park and the caverns and Natural Bridge in the Shenandoah Valley and museums such as the New Market Hall of Valor, To the Rescue Exhibit and the Science Museum in Roanoke. In the Horse Country stretching from Loudoun County to Albemarle County, children thrill at seeing horse shows, steeplechases and foxhunts. Lexington's Virginia Horse Center has a plethora of events interesting to children. And the jousting tournaments at Natural Chimneys in Augusta County are a real treat — for all ages, actually. But parents be warned: exposing your children to horse events may lead to your buying a pony or horse.

Much of the Blue Ridge is rural, which means that there's a county or local fair near almost any destination. What kid wouldn't be fascinated by the farm animals (often shown by kids their age) and the carnivals and games which usually accompany these highlights of the harvest season (see our Annual Events and Festivals chapter). Many resorts and inns in the Blue Ridge appeal to families, so you may be able to plan a trip to our neck of the woods without looking any farther than our chapters on Resorts, Other Accommodations and Bed and Breakfast and Country Inns — but think of all the temptations you'd miss!

Shenandoah Valley Region

Winchester

Winchester, in Frederick County, becomes a boom town every spring during the **Apple Blossom Festival** (see the Annual Events and Festivals chapter). Every year the festivities seem to begin a few days earlier, and there are many activities children will enjoy: the grand parade with its marching bands, baton twirlers, floats and horseback riders; the ongoing arts and crafts festival; the races and athletic events, and, of course, the circus. A few miles from town at the regional airport, aircraft owners from far and wide participate in a **Spring Fly-In** on the Sunday of the festival, and it's great fun to see their planes up close and watch them compete for prizes. In August, the Chamber of Commerce puts on the **Great American Duck Race** at Jim Barnett Park, a fun day of games, refreshments and, yes, duck races.

Middletown

The **Re-enactment of the Battle of Cedar Creek** takes place every October (see our Annual Events and Festivals chapter) at historic Belle Grove Plantation on the very battlefield where the fighting took place. The action involves a lot of drama and musket fire, even if children don't understand the tragedy of the event being remembered. Middletown's **Wayside Theatre** often has family comedies and musicals such as *Oliver* that are suitable for children.

Front Royal

The Blue Ridge's greatest resource is its natural beauty, and there's nothing better you can do for your children than to introduce them to nature. Starting at Front Royal, you can enter the magic world of the **Skyline Drive**, a road that squiggles along the crest of the mountains all the way to Waynesboro, where it joins the Blue Ridge Parkway (see the Blue Ridge Parkway and Skyline Drive chapter). The Drive and Parkway run through national parks where deer and other wild creatures will be easy to spot from your car. To make the experience even more special for your children (and you), plan to stay at one of the campgrounds or lodges in this unspoiled area.

In Front Royal's **Skyline Caverns**, three swift streams are stocked with fat trout that dart about in easy view. Youngsters will also marvel at the cave formations, including the unusual anthodites, or "cave orchids," for which Skyline is noted. Above ground is the **Outdoor Skyline Arrow**, a miniature train that carries children on a half-mile journey through a real tunnel (see our Other Attractions chapter).

Front Royal is where the north and south branches of the Shenandoah River join in their rush to the sea. The waterfront below the U.S. 522 bridge draws boaters, swimmers and fishermen during warm weather, and in August the surrounding towns join in the **Riverfest** (see Annual Events), with its canoe races, costume events, tug-of-war and other water games. The **Front Royal Canoe Company** (see Recreation) in Front Royal can put you and your family adrift on any summer day.

Bayse

The **Bryce Family Resort** offers a wide range of family accommodations and activities (see our Resorts chapter), including skiing, grass skiing, horseback and pony riding, mountain biking, Rollerblading and tennis. A large private lake with beach provides all sorts of water activities.

New Market

A visit to the **Hall of Valor Museum** at the New Market Battlefield Historical Park is a sobering but educational experience. A stirring film tells the story of 247 young military school cadets, perhaps about the age of your youngsters, march-

Photo: Wintergreen Resort

These three seem to ask, "What could be more fun than winter on the slopes?"

ing into a heated battle during the Civil War. Major Civil War battles are depicted in murals and life-size models, and the museum has some fascinating artifacts from the war.

Luray

It's a wonder this town doesn't fall into some subterranean passage. Grand and Luray caverns (and probably other undiscovered grottoes) riddle the underground like Swiss cheese. **Luray Caverns** has the world's only stalacpipe organ, as well as a **Car and Carriage Caravan** above ground, which contains antique cars, carriages, coaches and costumes dating back to 1625.

Hook up with Shenandoah Outfitters or the Down River Canoe Company. Either outfitter will rent you a canoe, raft or, better yet, inner tubes for a lazy day of floating on the Shenandoah.

Luray also has one of the state's largest reptile collections for kids who appreciate the creepy crawlies. The **Luray Rep-**

tile Center and Dinosaur Park on Va. 211 also has a petting zoo with tame deer, llamas and other creatures.

Harrisonburg

The **Rockingham Fairgrounds** has some sort of festival, fair or show going on almost every weekend, particularly at harvest time.

East of Harrisonburg is **Massanutten Mountain Resort**, a great place for families. During the winter, special programs help develop junior skiers into racers. Kids can also go sledding and skating, and summer brings fishing, hiking, horseback riding and mountain biking.

Mt. Solon

The centerpiece of **Natural Chimneys Park** is a group of rock towers, some of which are more than 120 feet tall. The park is also the site of jousting tournaments in June and August (see the Annual Events and Festivals chapter). This 150-year-old sport features riders of all ages.

Staunton

Staunton's greatest attraction for children is its fascinating **Museum of American Frontier Culture** (see our Arts and Culture chapter), where fields and livestock are tended exactly the way European and early American farmers used to do it. From cows to chickens to kittens, the animals will help make this a fun-filled day for children, and many festivals here throughout the year (see Annual Events and Festivals) are geared to families.

Waynesboro

Older children (and parents) will enjoy a visit to **Virginia Metalcrafters** showroom, where you can watch brass being molded, ground and polished. Outside of town are **Sherando. Lake State Park** and **Shenandoah Acres Resort** (where raft races for all ages are held in July), both excellent places for family fun (see the Recreation chapter for more information).

Lexington

History is a major reason families come to Lexington and Rockbridge County — Civil War history (Robert E. Lee and Stonewall Jackson), World War II history (George C. Marshall), agricultural history (Cyrus McCormick) and natural history (Natural Bridge). The beauty of the area is another reason families visit the area: the Blue Ridge Parkway, Virginia Horse Center (nearly 400 acres of rolling hills), farms (Cyrus McCormick's working farm), the **George**

Washington National Forest, canoeing or tubing down the Maury River, hiking **Woods Creek Park** and the **Chessie Nature Trail** and many trails off the Blue Ridge Parkway.

To keep children listening and involved during guided tours, the **Stonewall Jackson House** provides young visitors with small slates listing items in the house that children circle when they see the object. The **VMI Museum** has a special display of a typical cadet's room in the barracks that children are always fascinated by. **Little Sorrel**, Stonewall Jackson's war horse, is also mounted and on display in the Museum. The Virginia Military Institute cadets in uniform and the Friday afternoon full dress parades are always of special interest to children. Throughout most of the year (except during breaks and exams) cadet guides are available for tours of the VMI Post.

The **George C. Marshall Museum** has a scavenger hunt for children. For large pre-scheduled children's groups the museum staff has a program called "Try On A Piece Of History" in which pieces of uniforms are used to bring history alive.

Horses are an important part of Lexington and Rockbridge County and both children and adults are delighted with a narrated carriage ride of the historic downtown and residential districts of Lexington. The Virginia Horse Center hosts all kinds of horse shows, but the ones that are of particular interest to children are the miniature horse shows and the pony club shows.

The **Natural Bridge Wax Museum** figures always fascinate children. A special behind-the-scenes tour shows how the figures are made.

Special events that all members of the family enjoy include the **Rockbridge Re-**

gional **Fair** in July and the **Rockbridge Community Festival** in August. **Fridays Alive** concerts throughout the summer are great fun for the whole family.

Theatre at Lime Kiln, Lexington's summer professional outdoor theater, presents musicals, plays and concerts in "the most unusual theatre setting in the United States." The productions are often family-oriented and each year there are some special shows scheduled for children. For all that extra energy which children have, a stop at **Kids Playce Playground** and Lime Kiln Park is great. Picnic tables are available too. To top off the tour, everyone always enjoys stopping at **Sweet Things**, Lexington's homemade ice-cream parlor. You can even watch the homemade cones being made.

Roanoke Valley Region

Roanoke

Many families come to Roanoke via the Blue Ridge Parkway, since the Capital of the Blue Ridge is the largest metropolitan area off one of the most popular and beautiful roads in the United States. Cultural attractions and shopping await below in downtown Roanoke. The Mill Mountain Exit off the Parkway takes you down the mountain to Roanoke, which offers many cultural attractions for both adults and children alike.

Mill Mountain itself offers a nice campground, the scenic overlook of the **Mill Mountain Star** — a 100-foot-high manmade metal star that glows at night — and the **Mill Mountain Zoo**, a small but interesting zoo that children love. There, they can ride the Zoo Choo, see Ruby the Tiger or get acquainted with wildlife both exotic and indigenous to the area.

Shopping is a major reason tourists visit Roanoke. Roanoke's historic **city market** interests children with colorful seasonal produce peddled by farmers wearing straw-brimmed hats and arts and crafts sold by Floyd County flower children dressed in tie-dyed T-shirts. You never know what you'll find in the farmer's booths in the city market, but you can be sure it will be fresh, beautifully presented and an attraction unto itself. Whatever the season, kids will delight in everything from hand-made Easter eggs and Christmas greenery to fresh peaches and strawberries.

Take your kids into **Wertz's Produce**, next door to Gallery Three, at the city market. Children who have never been into an old-style general store with good food, candy and antiques will love visiting Wertz's. Owner Ezra Wertz is recognized in tourism circles as the most-photographed man in Roanoke! Across the street is **Good Things On the Market**, a candy store that's a must-see for kids of all ages. There, you'll find the childhood staples of gumdrops and licorice along with fancier, trendy candy and the latest gimmicks in the confectionery world, all packaged to delight any child. Candy-lovers also need to visit **Sweet Things** in the City Market Building, which has been bustling with activity since 1922. The large festival marketplace showcases shops, gifts, food, crafts and special events under a neon light sculpture. At the center is a culinary arcade, where more than a dozen restaurants offer a taste of American and International cuisine, so something will appeal to the younger set.

Children can soak up a bit of culture and knowledge here too. Towering above the city market is Center in the Square, the cultural complex of Roanoke, which was an old warehouse before being transformed into a home for the **Science Museum of Western Virginia, Roanoke Valley Historical Society and Museum, Mill Mountain Theatre**, the **Art Museum of Western Virginia** and the **Arts Council**. You can easily occupy your kids for the day visiting each of these attractions.

The most-visited place in Center in the Square is the Science Museum, which just celebrated its 25th anniversary. Interactive exhibits ranging from colorful lasers to holograms keep the kids busy, and afterwards you can catch the latest **Hopkins Planetarium** show. Both the museum and planetarium rate high on every child's list of what was fun to do in Roanoke. Its gift shop on the ground level is full of items large and small to intrigue every child's imagination.

At the History Museum a permanent exhibit offers the history of the area, emphasizing the railroad, which launched the city as a crossroads of transportation. Children enjoy seeing the miniature general store of yesteryear and an exhibit of vintage clothing. Special exhibits might range from D-Day to Elvis Presley's birthday. A gift shop on the ground level offers a treasure of books that are wonderful keepsakes.

The Art Museum also offers special exhibits for children such as cartoon originals. Its permanent collection of pictures and sculpture is worth a visit as well.

Call ahead to see what Mill Mountain Theatre has in store. This energetic theater group always has children in mind and offers special programming along with its general crowd-pleasers, ranging from *The King and I* to *Scrooge*. Its cast and directors are some of the best in the nation.

Three other museums outside the City Market area also definitely worth the trip. Just a few blocks up Salem Avenue you'll find the **Virginia Museum of Transportation**, where Roanoke proudly displays its railroad heritage in a restored freight station. Here, the kids will find history larger than life as they stand beside steam engines and vintage locomotives. They can climb aboard a caboose or stroll through a railway post office car and the largest rolling stock collection in the East. A true delight is the gift shop which is stocked with every child's dreams. Not far away is the **Harrison Heritage Museum**, which traces the history of the African-American experience in a renovated school. Its colorful displays of beautiful African artifacts are well worth a visit.

Kids who like bells and whistles will expend lots of energy at **To the Rescue**, the official national museum of the volunteer lifesaving movement. Formerly at Center, the exhibit has just moved to Tanglewood Mall. Here, children can fulfill all their emergency room and rescue fantasies with interactive exhibits, a simulated car wreck and documentary footage. Don't miss this gem in the city that gave birth to the volunteer rescue squad movement.

Kids will also not want to miss the **Grandin Movie Theatre**, one of the few ornate theatres the wrecking balls haven't destroyed. You can see classics and modern movies for the best prices in town. This cavernous, popcorn-scented architectural masterpiece will thrill children who have never seen anything like its tiled floors, mahogany candy cases and ornate decor.

Out of town, plan a 7-mile foray into nearby Roanoke County to see the **Virginia Explore Park**, Virginia's newest tourist attraction. It consists of reconstructed buildings and barns showing the lifestyle of yesteryear. Interpreters authentically demonstrate the lifeways of 18th-century pioneers. It's one of the area's most popular attractions for school children because of its beauty, pristine environment and showcase of what life used to be for our great-great-grandparents.

All these attractions are for the taking year-round. However, two big May festivals bring out the families and give kids something to talk about the rest of the year. The first weekend in May is famous for its combined **Chili Cook-off and Community School Strawberry Festival**. Thousands throng the city market, first to sample the chili and showmanship and then to visit the Strawberry Festival, where they sample homemade shortcakes and real whipped cream and assorted strawberry delicacies. The second fair-weather event is the major outdoor celebration of western Virginia, **Festival in the Park**. It's a two-week-long celebration of music, entertainment, food and fun and attracts several hundred thousand people to sample a incredible array of festivity. It happens the last weekend in May and the first weekend of June. Special children's programming is ongoing, with theater, drama, special acts and the fabulous **Children's Parade** where thousands of children decorate their bikes and march alongside gigantic helium balloons, "Macy's in Miniature," some say.

Great festivals take place monthly in Roanoke. The city is also is headquarters city for the **Commonwealth Games of Virginia**, where nearly 10,000 amateur athletes competed during July.

Dining out can be a treat for kids, especially at such places as **Macado's** downtown and the **Star City Diner**, which are outrageously decorated to be real child-pleasers. You can't miss **Star City** because of the hula-hoop waitress and Big Boy statues on the roof. And, in case your kids are really traditionalists who don't want to try new things and insist on the tried

and true, there's a **Chuck E. Cheese's** and **Discovery Zone**, both on Electric Road, with their standard fare of high-decibel dining.

There's enough to do in Roanoke to keep you and your family occupied for a solid week or so. Call the Roanoke Valley Convention & Visitors Bureau, **(800) 635-5535**, for its latest calendar of events and shopping, attraction and restaurant guides.

East of the Blue Ridge

Leesburg

Oatlands Plantation, south of Leesburg, has some marvelous activities for children, including sheep dog trials, steeplechases, Civil War Re-enactments, and Draft Horse and Mule Day, when the gentle giants of the horse world compete in obstacle races and log pulls.

The **Washington and Old Dominion Rail Trail** runs right through Leesburg and is a delightful place for biking and hiking.

Leesburg's magnificent **Morven Park** (see the Arts and Culture chapter) is the scene of many exciting horse activities, including steeplechases, horse shows and carriage driving competitions. The carriage museum on the grounds has items of special interest to children, including small sleighs and carts and a marvelous toy carriage collection.

Middleburg, Upperville and Warrenton

These hotbeds of the horse country have countless steeplechases and horse shows including the marvelous Warrenton Pony shows in the spring and fall. And **The Flying Circus** in Bealeton, south of Warrenton, puts on a different air show every weekend from May through October (see our Annual Events and Festivals chapter).

Sperryville

This is a good place to enter the Skyline Drive for an afternoon of hiking and wildlife watching. **Skyland**, just south of this entry point, has stables with horses that are gentle enough for children. If your children are big enough, you can take them on a memorable trail ride.

Culpeper

Culpeper is another county where life revolves around horses. The town of Culpeper has horse shows from early spring until fall. If your children are horse-crazy, they'll be ecstatic in this environment (see the chapters Other Attractions and Annual Events and Festivals.)

Madison County

At the **Wonderful World of Miniature Horses Theme Park** (see the Other Attractions chapter), horses no more than three feet tall dance and perform for spectators, jumping over obstacles wider than the horses are tall. Children will delight in these kid-sized equines, particularly when they ride the living carousel and get to pet the horses. The

park also has pot-bellied pigs, sheep and other animals.

Gordonsville

The **Exchange Hotel**, a restored railroad hotel that served as a military hospital during the Civil War, now houses a museum with many interesting artifacts from the war.

Montpelier Station

Madison's **Montpelier** estate is the scene of several festivals and steeplechase races.

Schuyler

If your children have seen *The Waltons* reruns — or even if they haven't — they'll enjoy the **Waltons Mountain Museum** west of Charlottesville (see our Arts and Culture chapter) dedicated to Earl Hamner and his wonderful television family. The museum, in the school where Hamner studied, is a grouping of sets from the series, with actual scripts, photos and memorabilia. Kids can see videos of special shows and interviews with Hamner and the cast.

Charlottesville

The **Virginia Discovery Museum** on the downtown mall is a dynamic place for families (see the Arts and Culture

Insiders' Tips

When traveling in the Blue Ridge with children, even on a short daytrip into the countryside, pack a change of clothes, some snack food and drinks.

chapter). Activities include hands-on exhibits, costumes, science programs and an art room especially for children. Special events are held throughout the year.

The **Community Children's Theatre** has been bringing affordable family entertainment to the Charlottesville Performing Arts Center for more than 40 years (see our Arts and Culture chapter).

If your kids are into sports, you've got a smorgasbord of events here. Athletic events at the University of Virginia run the full gamut from football to polo and are exciting outings for children.

Charlottesville is, of course, steeped in history, and many children will enjoy the "old-fashioned" houses and odd furnishings of landmarks such as **Monticello** and **Ash Lawn-Highland**. Try to attend when there's a special event (see our Annual Events and Festivals chapter) such as Kite Day at Ash Lawn-Highland, an early May occasion when children of all ages can come fly their kites and participate in contests.

Wintergreen

Wintergreen Four Seasons Resort is rated tops in the country by *Family Circle* and *Better Homes and Gardens* for its children's programs. **The Treehouse** is a center for day-long delightful activities that will free you to pursue the resort's many adult attractions. In winter, the resort offers innovative ski programs combining lessons with just plain fun. In the summer, programs introduce children to the wonders of the wild. Horse and pony rides, riding and vaulting (horseback gymnastics) lessons are available at the stables. During any season, the Wintergarden Spa is a delightful place for kids to swim. Other activities include hiking and biking on trails in the resort's 11,000 acres.

Lynchburg

Lynchburg is the major metropolitan city in this part of the Blue Ridge, and history and shopping beckon in many forms for the children to have an enjoyable day.

You wouldn't think that a shoe store would interest kids, but you'll want to trot them into the **Craddock-Terry shoe manufacturing plant and outlet** downtown so they can eyeball a pair of size 21 shoes! The more than 300,000 pairs of shoes includes a great children's selection (and a big selection of socks to go with them). The prices are often real bargains.

The **Farmer's Market** is another busy, bustling, wonderful place for young people.

Lynchburg's history lessons are full of surprises that kids will appreciate. For example, the **Pest House Medical Museum and Confederate Cemetery** takes them on a tour of Dr. John Jay Terrell's medical office with its 1860s hypodermic needles and primitive medical instruments. The amputating blades used on

Don't underestimate roadside overlooks and rest stops as interesting places for kids.

Insiders' Tips

Civil War soldiers always attract grave attention and bring the war down to a more human level that kids don't always get from a textbook.

Point of Honor, the restored home of Dr. George Cabell, also gives a slice of 19th-century life. Children are fascinated to hear that the name comes from the gun duels fought on its lawn! And most school children have heard Patrick Henry's "Give me liberty or give me death!" speech, so take them to **Red Hill**, which was home to the famous lawyer and his 17 children. They can see Henry's home, original law office, kitchen and garden as they were before his death. Before leaving Lynchburg, don't overlook **Poplar Forest**, Thomas Jefferson's summer home. It is being renovated and offers indoor and outdoor views of painstaking historical restoration.

Smith Mountain Lake

Smith Mountain Lake is a haven for children if you go prepared for the right places. Otherwise, you can wander the whole day over 500 miles of shoreline with disappointed children.

Start at **Hales Ford Bridge**, the center of lake life. Here, you can rent pontoons, Jet Skis or go parasailing. Call ahead to reserve so you won't be disappointed. If you want to go fishing, look up some good guides such as Bob King in the Fishing Chapter of this book. Although you can do some impromptu lake expeditions in your rented boat, you may want an expert to show you where the action is.

If it's rainy, the town has a terrific **arcade** with nearly 50 different video and skill games. The **ice-cream parlor** is right next door and you can eat your treat either sitting on the decking on a pretty day or inside if the mercury is rising. There are several nice gift shops for browsing including **Gifts Ahoy**, with toys they'll enjoy. **The Little Gallery** also has unique crafts and paintings, many lake-oriented.

Unless you know someone with a house at the lake, looking for a swimming spot can be frustrating. The shoreline is privately owned except for the **Smith Mountain Lake State Park**. You won't be disappointed if you go there. Relatively new, the beach is beautifully situated looking at the mountains, and a nearby campground and Turtle Island make an enchanting voyage from the beach for the little ones.

Bedford is about 20 miles from the park at the lake. Children can soak up history effortlessly at the **Bedford City/County Museum** with its Civil War artifacts and other well-displayed items. At Christmas, one of the biggest displays of lights in the United States is showcased here at the **Elks National Home**.

Franklin County

Right next to the lake is **Booker T. Washington National Monument**, centered around the famous educator's birthplace. A video on how a 9-year-old rose above slavery to become one of the most inspirational leaders of his time will fascinate everyone. The video addresses Washington's hard life and meager existence and is a historic sojourn into a time in America when slavery was a way of life. Booker T. also has a beautiful restored farm with lots of farmyard animals that will uplift you after viewing his triumph over hardship.

If your travels take you southeast of the Blue Ridge, it's definitely worth a trip to the **Blue Ridge Institute Museums at**

Ferrum College. There's an 1800 German-American working farmstead with log house, oven, outbuildings, pasture and garden that demonstrates the lifestyles of early colonists. Also visit the **Blue Ridge Institute** with its many exhibits and archives, which are internationally recognized for excellence. Exhibits have included walking sticks and canes and quilts.

New River Valley

Blacksburg and Radford

The New River Valley is synonymous with **Virginia Tech**, the state's largest land-grant university. It's a 45-minute drive down I-81 from Roanoke. Tech in itself is the major attraction in Blacksburg and one the children will enjoy touring. City children will enjoy the perfect farm animals and agricultural experimental stations which raise extraordinary farm livestock and hybrid crops, the likes of which you won't see anywhere else.

The most popular spot at Tech is the **Duck Pond**. Small children are enchanted by the pampered fowl who lord over the spot and hold court for visitors. Brazen at times, they've no qualms about coming to the kids to get a snack if you don't bring them a special treat. These ducks are definitely more educated than most and definitely more aggressive!

Arts and culture are also plentiful on campus, and taking your kids to the student galleries and scheduled events will enrich their cultural education.

One of the biggest attractions in western Virginia can be found right outside of Blacksburg, 20 minutes from U.S. 460, at the **Cascades State Park** in Pembroke. College students and people from all over the nation come to hike the trail to the fabulous Cascades waterfall. It's recommended for children who can hike 3 miles and is no fun for small ones.

If you're thinking about going swimming, the town pool at Blacksburg and the city pool at Radford, home to Radford University, are two of the nicest in the Blue Ridge. The park at Radford, beside the New River, is a joy for children. They can walk or bike beside the New River and then picnic in the gazebo. It's one of the most impressive, inexpensive things a family can do.

South of Radford is **Claytor Lake**, a man-made body of water lined with white sand beaches, boat rentals and a beautiful campground. It's a good base for sightseeing throughout the Valley. While dragging kids into gift shops might be their idea of dull, such places as Floyd County's **Cockram's General Store** will be a treat. Tins of canned possum and roadkill and other country eye-openers make this a must-see.

Alleghany Highlands

The biggest attractions for children here are the **Homestead Resort** and the

Remember your camera when planning outings with kids. Their wide-eyed expressions are priceless, especially if you're going to a farm or horse show.

Insiders' Tips

rugged beauty of the area. They also can visit the **Greenbrier Resort**, in White Sulphur Springs, West Virginia (see our Resorts chapter). Shops and snack bars are higher-priced than most, but fun nevertheless. For example, an ice-cream sundae at the shops surrounding the Homestead go for about $5, with prices at the Greenbrier slightly higher, but the ambiance is worth the extra cost just to hear them "ooh" and "ahh" at the fancy desserts and elegant surroundings. Both resorts have toy shops and boutiques with some rare finds you'd expect to see on Fifth Avenue. Some items are reasonably priced while others are outrageous. They're guaranteed entertainment for a Sunday afternoon.

If resorts aren't your family's thing, there's plenty of the great outdoors around here for camping, swimming and sightseeing. **Blue Bend** is a favorite swimming hole in the Monongahela National Forest in nearby Alvon, West Virginia (see the Recreation chapter). Some say the swimming spot got its name because that's the color swimmers turn when they hit the icy water. Kids'll love the idea.

Inside
Wineries

America's first true connoisseur of fine wine was the Virginia-born Thomas Jefferson. And so it's fitting that the region is now home to so many fine wineries. With few exceptions, the state's most highly acclaimed wineries are in the foothills of the Blue Ridge. This is no coincidence. Higher elevations ensure healthy growing conditions for grapes, minimizing summer heat and lengthening the growing season.

The Shenandoah Valley, both climate- and soil-wise, has been favorably compared to the Mosel Valley of Germany, a famous Riesling region, and the Piedmont is said to share many of the same characteristics with the Bordeaux region of France.

Thomas Jefferson experimented for 30 years with grape-growing and wine-making at Monticello, believing that Virginia provided a suitable environment for winemaking. But it wasn't until the 1980s that the wine-making industry really took off in the state. In 1973 Virginia had only 59 acres of grapes; by 1981 the total had grown to 581 acres. Today more than 1,400 acres of vines and 42 wineries are scattered across the Commonwealth.

Photo: Prince Michel Vineyards

The Prince Michel tour offers one of the most extensive wine museums in the nation.

The Wine Spectator calls Virginia "the most accomplished of America's emerging wine regions." Find out for yourself what all the fuss is about. Just follow the highway signs with a cluster of grapes on them.

The Blue Ridge is home to more than 30 wineries, half of them in the rolling farmland stretching from Culpeper to Charlottesville. Most are family-owned and operated establishments. If you're lucky, you'll be in the area when one of the wineries hosts a festival or open house. Rebec Vineyards in Amherst County throws a big Spring Open House the end of April; six wineries participate in the Nelson County Summer Festival at Oak Ridge in June; Wintergreen Resort hosts the Virginia Wine Festival in July; Chateau Morrisette in Southwestern Virginia holds summer and fall jazz concert series on its grounds, offering tastings, tours and gourmet lunches; and 15 wineries are represented at the late September Smith Mountain Lake Chamber of Commerce Wine Festival at Bernard's Landing Resort.

We recommend an excellent annual guide to Virginia's wineries which includes maps, complete directions and a calendar of events. It's available free from the Virginia Wine Marketing Program, VDACS, Division of Marketing, P.O. Box 1163, Richmond, Virginia 23209, or phone (804) 786-0481.

The following is a complete list of wineries of the Blue Ridge region, beginning with those in the Shenandoah Valley. Wineries are organized geographically, from north to south and east to west within regions.

Shenandoah Valley Region

DEER MEADOW VINEYARD

199 Vintage Ln.	(540) 877-1919
Winchester	(800) 653-6632

Owner Charles Sarle built his own winery and made his first commercial wines in 1987, after retiring from a career as a mechanical engineer. He had been a home winemaker for 10 years. He and his wife Jennifer operate the winery on their 120-acre farm southwest of Winchester. They make Chardonnay, Seyval Blanc, Chambourcin and "Golden Blush" — a wine from an American hybrid. They invite you to tour their winery and bring along a picnic lunch and a fishing pole. Deer Meadow Vineyard is open March through December. Tours are offered from 11 AM to 5 PM Wednesday through Sunday and most Mondays and holidays.

NORTH MOUNTAIN
VINEYARD & WINERY

Off Va. 623, Maurertown   *(540) 436-9463*

This 20-acre vineyard is situated on property in northern Shenandoah County that has been farmed since the late 1700s. The vineyard was established in 1982, when proprietor Dick McCormack planted some 8,000 vines of Chardonnay, Vidal and Chambourcin.

At the winery building, which was built in 1990 and modeled after a European-style farmhouse, you can taste some

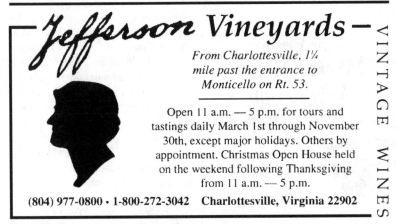

Jefferson Vineyards

VINTAGE WINES

From Charlottesville, 1¼ mile past the entrance to Monticello on Rt. 53.

Open 11 a.m. — 5 p.m. for tours and tastings daily March 1st through November 30th, except major holidays. Others by appointment. Christmas Open House held on the weekend following Thanksgiving from 11 a.m. — 5 p.m.

(804) 977-0800 • 1-800-272-3042   Charlottesville, Virginia 22902

of his wines for free. The winery produces several table wines, including a spiced apple variety. North Mountain is open from 11 AM to 5 PM on weekends and holidays for tours and tastings.

SHENANDOAH VINEYARDS
Off U.S. 11, Edinburg   **(540) 984-8699**

This is the Shenandoah Valley's first winery, growing 14 varieties of grapes on 40 acres. The winery itself is on the lower level of a renovated Civil War-era barn, which also houses a small gift shop and tasting room. Owner Emma Randel lives in the restored log house where her mother was born. In this peaceful setting, with sweeping moutain views, the winery produces Chardonnay, Riesling, Cabernet Savignon and several blends including Shenandoah Blanc, Shenandoah Ruby and Cabernet Blanc. The winery is open from 10 AM to 6 PM daily except Thanksgiving, Christmas and New Year's Day. Tours are given on an hourly basis from 11 AM to 5 PM.

GUILFORD RIDGE VINEYARD
Off U.S. 211, Luray   **(540) 778-3853**

On their four-acre Page County vineyard, owners John Gerba and Harland Baker grow hybrid grapes and Bordelaise wine-making methods to produce their Page Valley Red, Delilah (light red), Pinnacles (crisp white) and other wines. Call ahead to arrange a visit and purchases.

ROCKBRIDGE VINEYARD
Off Va. 252, Raphine   **(540) 377-6204**

Shepherd and Jane Rouse are the owners of this five-acre winery. Shep was the winemaker at Montdomaine, but is now trying his hand on his own patch of land between Staunton and Lexington. The Rouses produce Chardonnay, Riesling and two blends called St. Mary's Blanc and Tuscarora. Call in advance for tours.

East of the Blue Ridge Region

TARARA VINEYARD & WINERY
U.S. 15 and Va. 662
Leesburg   **(540) 771-7100**

R.J. "Whitie" and Michael Hubert own this 50-acre vineyard in Loudoun County and age their premium wines in a 6,000-square-foot cave overlooking the Potomac River. Winemaker Debbie

Dellinger produces Chardonnay, Charval, Cabernets, Cameo and Terra Rouge. Visitors can tour the cave and enjoy complimentary tastings 11 AM to 5 PM Thursday through Monday, Tuesday and Wednesday by appointment and weekends only in January and February. The vineyard grounds have picnic and meeting facilities.

LOUDOUN VALLEY VINEYARD
Va. 9, Waterford   (540) 882-3375

This 25-acre vineyard has one of the best views in the area, and owners Hubert and Dolores Tucker have capitalized on it. Their glass-walled tasting room overlooks the Short Hill Mountains and the vineyards, land where Mosby's Rangers camped during the Civil War. The Tuckers produce Chardonnay, Riesling, Cabernet Sauvignon, Merlot and Zinfandel wines. Tours are available 11 AM to 5 PM weekends and weekdays by appointment year round.

WILLOWCROFT FARM VINEYARDS
Off U.S. 7, Leesburg   (540) 777-8161

Small but selective describes this five-acre vineyard on top of Mount Gilead.

The winery is housed in a rustic barn with a splendid view of the nearby Blue Ridge. Owners Lewis and Cindy Parker create some of the Piedmont's finest Cabernet Sauvignon, Chardonnay, Riesling, Seyval and Cabernet Franc. Each September, they invite the public to help harvest grapes, a special, hands-on experience few people have the opportunity to enjoy. The vineyard is open 11 AM to 5 PM Wednesday through Sunday and by special appointment at other times.

SWEDENBURG WINERY
Off U.S. 50, Middleburg   (540) 687-5219

Named after its proprietors, Wayne and Juanita Swedenburg, this family vineyard consists of more than 15,000 grapevines on the 130-acre Valley View Farm, which has been under continuous cultivation for more than 200 years. The winery produces European-style premium wines, including Cabernet Sauvignon, Pinot Noir, Chardonnay, Riesling and Chantilly. Swedenburg hosts the annual Vinifera Wine Growers Association Festival (last Saturday of August) featuring more than 20 Virginia wineries. There's plenty of room to stretch out here and have a picnic, and you may even want to bring your fishing pole and wet a hook in the farm's pond. The vineyard is open from 10 AM to 4 PM daily.

MEREDYTH VINEYARDS
Va. 628, Middleburg   (540) 687-6277

This pretty Fauquier County vineyard is among the most prized in Virginia, with excellent offerings of Seyval Blanc, Cabernet Sauvignon, Riesling and Chardonnay. Meredyth is situated on a 56-acre farm outside of Middleburg along the edge of the Bull Run Mountains, foothills to the Blue Ridge that are also among the oldest mountains in the world. The

OAKENCROFT
VINEYARD AND WINERY

TOURS • TASTINGS • SALES
11-5, 7 days a week April-Dec. Other months by
appointment only 3 1/2 miles west on Barracks Rd.
(804) 296-4188 Charlottesville, VA

Archie Smith family opens the vineyard for public tours from 10 AM to 4 PM every day of the year except Christmas, Thanksgiving and New Year's Day. The vineyard store is open from 10 AM to 5 PM daily.

PIEDMONT VINEYARDS AND WINERY
Va. 626, Middleburg   (540) 687-5528

Virginia's first commercial vinifera vineyard is on Waverly, a 37-acre pre-Revolutionary War farm. Wines produced are Chardonnay, Semillon, Seyval Blanc, Hunt Country White and Cabernet Sauvignon. The winery is open for tours and tastings 10 AM to 5 PM daily except Thanksgiving, Christmas and New Year's Day. There's a picnic area on the grounds for the use of visitors.

NAKED MOUNTAIN VINEYARD
Off U.S. 55, Markham   (540) 364-1609

This chalet-like winery sits on the east slope of the Blue Ridge, east of Front Royal in Fauquier County. A picnic area on the five-acre vineyard offers sensational views. Owners Bob and Phoebe Harper produce Chardonnay (one of the best in Virginia, according to some), Riesling,

Sauvignon Blanc and Cabernet Sauvignon. They use traditional methods of winemaking — including fermentation in French oak barrels. The winery has a spacious tasting room on the second floor surrounded by a deck. Tours are offered from 11 AM to 5 PM weekends and holidays during January and February; Wednesday through Sunday (and holidays) March to December. For groups of 10 or more, call ahead for an appointment.

LINDEN VINEYARDS
Off U.S. 55, Linden   (540) 364-1997

Linden has 12 acres of vines and leases six additional acres at Flint Hill to produce about 4,000 cases a year of Chardonnay, Seyval, Cabernet, Sauvignon Blanc and Riesling-Vidal. The latter is a blend that does not require aging and produces a young, fresh wine, with 48 percent Vidal and 52 percent Riesling. The small, well-designed winery, which was started in the spring of 1987, includes a comfortable tasting room with a view of the vineyards against a mountain backdrop. The grounds have picnic areas. Tours are offered 11 AM to

5 PM on weekends January through March and Wednesday through Sunday from April through December. The winery is also open most holiday Mondays, but is closed Thanksgiving, Christmas and New Year's Day.

OASIS VINEYARD
U.S. 522 and Va. 635
Hume   *(540) 635-7627*

This vineyard and winery is on a spectacular stretch of land facing the Blue Ridge Mountains. The winery produces Chardonnay, Riesling, Merlot, Gewurztraminer, Cabernet Sauvignon and two types of Champagne, using the traditional *methode champenoise*. Owners Dirgham Salahi and his Belgian-born wife Corinne purchased the property in the mid-1970s and planted French hybrid grapes as a hobby. They soon learned that the soil was well-suited for wine grape growing and turned their hobby into a business. Although much of Oasis' wine is sold at the winery, it is also carried by some independent vintners and served by many restaurants in Washington, D.C. Tours are offered daily from 10 AM to 4 PM, but sales are available until 5 PM.

FARFELU VINEYARD
U.S. 522, Flint Hill   *(540) 364-2930*

This small winery near Oasis Vineyard has been revitalized in recent years. It was one of the first Virginia wineries to receive a commercial license as a farm winery and produced its first wines in 1975. Owner Charles Raney, a former United Airlines pilot, produces Cabernet Sauvignon, Chardonnay and red and white picnic wines. Tours and tastings are available from 11 AM to 5 PM daily, but Raney asks that visitors telephone in advance.

GRAY GHOST VINEYARDS
U.S. 211, Amissville   *(540) 937-4869*

This fledgling vineyard was opened in the spring of 1994 on nine acres of land in Rappahannock County. Owners and winemakers Charyl and Al Kellert produce Chardonnay, Cabernet Sauvignon and Vidal Blanc. The winery is open for tours 11 AM to 5 PM weekends.

ROSE RIVER
VINEYARDS AND TROUT FARM
U.S. 33, Syria   *(540) 923-4050*

This is a 177-acre farm winery in Madison County that borders Shenandoah National Park on the east. Picnic sites and hiking trails are available to visitors. From the winery cellars come Cabernet Sauvignon, Chardonnay, Mountain Peach, Mountain Blush and other wines. The farm also raises trout, which are available for purchase at most times either fresh or smoked. Tours are offered 10 AM to 5 PM weekends from April to November, 10 AM to 5 PM daily during October and at other times by appointment.

PRINCE MICHEL DE VIRGINIA VINEYARDS
U.S. 29, Leon   *(800) 869-8242,*
                            (540) 547-3707

Prince Michel de Virginia Vineyards, the largest wine producer in the state, is just south of Culpeper. So popular are its wines that the vineyard sells out every year.

Prince Michel is also the only Virginia winery with an extensive museum about wine and an exclusive restaurant with a French chef. The winery's owner, Jean Leducq, made his fortune in the industrial laundry industry and now lives in Paris. His dream to have his own winery came true in 1983 in the Blue Ridge foot-

PRINCE MICHEL
DE VIRGINIA

VINEYARDS & RESTAURANT

Just 10 Miles South of Culpeper on Route 29 South

Wine Museum, Shop & Restaurant
(540) 547-3707 or (800) 869-8242

Tours & Tastings Daily, 10-5, Free Admission
Restaurant: (540) 547-9720 or (800) 800-WINE

hills. In deference to Leducq's French background, all the employees at Prince Michel receive French language instruction.

The museum's diverse collection includes photos showing the process of grape-crushing. Some shots taken in Burgundy show two naked men in a barrel with the grapes, stirring and ventilating them. (Rest assured, this is not a technique applied at Prince Michel!) There's also a collection of every Mouton Rothschild label from 1945 to 1984, many of which were designed by famous artists such as Picasso, Salvador Dali and Georges Roualt.

The winery also has a special room for viewing a video documentary about the history of wine, the process of making it and about Prince Michel de Virginia Vineyards.

A self-guided tour takes visitors throughout the winery and features displays that describe the wine-making process. The tour ends at the gift shop, which sells everything from elegant wine canisters to scarves, wine-related jewelry and, of course, the wine itself. Visitors can

sample wine or drink it by the glass at an attractive bar inside the gift shop.

Prince Michel produces about 40,000 to 45,000 cases a year, though it has the capacity to produce nearly double that amount. Some of the vineyard's award-winning wines include Le Ducq Meritage, Chardonnay, White Burgundy, Blush de Michel and VaVin Nouveau. Rapidan River Vineyards, also in Leon, is one of the Prince Michel family of vineyards. It produces fine Rieslings and Gewurztraminer. For information, call (540) 547-3707.

Prince Michel is open to visitors from 10 AM to 5 PM daily except major holidays and hosts the annual Fete des Vendanges harvest festival in October.

Read more about the Prince Michel Restaurant in our Restaurants chapter or call (800) 800-WINE for reservations.

MISTY MOUNTAIN VINEYARDS INC.
Madison   **(540) 923-4738**

According to *The Wine Spectator*, Misty Mountain's owner Michael Cerceo produces some of the state's best red wines in his 19th-century refurbished barn.

Cerceo, a physicist, makes about 3,500 cases of wine a year from his 12 acres of vines, barrel-fermented Chardonnay, Merlot, Cabernet Sauvignon and Riesling. Tours are offered from 11 AM to 4 PM Monday through Saturday and on Sunday by appointment. Tours are offered by appointment only November through January.

AUTUMN HILL
VINEYARDS/BLUE RIDGE WINERY
Va. 603, Stanardsville   (804) 985-6100

This is a small, award-winning winery on the plateau of a hill northwest of Charlottesville. Owners Avra and Ed Schwab left Long Island for Virginia in the mid- 1970s. Ed, who ran an interior design firm, had grown weary of the rat race. Deciding to try wine-making, the couple planted the first stage of their vineyards in 1979. Their European-style wines include Chardonnay, Riesling, Blush and Cabernet Sauvignon. The winery is open to visitors only two weekends: the last weekend in March and the first weekend of November.

HORTON CELLARS
6399 Spotswood Tr., Gordonsville (540) 832-7440

In the early 1980s Dennis Horton searched the vineyards of southern France for grapes that would thrive in Virginia's warm climate. He settled on the Viognier, a variety used in some of the world's finest wines. He and his business partner Joan Bieda harvested the first crop from their 55 acres in Orange County in 1991 and made it into wine at Montdomaine Cellers, a noted Cabernet producer south of Charlottesville. In 1993 the vineyard made the first crush at its new underground stone cellars and offered tastings in a delightful vaulted-ceiling tasting room. Horton's Viognier and other Rhone varieties have done well in national competitions, but try the Norton, as well. This native Virginia grape produced Monticello's prize-winning clarets in the 1800s. The vineyard, which is on U.S. 33 between Barboursville and Gordonsville, is open year round, with tours and tastings from 11 AM to 5 PM daily.

BARBOURSVILLE VINEYARDS
Va. 777, Barboursville   (540) 832-3824

The giant Italian wine firm Zonin owns this winery outside Charlottesville, which includes a cattle farm and the imposing ruins of a mansion designed by Thomas Jefferson for Virginia governor James Barbour. The site is a registered Virginia Historic Landmark and has many prime picnic spots. The winery produces 10,000 cases of wine a year from 75 acres of grapes. According to *The Wine Spectator*, the whites are clean and crisp, while the reds are light and fruity in style. Wines include Chardonnay, Riesling, Sauvignon Blanc, Cabernet Blanc, Pinot Noir, Traminer Aromatico, Malvaxia, and an award-winning Cabernet Sauvignon Reserve 1988. Tours are available on Saturdays from 10 AM to 4:30 PM. Tastings and sales are offered 10 AM to 5 PM Monday to Saturday and 11 AM to 5 PM on Sunday.

BURNLEY VINEYARDS
Va. 641, Barboursville   (540) 832-2828

This is one of oldest vineyards in Albemarle County, producing Chardonnay, Cabernet Sauvignon, Riesling, Rivanna White, Rivanna Red, Rivanna Sunset (blush) and Daniel Cellars Somerset (dessert) wines. Lee Reeder and his father planted the first vines in 1976, the year after nearby Barboursville Vineyards opened. In 1984 father and son

CHÂTEAU MORRISETTE

Restaurant • Winery Tours • Black Dog Jazz Concerts
Catering • Outside Dining • Picnic Lunches • Receptions
Banquets • Nicholas The Dog • Wine Tasting

Meadows of Dan, VA
(540) 593-2865

started their own winery. Today they produce about 5,000 cases a year from grapes grown on their own 20 acres and from Ingleside and North Mountain Vineyards. Tours are available and tastings are offered in a room with a cathedral ceiling and huge windows overlooking the countryside. The winery is open 11 AM to 5 PM daily March through December and weekends in January and February. Group tours or evening visits can be arranged in advance.

JEFFERSON VINEYARDS LTD.

Va. 53, Charlottesville (804) 977-3042
(800) 272-3042

Between Monticello and Ashlawn, this vineyard is situated on the same stretch of rolling land once owned by Filippo Mazzei, the 18th-century wine enthusiast who helped convince Thomas Jefferson to plant vines.

Italian viticulturalist Gabriele Rausse from the University of Milan was hired to grow grapes and make wine here in 1981. Rausse was Barboursville's first wine grower and has worked with growers statewide for 15 years. Today he produces Pinot Grigio, Pinot Noir, Cabernet Sauvignon, Chardonnay and Riesling at Jefferson Vineyards. Tours are available 11 AM to 5 PM daily March through November and by appointment from December through February. Manager Charles Taylor also books private parties in the tasting room.

The winery has a small gift shop and a pleasant picnic area under a grape arbor. On the Thomas Jefferson Parkway is the vineyard's market, which sells all the wines made at the vineyard, along with homemade breads, imported cheeses, crackers, sandwiches, cookies and fresh produce when in season.

OAKENCROFT VINEYARD AND WINERY

Va. 654 to Garth Rd.
Charlottesville (804) 296-4188

Owner Felicia Warburg Rogan heads the Jeffersonian Wine Grape Growers Society, a group that won Charlottesville the title of Wine Capital of Virginia and initiated the annual Monticello Wine and Food Festival about 14 years ago. The winery is situated on a bucolic farm west of the city, with a lake in front and rolling hills behind. A big red barn houses the winery, tasting room and gift shop. The winery produces Chardonnay, Blush, Cabernet Sauvignon, Countryside White-Seyval Blanc, Sweet Virginia and Jefferson Claret and Merlot. Tours are given April through December seven days a week from 11 AM to 5 PM. In March tours are conducted on weekends only from 11 AM to 5 PM, and tours in January and February are by appointment only.

MONTDOMAINE CELLARS

Va. 720, Charlottesville   (804) 971-8947

One of Virginia's largest wineries, Montdomaine produces 10,000 cases annually from its 40 acres of vines. Bearing the Montdomaine label are fine Chardonnays, Cabernet Sauvignons and Cabernet Francs. Winemaker Owen Smith is particularly known for his Rhone wines, produced at Horton Cellars. The winery, a 1993 Governor's Cup winner, is owned by Horton Vineyards.

Montdomaine's winery building is partially built into a hillside to provide natural cooling. Visitors are welcome for tours and tastings 12 AM to 5 PM March through December. The vineyard is about 10 miles from the Thomas Jefferson Visitors Center off I-64.

TOTIER CREEK VINEYARD

Va. 720, Charlottesville   (804) 979-7105

This family-owned vineyard was planted in 1982 and '83. Owner/vintner Jamie Lewis uses Virginia white oak barrels to age his wines, which include three types of Chardonnay, Merlot, Cabernet, Riesling and Blush (a blend of Riesling and Merlot). Totier Creek wines are only available at the vineyard or at wine festivals.

The vineyard is 10 miles south of Charlottesville in the Green Mountain range, a series of foothills east of the Blue Ridge. Tours and tastings are conducted 11 AM to 5 PM Tuesday through Saturday

and noon to 5 PM on Sundays. Bring a picnic lunch to enjoy on the winery deck.

AFTON MOUNTAIN VINEYARDS

Afton   (540) 456-8667

This winery lies on a southeastern slope of the Blue Ridge at 960 feet, just minutes from the end of Skyline Drive and the beginning of the Blue Ridge Parkway near Afton, a village known for its antiques and mountain crafts. The winery and vineyards — nine acres of vines that are among the most mature in Virginia — offer magnificent views of the Rockfish River Valley and the mountains immortalized in Edgar Allan Poe's *Tale of the Ragged Mountains*. Wines include Chardonnay, Cabernet Sauvignon, White Zinfandel, Gewurztraminer, Riesling and Sweet Afton Semillion Apple Wine. Winter wines include Merlot and Pinot Noir. The winery is open for tours and tastings 10 AM to 5 PM Friday to Monday during January and February and 10 AM to 6 PM Wednesday to Monday the rest of the year.

WINTERGREEN VINEYARD & WINERY

Va. 664, Nellysford   (804) 361-2519

In the beautiful Rockfish Valley adjacent to Wintergreen Four Seasons Resort, this Nelson County vineyard and winery offers spectacular views during all seasons of the year. Part of the original High View plantation built by the Rodes family, the land has been in agricultural use since the early 1800s, in turn producing tobacco, wheat, barley, hay, apples and now grapes. Award-winning wines include Chardonnay, Cabernet Sauvignon, Riesling, Blush, Three Ridges White, Governor Nelson White and Mill Hill Apple wine. The facilities are open for free tours and tastings daily from 10 AM to 6 PM (winter hours are noon to 5 PM, closed Tuesday). The winery has a picnic area and gift shop. Exit the Blue Ridge Parkway at Milepost 13, turning onto Va. 664 E. The winery is 5 miles on the left.

CHERMONT WINERY INC.

Esmont   *(804) 286-2211*

This small winery in the rolling hills of southern Albemarle County was established in 1978 by Josh Sherman, a career pilot and retired Navy captain. Sherman planted 10 acres of Chardonnay, Riesling and Cabernet Sauvignon grapes over a period of three years, making his first wine in his basement in 1981. He has since built a winery with a large tasting room. The winery produces Chardonnay, Riesling (dry and semisweet) and Cabernet Sauvignon. Tours are offered noon to 5 PM Tuesday through Saturday most of the year, Sunday year round by appointment and any day January through March by appointment. The winery is closed on major holidays.

MOUNTAIN COVE VINEYARDS

Lovingston   *(804) 263-5392*

In 1974 Mountain Cove owner Al C. Weed II became the first person in Central Virginia to plant grape vines. A native of Brooklyn, New York, Weed left a career in investment banking and moved with his family to the Nelson County farm in 1973. He planted French hybrid grapes, believing that they were more hardy and prolific than other vines. Today he produces several blends called Skyline White, Skyline Red and Skyline Rose, as well as a tasty peach wine called LaAbra Peach. Weed built most of the winery and the log cabin tasting room himself. The vineyard is open daily 1 PM to 5 PM April through December and 1 PM to 5 PM

Vintage Varietal Wines Produced in the Shadow of the Blue Ridge Mountains.

3659 South Ox Rd., Edinburg, Virginia 22824
Hrs: 10 am - 6 pm Daily 10 am - 5 pm Jan, Feb, March
540-984-8699

Wednesday through Sunday from January to March. From Lovingston, follow U.S. 29 N. Turn left on Va. 718, right on Va. 651. The winery is on the right.

REBEC VINEYARDS

Amherst   *(804) 946-5168*

This five-acre family-owned winery is about halfway between Charlottesville and Lynchburg on U.S. 29. Richard and Ella Hanson once could laughingly boast that their winery was the smallest in Virginia, but that's no longer the case. Nor does size necessarily equate to quality. The Hansons produce White, Blush, Chardonnay, Cabernet Sauvignon and Riesling. Since 1991 Rebec Vineyards has hosted the Virginia Garlic Festival, an October event which features the crowning of a garlic queen, a garlic-eating contest, live music, good food and a lot of Virginia wine.

The Hanson house, built in 1742, has been home to the descendants of three Virginia governors: Thomas Nelson, William Crawford and William Cabel. The winery is open for tours 10 AM to 5 PM daily March 15 through December and by appointment from December 15 to March 15.

STONEWALL VINEYARDS
Concord   *(804) 993-2185*

This family-operated winery is halfway between Appomattox and Lynchburg. From their 10 acres of vinifera, French and American hybrids, owners Larry and Sterry Davis and winemaker Bart Davis produce Claret, Cayuga White, Chambourcin, Vidal Blanc and Pyment, a medieval blend of wine, honey and spices. Tours are offered 11 AM to 4 PM Wednesday through Sunday from March to December and by appointment at other times. A good time to visit is in May, during Mayfest, an annual celebration of wineries, foods, crafts and live music. In mid-October, the winery hosts Jazz on the Lawn, an event featuring gourmet food, live music and, of course, plenty of wine. Call for the exact dates, because they vary from year to year.

Southwest Virginia

TOMAHAWK MILL WINERY
Chatham   *(804) 432-1063*

Walter Crider has a unique setting for a winery — a historic water-powered grist mill overlooking the mill pond. In this bucolic setting you can taste his

Chardonnay wine 9 AM to 5 PM on Saturdays from March through December 24, and other times by appointment. From U.S. 29 between Gretna and Chatham turn west on Va. 649 for 8.5 miles.

CHATEAU MORRISETTE WINERY INC.
Meadows of Dan   *(540) 593-2865*

This winery commands a view from a hilltop 40-acre farm bordering the Blue Ridge Parkway in Floyd and Patrick counties. Since 1983 wines have been made here in a traditional European style, using stainless steel tanks for fermentation and French and American oak for aging. The winery, built of native stone and wood with an underground wine cellar, resembles a miniature German castle. Facilities include a tasting room, restaurant and a large deck for picnicking.

Chateau Morrisette hosts a monthly "Black Dog" jazz concert series every summer from June to October. Live jazz, tastings, tours and gourmet lunches make this an exciting event.

Tours, tastings and sales of the winery's Chardonnay, Merlot, Black Dog, Black Dog Blanc and Sweet Mountain Laurel are available 11 AM to 4 PM daily except major holidays.

Inside
Other Attractions

The Blue Ridge area has so many diverse attractions that a few deserve a chapter of their own: Covered Bridges, Zoos, Caverns, Horse Country and Spectator Sports.

Covered Bridges

Virginia's first covered bridges were built around 1820, and during the following century hundreds were erected. Happily, a few of these favorite courting spots of yesteryear have been preserved. Of the seven covered wooden bridges accessible to the public, the Blue Ridge claims the bridge deemed the oldest and most unusual, Humpback Bridge in Covington, Alleghany County. Don't forget your camera. Here's a rundown of these beauties, from north to south.

MEEMS BOTTOM BRIDGE

North of Harrisonburg and less than a half-mile from busy I-81, visitors can step back in time at Meems Bottom Bridge, a 204-foot, single-span Burr arch truss over the north fork of the Shenandoah River, 2 miles south of Mount Jackson on U.S. 11. It takes its name from the Meems family who owned the Strathmore estate west of the Shenandoah River. The original 1893 structure was rebuilt in 1979, almost three years after arsonists burned it. It had been

Some of the smallest horses in the world can be found in Madison at the Wonderful World of Miniature Horses.

burned before, in 1862, when Stonewall Jackson went up the valley ahead of Union general John C. Fremont, prior to the battles of Harrisonburg, Cross Keys and Port Republic. The bridge was rebuilt, only to be destroyed again by a flood in 1870. The one-lane bridge is open to automobile traffic, and is a good side excursion from New Market, which lies 6 miles to the south and is a major destination for Civil War buffs.

HUMPBACK BRIDGE

Known as the "Granddaddy of them all," Humpback is Virginia's oldest standing covered bridge and the nation's only surviving curved-span covered bridge. Built in 1835 as part of the Kanawha Turnpike, it is a graceful, 100-foot arched span with an eight-foot rise over Dunlap Creek in Alleghany County, within viewing distance of I-64, off the Callaghan Exit between Covington, Virginia, and White Sulphur Springs, West Virginia. Its hump-like design is unique in the western hemisphere. Only one other bridge, in France, is similarly constructed.

During autumn, the Humpback Wayside, between Virginia's breathtaking Allegheny and Blue Ridge Mountains, is a popular picnic area. Visitors can stroll through the bridge and wade in the shallow creek below to admire the bridge's hand-hewn oak timbers. Milton Hall, a historic bed and breakfast inn with gorgeous gardens, is close by.

SINKING CREEK BRIDGES

Near the beautiful Appalachian Trail in the New River Valley's Giles County stand two modified Howe trusses built across Sinking Creek, north of Newport. Built in 1912 and 1916, the 55-foot Link's Farm Bridge and 70-foot Sinking Creek Covered Bridge were left in place when a

modern bridge was built in 1963. The Newport countryside is worth exploring for its quaint, country setting and is considered choice farm real estate by professors at nearby Virginia Tech. Northwest is Mountain Lake Resort, made famous by the movie *Dirty Dancing*.

Zoos and Animal Farms

Complementing all the natural sites in this area are several zoos and animal attractions that both children and adults will find fascinating.

THE WONDERFUL WORLD OF MINIATURE HORSES THEME PARK

Off U.S. 29, Madison   (540) 948-4000

Imagine full-grown horses no taller than a yardstick! That's what you'll find at Morgan and Georgeanna Gibbs' wonderland, just 25 miles north of Charlottesville in Madison County. These miniature horses dance, prance and show off for about 20,000 visitors a year. They all have mythical names, like Hercules and Thor. In the show, they follow Georgeanna's instructions and jump over obstacles that are wider than the horses are tall! Children can delight in riding the living carousel or a hay ride or train ride.

Some of the other exotic pets at Wonderful World are potbellied pigs, a breed of sheep dating to biblical times and a monkey named Ooh! that rattles his cage.

If you find it difficult to tear yourself away from the horses, you can arrange to take one home. The park sells about 20 colts and fillies a year; prices start at $2,500 and can go to several hundred thousand dollars.

The theme park is open on weekends from May through Memorial Day, Wednesday through Sunday from Memorial Day to Labor Day and weekends from Labor Day through mid-October. Hours are 10 AM to 5 PM Wednesday through Saturday and noon to 5 PM Sunday. Call for show times. Admission is $5.75 for adults, $5 for senior citizens and $3.50 for children. Group and birthday party reservations are available.

NATURAL BRIDGE ZOO

*U.S. 11 off I-81 at
Exit 175 or 180*   *(540) 291-2420*

Next to Natural Bridge Village and Resort, this 25-acre zoo is also an endangered species breeding center. It has the largest petting area in Virginia and elephant rides for the kids. For two decades the zoo has been raising generations of endangered species, including four generations of the scarlet macaw, Siberian tigers, ring-tailed lemurs and Himalayan bears. For $2.50, on weekends, children can ride Asha, the African elephant. Enjoy the thrill of mingling with tame deer, gentle llamas and cute, fuzzy miniature donkeys. The family also will enjoy large covered picnic pavilions and a well-stocked gift shop. Hours of operation are 9 AM to 6 PM seven days a week. Admission is $6 for adults and $4 for children ages 3 to 12.

MILL MOUNTAIN ZOO

*Off Blue Ridge Pkwy.
Roanoke*   *(540) 343-3241*

On top of Roanoke's Mill Mountain, off the Blue Ridge Parkway and alongside the famous star, is a three-acre zoo operated by the Blue Ridge Zoological Society of Virginia. Its main star is Ruby the Tiger, who received local and national attention during a two-year fund drive to build a new habitat at the zoo. Thanks to recent donations, Ruby also has her own watering hole for use in the summertime. In addition to Ruby, 43 species of native and exotic animals live at the zoo. A popular attraction is the prairie dogs, who pop up and down out of their burrows, much to the delight of schoolchildren. Other residents are Japanese snow monkeys, tree kangaroos, red pandas and white-naped cranes.

The zoo is open to the public daily (closed Christmas Day) 10 AM to 5 PM. Admission is $3.50 for adults, $2 for children younger than 12 and free to those younger than 2. The Roanoke Jaycees operate a miniature train with an additional fee. The zoo's concession and souvenir stand are open during peak season.

Photo: Lynchburg Museum

An interior shot of the Point of Honor in Lynchburg.

Picnic facilities, a wildflower garden and a breathtaking overlook view of Roanoke are nearby. You can get to the zoo off I-581; follow the signs off the Elm Avenue Exit to Jefferson Street and take a left on Walnut Avenue over the bridge.

Caverns

America's history doesn't stop at ground level. There's another world down under, with a history millions of years old. Exploring caves, called spelunking, is a unique experience — surrounded by an unearthly silence, you can hear the steady drip of calcite solution as it forms stalactite icicles and stalagmite gardens at the modest rate of one inch every 125 years. Cave temperatures average 54 degrees year round, so a sweater is a good idea. Under Virginia's outer skin are so many miles of caves that a number of them have never been completely explored. The Blue Ridge region of the Appalachians has the highest number of caves in North America. Six are easily accessible from major interchanges of the Skyline Drive or I-81.

Thomas Jefferson, an early Blue Ridge spelunker, wrote about Madison's Cave (closed to the public) near Grottoes in his "Notes on the State of Virginia." All the caverns have interesting histories — stories of Native Americans, soldiers, and adventurous children who stumbled across passageways leading to hitherto unseen wonders.

Unfortunately, some caves bear the scars of souvenir hunters, a practice that has been halted by the Virginia Cave Act. Explorers of wild caves now know to "take nothing but pictures, leave nothing but footprints." On a hot day, you can't beat the caverns' natural air conditioning as you tour the impressive formations and age-old waterways.

If commercial caves are too tame for you, get down and dirty in one of Virginia's many wild caves with Highland Adventures, P.O. Box 151, Monterey, Virginia 24465, (540) 468-2722. The outfitter supplies helmets, lamps and guides; you provide the old clothes (remember, caves are damp and average 54 degrees year round) and knee pads for crawling.

SKYLINE CAVERNS

Off I-66 at Exit 6
Front Royal　　　　　(540) 635-4545

Sixty-million-year-old Skyline Caverns, at the foothills of the Blue Ridge near the Skyline Drive, has a unique solarium entrance, where green shrubs border the cave to create a most attractive welcome. Three running streams traverse the core of the cave, stocked with trout as an experiment in adaptation. Fat and thriving, they require chopped pork each week to make up for a lack of vitamin D. Another unusual aspect is anthodites, called "orchids of the mineral kingdom," the only such rock formations in the world. They grow at a rate of one inch every 7,000 years!

Skyline is noted for its simulated scenes of reality, such as the Capitol Dome, Rainbow Trail and the Painted Desert. Kids enjoy the outdoor Skyline Arrow, a miniature train that carries them on a half-mile journey through a real tunnel. Skyline Caverns, near the north entrance of Shenandoah National Park, is open year round, with hours depending on the season. From June 15 through Labor Day, the hours are 9 AM to 6:30 PM. Admission is $10 for adults and $5 for children ages 7 to 13.

SHENANDOAH CAVERNS

Off I-81 at Exit 269　　　(540) 477-3115

Shenandoah Caverns, taking its name from the Native American word for "daughter of the stars," was discovered in 1884 during the building of the Southern Railway. The grotto is an estimated 11 million years old and is the closest underground attraction to I-81. It's also the only one in Virginia with an elevator, an advantage to visitors who are handicapped, elderly or just plain tired. Bacon Hall, a formation named for its hanging

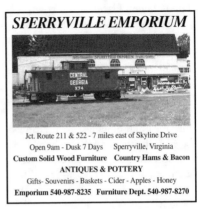

slabs of striped iron oxide and calcite, has been featured in National Geographic. Other notable points on the tour are the Grotto of the Gods, Vista of Paradise and Rainbow Lake. Nearby attractions include Skyline Drive, New Market Battlefield and its two Civil War museums, Tuttle & Spice 1880 General Store and the Meems Bottom covered bridge. Shenandoah Caverns is open year round; hours depend on the season. Admission is $8 for adults and $4 for children ages 8 to 14. Group rates are available upon request.

LURAY CAVERNS

U.S. 211, 15 minutes off I-81
at Exit 264, Luray　　　(540) 743-6551

Luray Caverns, the largest known cave on the East Coast, is a colorful natural cathedral with the world's only Stalacpipe Organ. Stalactites are tuned to concert pitch and accuracy and are struck by electronically controlled, rubber-tipped plungers to produce music of symphonic quality. An hour-long conducted tour transports visitors through a wonderland of vast chambers, some 140 feet high. Memorable formations include the Fried

Eggs, the enormous Double Column and Pluto's Ghost. Placid, crystal-clear pools such as Dream Lake reflect the thousands of stalactites above. One of the largest chambers, the Cathedral, has been the setting for more than 250 weddings. A wishing well has produced more than a half million dollars for charity. Topside, there's a gift shop and restaurant. Don't miss the Luray Singing Tower, a carillon of 47 bells, the largest weighing 7,640 pounds, the smallest 12 pounds. Recitals are given seasonally. A self-guided tour of the Historic Car & Carriage Caravan is included in the caverns admission.

The central entrance to Skyline Drive is only 15 minutes from the caverns, which are open year round. Hours are seasonal. Admission is $11 for adults and $5 for children ages 7 to 13. Adults older than 62 and armed forces personnel on active duty pay $9. Children ages 6 and younger are admitted free.

ENDLESS CAVERNS

Off I-81 at Exit 257
New Market   *(540) 740-3993*

On October 1, 1879, two boys and their dog chased a rabbit up the slope of Reuben Zirkle's farm. The rabbit disappeared under a boulder. The boys moved the boulder, and before their astonished eyes appeared a great shaft of Endless Caverns. No end has ever been found to the labyrinth of winding channels and vast rooms, which now are lighted artfully and dramatically for visitors. Snowdrift and Fairyland are two of the most popular formations. Of all the caverns, Endless is the one that makes you feel as if you're venturing into uncharted, rugged territory, and its outdoor scenery is the most beautiful. Just as interesting are the historic native limestone buildings constructed during the 1920s. On the

wide porches of the Main Lodge, visitors are invited to rest, rock and relax while enjoying a sweeping view of the Shenandoah Valley. The stone lodge is cooled in the summer and warmed in winter by air from the caverns. Nearby, Endless Caverns' 100-site campground sits at the foot of Virginia's Massanutten Mountains, adjoining George Washington National Forest. On I-81, you can't miss the sign for Endless Caverns — it's the largest outdoor billboard in the Eastern United States, standing 35 feet high and 500 feet long. Endless Caverns is open year round except Christmas. Hours from March 15 to June 14 are 9 AM to 5 PM; June 15 to Labor Day, 9 AM to 7 PM; after Labor Day to November 14, 9 AM to 5 PM; and November 15 to March 14, 9 AM to 4 PM. Admission is $9 for adults and $4.50 for children ages 3 to 12.

GRAND CAVERNS

Off I-81 at Exit 235
Grottoes   *(540) 249-5705*

Grand Caverns, within Grand Caverns Regional Park, is one of the oldest and most spectacular caverns in the Shenandoah Valley. The public has been coming here since 1806, including Thomas Jefferson, who rode horseback from Monticello to see the site. During the Civil War, General Stonewall Jackson quartered his troops within this massive stone fortress after the Battle of Port Republic. Union soldiers also visited the cave. Their signatures still can be seen penciled on the walls. In better times, the Grand Ballroom, which encompasses 5,000 square feet, was the scene of early 19th-century dances for the socially prominent. Cathedral Hall, 280 feet long and 70 feet high, is one of the largest rooms in Eastern caverns. Massive columns and the rare "shield" formations, whose origins are a mystery to geologists, are highlights.

Grand is a hauntingly beautiful cave, and its origins are mysterious. Its unique vertical bedding is believed to be the result of Africa's collision with Virginia millennia ago.

It's open 9 AM to 5 PM on March weekends, and seven days a week April through Halloween. Admission is $9 for adults and $6 for children ages 3 to 12. Discounts are offered to AAA Auto Club, senior citizens and active military.

NATURAL BRIDGE CAVERNS

U.S. 11 off I-81 at
Exit 175 or 180   *(540) 291-2121*

Here's a cavern with its own ghost! For more than 100 years, people have been hearing the plaintive voice of a woman deep within the limestone passages. The first time it happened in 1889, men working in the caverns abandoned their ladders, fled and refused to go back. Their tools and lanterns were found in 1978. The last time the ghost was heard was as recently as 1988, when six people on the last tour of the day heard a distinct moaning sound, which continued throughout the guide's narrative. In all cases, it is documented that those present had an eerie feeling and fled the premises without hesitation. The caverns, at Virginia's Natural Bridge complex, offer a guided, 45-minute tour 347 feet underground.

Topside, see Natural Bridge and the Wax Museum. The pathways are winding and steep in areas, so walking shoes are suggested. The Caverns Gift Shop is the largest in the valley, with 10,000 square feet of space and rock and mineral candies which are sure to delight youngsters. Colonial-style Natural Bridge Hotel features sumptuous buffets.

The cavern is open March through November, 10 AM to 5 PM daily. Admission is $7 for adults, $3.50 for children ages 6 to 15, and a special combination ticket to see all three attractions is $15 for adults and $7.50 for children ages 6 to 15.

DIXIE CAVERNS

5753 W. Main St., Salem   *(540) 380-2085*

Dixie Caverns' tour guides first take visitors up the mountain instead of down into it, pointing out the spot where a dog fell through a hole and led to the discovery of the caverns. The pet's owners also found evidence that the Native Americans of Southwestern Virginia used the cave for shelter and food storage. Some of the most popular formations on the cavern tour are the Turkey Wing, Magic Mirror and Wedding Bell, where dozens of couples have been united. Outside, there's also lots to do and see. The Dixie Caverns Pottery displays thousands of gifts. There's also a special basket shop, a shop named Christmas in Dixieland and a Rock and Mineral Shop, with its famous polished-stone wheel. The campground is open all year for RVs and campers. For fishermen, the Roanoke River is nearby. The caverns are also open year round from 9:30 AM to 5 PM daily. Admission for adults is $5.50, $3.50 for children 5 to 12. Dixie Caverns is just south of Roanoke off I-81 at Exit 132.

Spectator Sports

Although most sports-minded visitors are in the Blue Ridge to play, some want to watch others play. The area has a lot to offer in college competition, especially basketball and football. You'll want to get tickets early, because the locals are avid fans. You can attend most horse shows and steeplechases on the spur of the moment, and the excitement is well worth the admission (see Horse Country Activities in this chapter).

Baseball

THE VALLEY BASEBALL LEAGUE
Harrisonburg   *(540) 568-3552*

One of the oldest amateur baseball leagues in the country, the Valley League is sanctioned by the NCAA because it features college players, many of whom go on to play professional ball. Front Royal, Harrisonburg, New Market, Staunton, Waynesboro and Winchester have franchised teams in the circuit. Starting the first weekend in June, there are 40 regular season games, then best-of-five finals and finals. Games are played every day of the week, beginning about 7:30 PM.

SALEM AVALANCHE
1004 Texas St., Salem   *(703) 389-3333*

A Class A team for the Colorado Rockies, the Buccaneers live happily in the sports-crazed Roanoke Valley City of Salem, where they have a new, state-of-the-art stadium. Beginning in April, 140 games are on the agenda until September, half at home at Salem Ballpark, the new stadium. You can hear the Avalanche games on WROV, WBNK and WFNR radio stations. General admission is $3. Take Salem Exit 141 off I-81.

LYNCHBURG HILLCATS
City Stadium, Lynchburg   *(804) 528-1144*

Lynchburg has had a baseball team in its midst for more than 100 years. Since 1966 this group has been in the class A level of the Carolina League, along with other Virginia cities such as Salem and Woodbridge. The Lynchburg team has been affiliated with many different clubs along the way including the New York

Mets and the Boston Red Sox. Now, however, they are affiliated with the Pittsburgh Pirates. The team plays in City Stadium, which has a capacity of 4,000. They play 140 games per season, half of them at home. All games are broadcast on radio station WLNI. General admission is $4.

College Sports

JAMES MADISON UNIVERSITY BASKETBALL
Harrisonburg   *(540) JMU-DUKE*

JMU has 27 intercollegiate teams, but charges admission only to football and basketball games. When the men's basketball team plays at home, the whole town turns out or tunes in. The Dukes have advanced to post-season play five of the past seven seasons under coach Charles G. "Lefty" Driesell, who won his 650th game during the 1994-95 season. The JMU women have made five NCAA basketball playoff appearances. Games are played at the Convocation Center on the east side of I-81.

JMU's football team has been in three NCAA playoffs and made the 1994 NCAA I-AA final eight. The baseball squad is the only Virginia team to have played in the College World Series. Other nationally ranked sports at the college are field hockey (1994 national champions), archery (three national championships), men's lacrosse (1994 NCAA final eight, five NCAA playoffs), women's lacrosse and soccer.

Women's lacrosse and men's and women's soccer teams play at the new Reservoir Street Field (capacity 1,860) on the east campus. Baseball's home is Long Field (capacity 1,200), and football is played at Bridgeforth Stadium (capacity 12,800).

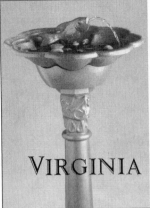
UNIVERSITY OF VIRGINIA FOOTBALL, BASKETBALL AND OTHER SPORTS

Charlottesville	*(804) 924-UVAI*
In state	*(800) 542-UVAI*

Football games at Scott Stadium have become so popular that it's hard to get tickets at the last minute. The Cavaliers chalked up eight consecutive winning seasons through 1994. For that reason, orange-garbed UVA alumni flock to the games in record numbers, hollering "Wahoo-Wah!" at all the right moments. If you want to be a part of this scene, call the above numbers for tickets now.

In the 1994 to '95 season, the men's basketball Cavaliers tied for the Atlantic Coast Conference regular season championship and advanced to the final eight of the NCAA tournament. The women's team won the Atlantic Coast Conference regular season championship in 1995. Under head coach Debbie Ryan, the women advanced to the final four in NCAA tournaments in the 1990, '91 and '92 seasons, advanced to the final eight in '93, to the Sweet 16 in '94 and to the final eight in 1995. Basketball games are played inside the 8,457-seat University Hall.

If you're a soccer fan, you can watch one of the top teams in the nation play home games at UVA. The men's soccer team won the last four NCAA Division I championships (1991 to 1994) and the women's team advanced to the final four in 1991. The Klockner Stadium for soccer and lacrosse opened in the fall of 1992. The Klockner Group donated $1.2 million to the construction of the stadium. Klockner, with headquarters in Germany, is a well-known industrial conglomerate with textile plants throughout the United States, including one in Gordonsville.

Lacrosse is another winning sport at UVA. The women's team advanced to the NCAA Tournament's Final Four each of the last four years and the NCAA Division I championship in 1991 and 1993. The men's team was the runner-up in the 1994 NCAA Division I tournament.

UVA hosts the Cavalier Classic Golf Tournament every spring, drawing some of the top players in the country to Charlottesville's Birdwood Golf Course.

VIRGINIA TECH HOKIE BASKETBALL

U.S. 460 By., off I-81   (703) 231-6726

Virginia Tech basketball soared to new heights in 1994-95 when the Hokies won their second National Invitation Tournament championship is New York's Madison Square Garden. Coach Bill Foster's Techmen defeated Marquette, 65-64, in overtime in the title game when Shawn Smith made two free throws with 0.7 seconds left on the clock. Ironically, Tech's first NIT championship came in overtime in 1973 with a 92-91 win over Notre Dame. Tech is a Division I school that will begin competing in the Atlantic 10 Conference in 1995-96. The Hokies have an illustrious history in their home arena, Cassell Coliseum, having won 339 of 415 games played there. The Hokies have never had a losing season at home in 34 years. Two of Tech's most famous players are Dell Curry, currently a star with the Charlotte Hornets, and Bimbo Coles, who plays for the Miami Heat. Cassell Coliseum is just off U.S. 460 Bypass adjacent to the football stadium, Lane Stadium/Worsham Field, near the heart of the Tech campus.

VIRGINIA TECH HOKIE FOOTBALL

Virginia Tech, Blacksburg   (540) 231-6726

Virginia Tech Football is BIG in western Virginia — so big that if you want to catch a game, go as early as you can to avoid the traffic jams on the less-than-adequate roads leading off I-81 onto U.S. 460 to Lane Stadium (capacity 51,000). Thousands of tailgating fans will join you in the parking lot. It's simply the main event for this part of the Blue Ridge, with wild, roaring crowds and lots of pageantry and fun!

For those interested in the game itself, be aware that Tech is in the Big East Conference. Its mascot is a turkey sporting maroon and orange. A 1990 game with the University of Virginia, the Gobblers' archrival, set a stadium record of 54,157, the largest crowd ever to see a football game in the state. Famous Tech football player graduates include Bruce "The Sack Man" Smith, who won the Outland Trophy in 1984; George Preas with the Baltimore Colts; Ricky Scales with the Houston Oilers; Don Strock of the Miami Dolphins; and Bill Ellenbogen of the New York Giants. To get to Lane Stadium, get off I-81 to the Blacksburg Exit and take U.S. 460. Just follow the crowd!

Hockey

THE ROANOKE EXPRESS

Hockey Roanoke Inc.
4502 Starkey Rd. S.W.
Roanoke   (540) 989-GOAL

Roanoke's new professional hockey franchise is selling out the house ever since it replaced the Roanoke Rampage. The season runs from October through March at the Roanoke Civic Center on Tuesday, Friday and Saturday, with a few exceptions. The team performs in the East Coast Hockey League, which includes 19 teams from nine different states.

Season tickets are available. Individual tickets are $4 to $8 a person. There is no lack of action, both on the ice and in the stands. Bring the entire family!

Race Car Driving

NEW RIVER VALLEY SPEEDWAY

Radford   (540) 639-1700

Once known as Pulaski County Speedway, this track now named the New River Valley Speedway. A NASCAR-sanctioned event, racing takes place on a paved, oval track that is $4/10$-mile long.

Every Saturday night from April to September, the Speedway packs in visitors from all over the New River Valley. The featured division is late-model stock, but other divisions include limited sportsman, modified-mini, ministock and pure stock.

A family atmosphere prevails, with more than 1,000 children showing up each Saturday. And, no matter what your preconceptions about racing are, this is a sport for everyone to enjoy. Doctors, lawyers, farmers and schoolteachers all make the Speedway a part of their weekends! Admission is $10 for adults and $1 for children 12 and younger.

Horse Country Activities

The Shenandoah Valley has always had a rich horse culture, stemming from the days when settlers depended on their equines to till their fields and carry them from place to place. East of the Blue Ridge, stretching from Loudoun to Albemarle counties, is Virginia Hunt Country, an area devoted to a centuries-old sport — riding to the hounds — and the accompanying lifestyle. Because of this singularity of purpose, the area has managed to keep development at bay, preserving large estates and horse farms. If you consider foxhunting a cruel sport, keep in mind that only one percent of the foxes hunted are caught. Most hunts end with the fox slipping into a den or eluding the hounds entirely. Nowhere do foxes have a finer life, because the locals protect their dens and put out medicated food to keep them healthy. The sport, you see, is in the chase, not the kill. It's a beautiful sight to see a stream of hounds pouring out into a broad field followed by a kaleidoscope of multicolored horses and riders clad in red coats. You can witness that here.

Natural adjuncts to foxhunting are horse shows and steeplechases, activities that are easily accessible in this region and thrilling to watch. Attending a horse event not only gives you a chance to see beautiful country and fine horses, but to people-watch. The Hunt Country is crawling with celebrities from politics or the entertainment industry who have homes in the Middleburg-Upperville or Charlottesville areas. Here are some of the most popular places to catch the action (see our Annual Events chapter).

Foxhunting

The area hosts more than a dozen historic hunts, which go out several times a week from fall through spring, including holidays. If you want to watch the blessing of the hounds or follow the chase by car, plan ahead. Call the Master of Foxhounds Association in Leesburg, (540) 771-7442, during weekly business hours and ask for the hunt schedule in the area you plan to visit. At least once a year, the Middleburg Hunt meets at the Red Fox Tavern in Middleburg and rides down Main Street, hounds and all. Contact the Red Fox (in our Bed and Breakfast Inns and Country Inns chapter) for details.

Horse Shows

PAPER CHASE FARM
U.S. 50, Middleburg   *(540) 687-5853*

Just head east on U.S. 50 from Middleburg and you'll spot the impressive rings, jumps and barns of Paper Chase, a facility owned and managed by the daughter of *USA Today's* founder. About two dozen weekend or Sunday shows are held here each year. Check it out when you visit Middleburg.

THE ROANOKE VALLEY HORSE SHOW

Junior League of
Roanoke Valley   (540) 774-3242

Rated "A" by the American Horse Show Association, this show has been a national standout in horse-lovers' country for more than 20 years. Sponsored by the Junior League of Roanoke Valley and Roanoke Valley Horsemen's Association, it is held in June and attracts more than 1,000 entries nationwide for a purse of over $250,000 and grand prix of $75,000. It's the only indoor, air-conditioned show in Virginia and continues to be one of the top multibreed shows in the United States. This is a truly special community effort which over the years has plowed more than $1million back into community projects.

UPPERVILLE COLT AND HORSE SHOW

U.S. 50, Upperville   (540) 347-2612

Upperville, the nation's oldest horse show and a major event on the "A" horse show circuit, takes place here the first week in June. Since 1853 local breeders and the country's best hunter and jumper riders have been strutting their stuff in white-railed rings shaded by enormous oaks that are older than the show itself. Spectators watch from the rail or from sheltered stands. Admission during the week is free, $5 for the Sunday Jumper Classic.

WARRENTON HORSE SHOW

U.S. 29 Busi.
Warrenton   (540) 347-2612

Founded in 1899, the Labor Day Warrenton Horse Show is one of the few major horse shows in which only one ring is utilized. Find a seat, stay put and let the action unfold before you. The grounds are also home to the annual Pony Show in late June and the Summer's End show in August. Tickets to the Labor Day Show are $3 plus $1 for the shaded grandstand; the other two shows are free.

COMMONWEALTH PARK

U.S. 522, Culpeper   (540) 825-7469

Though it's off the beaten path, this horse center has 900 stalls and eight competition rings, which are busy most of the time with hunter/jumper and cutting horse shows and a couple of horse trials. More than 30 events are scheduled each year, attracting the Olympic-class riders who live in the area.

OLD BLUE EQUESTRIAN SPORTS CENTER

Off Va. 151, Afton   (540) 456-8711

Author Rita Mae Brown, who was active in forming Charlottesville's Piedmont Women's Polo Club, is also the driving force behind Old Blue, named for George Washington's favorite horse. The center, which faces the Blue Ridge Mountains and is skirted by the Rockfish River, is an idyllic setting for horse shows, clinics, polo and foxhunting. In 1993 the center revived the Oak Ridge Fox Hunt Club, founded in 1887. As a spectator you can catch a horse show, polo match or the start of a foxhunt. The center usually hosts the Spring Fling Horse Show in May, the Summer Show in June, and the Oak Ridge Fall Festival Jumper Classic in October. Opening meet for the Oak Ridge Fox Hunt Club is the end of October. Call to see what's going on during your visit to the area.

VIRGINIA HORSE CENTER

Off I-64 W. at Exit 55
Lexington   (540) 463-2194

A showcase for the Virginia horse industry and one of the top equine facilities in the United States, the $12 million Virginia Horse Center is home to several premier national horse shows and three-day events, as well as the annual Virginia Horse Festival in April.

The indoor arena complex has 4,000 spectator seats and a 150-foot by 300-foot show arena. The facility can house 610 horses in permanent stalls and more than 100 in portable interior stalls. The center has two winterized barns, an enclosed schooling area, an on-grounds restaurant and 48 camper hookups. Outdoor facilities include the lighted Wiley Arena, four all-weather dressage arenas, a speed events ring, a pavilion, pre-novice through preliminary cross-country courses, and a 5-mile hunter trial course.

With all these amenities, there's something going on almost all the time. In addition to horse competitions, the center hosts living-history Civil War encampments, Jack Russell Terrier races, therapeutic riding demonstrations and foxhound demonstrations.

From I-81, take Lexington Exit 191, proceed on I-64 W. to Exit 55, then follow signs for 2 miles to the center. Tours are offered, but be sure to call beforehand.

Combined Training

Combined training, also called three-day eventing or horse trials, is a discipline dating back to the training of war horses in Europe. It's also one of the most exciting horse sports to watch. Dressage, performed on the first day, is the ballet of horse sports, requiring great discipline. On the second day is an endurance phase involving long gallops and jumping a big, solid cross-country course. The third day, horses are asked to jump a very structured course of fences to test their agility, soundness and willingness after the stress of the cross-country. The Blue Ridge area hosts several world-class events.

MORVEN PARK HORSE TRIALS
Morven Park, Leesburg   (540) 777-2890

During the final week in September, you can catch the action over cross-country jumps designed by Olympian Bruce Davidson. Davidson is often in the competition, along with other world-class competitors. The backdrop for the event is a splendid white-columned mansion, once the home of Virginia governor Westmoreland Davis and his spunky, side-saddle-riding wife. Treasures that the couple collected during a lifetime of world travel are on display in the mansion. The mansion, gardens, the Museum of Fox-hounds and Hunting, and the Carriage Museum are open during the event. Admission to the trials is free.

MIDDLEBURG HORSE TRIALS
Glenwood Park, Middleburg   (540) 687-6395

Top riders use this event, held the final weekend in September, to season their young horses. The Middleburg area is home to many Olympic riders, so the level of competition is high. At Glenwood Park, which is also a steeplechase and horse show venue, spectators can see almost all the course from the stands. Admission to the trials is free.

VIRGINIA HORSE TRIALS

Three-day events are held at Lexington's Virginia Horse Center in the spring and fall (see Horse Shows in this chapter).

Combined Driving

One of the most colorful and elegant equestrian sports is competitive carriage driving. Competitions are often paired with three-day events, because of their similarity. On the first day, drivers ex-

Photo: Va Dept. of Tourism

Shenandoah Caverns, near New Market, offer a world of subterranean beauty.

ecute a series of dressage movements, much like a skater's compulsory figures. The second day is devoted to the marathon, a grueling cross-country dash through streams and around natural and man-made obstacles. In the third phase, drivers dressed in formal attire wheel their teams through an intricate pattern of cones. Local driving clubs also get together for pleasure rides or driving shows, such as the fall show at Middleburg's Foxcroft School (see the Annual Events chapter). The Piedmont Driving Club in Boyce, (540) 955-2659, is your best source for information.

Endurance Riding

This is now an Olympic sport, but it's not the easiest competition for spectators to watch. The June Old Dominion 100-mile Ride, (410) 867-2145, bears mentioning because it is one of the most respected competitions in the country and is often a tune-up for the Olympics or World Championships. Riders camp overnight with their horses at the 4-H Center in Front Royal in preparation for a 5 AM start. Each rider has 24 hours to cover 100 miles of rugged terrain and is pulled from the competition if his horse fails to pass the frequent veterinary checks along the way. If you want to put out a little effort, you can hike to one of the veterinary checks or the river crossing to watch the horses come through. You probably won't want to hang around for the finish. The winners come in as darkness is falling, and the rest straggle in throughout the night.

Jousting

Maryland's state sport also has a following in Virginia. Though it's patterned after the rivalry of knights of old, today's sport is done not in armor but in T-shirts and jeans. Despite their informal dress, you have to admire the skill of the riders who, at a gallop, thread their lances through a series of rings.

HUME RURITAN JOUST
Va. 688 off I-66, Hume   (540) 364-1700
The August Ruritan Joust has been going on at the old school grounds on the edge of Hume for more than 30 years. Bring a blanket and a cooler for an afternoon of watching, but save room for the *piece de resistance*, the barbecue, which has been cooking underground all night.

The local women serve it up with all the fixings (see our Annual Events chapter).

Hunt Country Tours

TRINITY EPISCOPAL CHURCH ANNUAL STABLE TOUR
U.S. 50, Upperville   (540) 592-3343
A dozen farms open their stables every year for this Memorial Day weekend event, which draws busloads of tourists. It's a rare opportunity to see places where horses live better than people, including philanthropist Paul Mellon's Rokeby Farm and Redskin owner Jack Kent Cooke's Kent Farm. Proceeds of the tour go into the church's outreach budget and a program to feed the hungry in Washington, D.C. Tickets, good for both days, are $13 in advance, $15 the day of the tour.

HISTORIC GARDEN WEEK
(804) 644-7776
Tours often include the homes of wealthy horsemen who have interesting stables and horses. One year, the Middleburg tour visited an estate with extensive training grounds for the family's Olympic hopefuls. The Warrenton Hounds were shown off at another stop. Tickets are $12 per tour, $4 per house.

Polo

MIDDLEBURG POLO
U.S. 50 W. to Va. 624
Middleburg   (540) 777-0775
Kent Field is one of the oldest polo pitches in the area. It bore the name of Phipps Field, for the famous New York racing family, through the ownerships of Paul Mellon and Senator John Warner. Redskins football team owner Jack Kent Cooke now owns it; hence the name

change. Against the pretty backdrop of Goose Creek, teams play Sunday afternoons from mid-May to September. The atmosphere is relaxed and the action fast paced. Admission is $5 per person.

VIRGINIA POLO CENTER

Old Lynchburg Rd.　　　*(804) 979-0293*
Charlottesville　　　　*(804) 977-POLO*

The University of Virginia turns out some of the finest intercollegiate polo players in the country. Interest runs high among the student body when the UVA polo team plays arena polo at the Virginia Polo Center on Friday nights during the school year.

Polo's also a popular sport among the horsey set in Charlottesville. The Charlottesville Polo Club defends itself against area teams at the center from mid-May through September. So does the Piedmont Women's Polo Club, launched several years ago by best-selling author Rita Mae Brown. Call for admission and times.

BLUE RIDGE POLO CLUB

Off Va. 151, Afton　　　*(540) 456-8711*

Author Rita Mae Brown now wields a mallet with the Blue Ridge team based at the Old Blue Equestrian Sports Center (see "Horse Shows" in this chapter). Arena games are played Friday evening at 5:30 PM, late May through October; games on the grass field near the Rockfish River are played Sunday at 3:30 PM May through October. Admission is $3. This is a fine opportunity for tailgating or a picnic in the facility's shaded picnic areas.

ROANOKE SYMPHONY POLO CUP

Green Hill Park　　　*(540) 343-9127*

Roanokers' opportunity to "Ponder the Ponies and Promote the Notes" has gone professional to include U.S. Polo Association-ranked teams in its match. This year's event will feature Team Michelob of St. Louis, matched against another pro team, as yet to be announced. Each October (the 1995 event is October 7), the crowds travel farther from throughout the Mid-Atlantic and Northeast regions to attend this festive fund-raiser for the Roanoke Symphony. The polo tournament not only provides a unique cultural experience but also allows patrons of the arts to enjoy good food and fun together. Proceeds benefit the Youth Symphony and educational programs.

General admission is low (about $10) so that the revelry is accessible to everyone. However, you may rent tables for "tailgate" parties and tents for private groups. These costs range from approximately $170 to $1,450, depending on the size of tent or table you choose. Concessions are available during the activities. Tent and tailgate patrons have their names listed in the program as a gesture of appreciation.

Point-to-Point and Steeplechase Races

While both feature races over fences, steeplechases generally offer big money

---

Virginia's state dog is the American foxhound. Ask folks around Middleburg and Upperville about the Great Foxhound Match there at the turn of the century. The American hounds handily out-hunted the British hounds.

prizes and are sanctioned by the National Steeplechase Association. Point-to-points are sponsored by local hunts. While they often have topnotch steeplechase horses and riders in the field, point-to-points are usually attended by folks in mud boots and jeans. The fancy clothes and hats are saved for steeplechases. Either is good fun and a perfect excuse to prepare a sumptuous tailgate lunch.

Virginia has more steeplechases (about two dozen) than any other state and as many point-to-points. Contact the Virginia Steeplechase Association in Middleburg, (540) 687-3455, for a schedule. If you're visiting the Blue Ridge between March and November, you can catch a race almost any Saturday. Here are the biggest races (see the Annual Events chapter for others).

THE VIRGINIA GOLD CUP RACES
Great Meadow, The Plains   (540) 347-2612
For the past decade, this 70-year-old classic has been run at Great Meadow, an excellent facility owned by newspaper magnate Arthur Arundel. It seems that all of Capitol Hill attends this see-and-be-seen event, and there are lavish tailgate parties in full swing long before the first race at 1 PM. All tickets are sold in advance, and you should arrive when the gates open at 10 AM to get a parking place, see the pre-race demonstrations and cruise the booths. General admission parking, which admits up to six, is about $40. The Gold Cup takes place the first Saturday in May, Kentucky Derby Day.

Great Meadow is also the venue for the International Gold Cup the third Saturday in October. It's the third largest race in Virginia, after the Virginia Gold Cup and Foxfields. General admission parking, which admits six people, is about $40 in advance, $45 the day of the race. The Great Meadow Exit off I-66 is well marked.

FOXFIELD RACES
Garth Rd., Charlottesville   (804) 293-9501
Foxfield hosts two major steeplechase meetings each year, events that draw top 'chasers and 20,000 spectators from as far away as New Jersey. Races are traditionally held the last Saturday in April and the last Sunday in September. The seven-race card starts at 1 PM and features flat and jumping races.

Although hot dogs and soft drinks are sold at the course, sophisticated tailgate parties have become the norm. The scene is straight out of *Town and Country* magazine, with women in hats and smart outfits and men in natty tweeds. It's not unusual to see folks sipping champagne and nibbling caviar from silver plates on the back of a Rolls or BMW.

General admission costs $12 in advance and $15 at the gate, with an extra $5 for parking. Depending upon location, you can also reserve a parking spot for anywhere from $55 to $200, which includes four admission tickets.

The Foxfield Race Course is 5 miles west of the Barracks Road Shopping Center.

Horse events are often informal, with horses milling about at show in-gates or being led through crowds to saddling enclosures at steeplechases. Be sure to keep your dogs leashed and your children (and yourself) clear of the horses' feet.

Insiders' Tips

Foot Hunting

THE BOAR'S HEAD
INN & SPORTS CLUB

Charlottesville   (800) 476-1988
                             (804) 296-2181

The Boar's Head Inn & Sports Club, west of Charlottesville, hosts this old English sport — older than foxhunting — the Saturday after Thanksgiving every year. The master and hunt staff, dressed in the green hunting jackets, white trousers and green caps of the Farmington Beagle Club, meet at the Boar's Head Inn at 3 PM for a day of sport open to the public. The hounds are cast on the scent of a rabbit, and the field follows on foot through 53 acres of the Inn grounds. After the hunt, the Inn serves its traditional hunt tea.

On Thanksgiving morning many Inn guests congregate at 10 AM at Grace Episcopal Church in Cismont for the age-old "blessing of the hounds" and the start of the Farmington Hunt. It's impossible to follow this hunt on foot, but guests are welcome to "hilltop," catching glimpses of the action from their cars as the hunt runs along or across country roads. From noon to 8 PM, the Inn serves a grand Virginia Thanksgiving feast in the Old Mill Room.

Inside
Annual Events and Festivals

Not a season passes in Virginia's Blue Ridge and its foothills that some group isn't finding a way to celebrate it. You will have plenty to do each month all around the 14-county region: craft shows, antique sales, historic commemorations, agricultural fairs, horse shows and races, athletic competitions and some of the best fun you'll find anywhere in traditional holiday observances. Imagine the Shenandoah Valley sky ablaze with fireworks on Independence Day or conjure up a sense of patriotic pride as this history-rich region celebrates the birthdays of such famous Americans as Thomas Jefferson, George Washington, James Madison and the South's famous generals, Robert E. Lee and Stonewall Jackson.

Let your tastebuds lead the way as folks gather around to sample their favorite foods served with a big helping of fellowship. The Virginia Chili Cook-off in Roanoke is one such event, and the Highland Maple Festival in Monterey (with syrup-making demonstrations and plenty of maple-flavored goodies) is another. Other gatherings pay homage to such diverse edibles as garlic (and its humble brother, the ramp), apples in every form (especially apple butter!), wine, tomatoes, molasses, poultry and more. Fall festivals usually feature the entire harvest — so save up your calories.

Music is almost always on the program, running the gamut from hoedowns to symphonies. Don't miss the Old Fid-

Photo: Ferrum College

Many Blue Ridge festivals hold sack races for kids.

dler's Convention — the original and largest such event — and other cultural extravaganzas. Many activities are held at the region's beautiful historic mansions, such as Montpelier, Monticello and Ash Lawn-Highland.

In the Hunt Country from Leesburg to Charlottesville, steeplechases are a sporting and social staple. Informal point-to-point races in early February lead into the spring 'chasing season, which features race meetings in such wonderful venues as Leesburg's Oatlands Plantation and Morven Park, Middleburg's Glenwood Park, Charlottesville's Foxfields and Montpelier, and Great Meadow, in The Plains. After a summer hiatus for horse shows, including the historic Warrenton Horse Show and the Upperville Colt and Horse Show (the country's oldest show), steeplechasing resumes in the fall (see the "Hunt Country" section of our Other Attractions chapter).

The list that follows is a sampling of some of the bigger events — and a lot of smaller ones too — that can entertain you for a weekend or longer.

January

MASSANUTTEN SKI
WEEKEND EXTRAVAGANZAS
Harrisonburg   *(540) 289-9441*
Throughout the winter Massanutten Resort features special ski and snowboard weekends with different themes, activities and competitions.

BIRTHDAY CONVOCATION
FOR ROBERT E. LEE
Lexington   *(540) 463-3777*
The venerable general is saluted on his birthday, January 19, at Lexington's Lee Chapel.

BIRTHDAY CELEBRATION
FOR STONEWALL JACKSON
Lexington   *(540) 463-3777*
The South's second-greatest hero gets his due at this city-wide festival January 21, beginning on the grounds of Washington and Lee University.

CHARLOTTESVILLE AND UNIVERSITY
SYMPHONY ORCHESTRA
Charlottesville   *(804) 924-3984*
The Charlottesville Performing Arts Center hosts concerts on Sundays at 3:30 PM and 8:30 PM. They also perform in early March and late April.

VIRGINIA SPECIAL OLYMPICS
Wintergreen   *(804) 325-2200*
Wintergreen Resort hosts this annual snow-skiing competition for mentally challenged athletes.

HUNT COUNTRY
WINTER ANTIQUES FAIR
Leesburg   *(540)777-3174*
Thirty-five selected exhibitors from New England to the Carolinas offer 17th-to 20th-century furniture, porcelain, jewelry and other collectibles.

GALAX MOUNTAIN MUSIC JAMBOREE
Galax   *(540) 236-4885*
Come join the jamboree by watching cloggers and listening to that down-home bluegrass music. This event is held monthly at the Rex Theater.

February

GEORGE
Winchester   *(540) 662-6550*
An open house at George Washington's Office Museum is held every February on the weekend closest to Washington's birthday.

AFRICAN-AMERICAN HERITAGE MONTH

Staunton   (540) 332-7850

The Museum of American Frontier Culture hosts this examination of black contributions to early American growth.

LOUDOUN COUNTY
CIVIL WAR ROUNDTABLE

Leesburg   (540) 338-7550

Winter's a good time to attend this ongoing meeting, which features an address and discussion by various Civil War authorities.

CASANOVA HUNT POINT-TO-POINT

Casanova   (540) 347-5863

The Virginia point-to-point season precedes the more formal steeplechase season, giving amateur riders and inexperienced horses (not necessarily as a team) a chance to gain experience. Casanova, near Warrenton, is generally held the last Saturday. The meet opens the season and is greeted with great enthusiasm despite the cold, blustery weather.

WARRENTON ANTIQUE SHOW

Warrenton   (540) 439-8197

Collectors and stir-crazy locals brave the cold for this Fauquier County affair, held at the Pearson Armory.

VALENTINE'S DAY WEEKEND

Wintergreen   (804) 325-2200

Parties, special ski challenges and events for the kids top off this annual festival at Wintergreen Resort.

March

GUN SHOW

Harrisonburg   (540) 434-0005

The Rockingham County Fairground hosts this annual weapons display in late March.

SHENANDOAH VALLEY QUILTS EXHIBIT

Staunton   (540) 885-0897

This month-long exhibit (with weekend demonstrations) of one of America's oldest crafts is held at the Woodrow Wilson Birthplace and Museum.

ST. PATRICK'S DAY PARADE

Staunton   (540) 885-8504

Staunton shows its Irish roots at this popular event.

1996 GOP MOCK ELECTION

Lexington   (540) 462-4057

Washington and Lee students predict who the party not in the White House will nominate in 1996. The election will be held March 1 and 2 at W&L.

ST. PATRICK'S DAY PARADE

Roanoke   (540) 981-2889

Downtown Roanoke "sports the green" during this weekend parade.

CONFEDERATE WINTER CAMP

Newbern   (540) 674-4835

Experience camping during the Civil War period through demonstrations by Confederate re-enactors. See them outside the Wilderness Road Regional Museum. A true Irish meal is served in celebration of St. Patrick's Day.

HIGHLAND COUNTY MAPLE FESTIVAL

Monterey   (540) 468-2550

This festival is celebrated across Highland County, that rugged, gorgeous region bordering West Virginia west of Staunton. During the festival, you can visit local sugar camps and watch the actual process of syrup-making. There's also an arts and crafts show, a maple queen contest and ball, dances, including the maple sugar hoedown, and plenty of opportunities to scarf down pancakes with maple syrup, maple donuts and fresh fried trout.

WHITETOP MOUNTAIN MAPLE FESTIVAL

Mount Rogers National
Recreation Area (540) 388-3294

Usually held on two weekends in late March, this festive event features live country and western music, tours of maple tree tapping areas, arts and crafts and pancake dinners.

April

HISTORIC GARDEN WEEK

Locations throughout
Virginia (804) 644-7776

This late April event throws open the doors of more than 200 private homes and gardens throughout the Commonwealth for tours. Many Blue Ridge area cities participate in this statewide event, which is always held during the last full week of April. Charlottesville, Staunton, Harrisonburg, Roanoke and the Front Royal area are popular touring areas.

OLD TOWN EASTER EGG HUNT

Winchester (540) 665-0079

Held on the Saturday closest to Easter, this egg hunt delights youngsters from age 2 to 7. It takes place on the lawn next to the Godfrey Miller Center in downtown Winchester.

ANTIQUE BOTTLE AND COLLECTIBLE SHOW

Harrisonburg (540) 434-1129

For 25 years, this event at the Rockingham County Fairgrounds has entertained collectors and browsers.

SPRING IN THE VALLEY ARTS & CRAFTS SHOW

Salem (540) 375-8235

Come see the many crafts on display during this show, sponsored by the Virginia Mountain Crafts Guild.

CHAMPAGNE AND CANDLELIGHT TOUR

Charlottesville (804) 293-9539

This enchanting evening tour of the Ash Lawn-Highland home of President James Monroe is always held during Historic Garden Week. Period music is performed during tours of the Federal-style home and beautiful gardens, which are illuminated with 2,000 candles.

The James River Bateau Festival is held every June in Lynchburg.

THOMAS JEFFERSON
BIRTHDAY COMMEMORATION
Charlottesville   *(804) 295-8181*

Admission to Monticello's grounds and gardens is always free on April 13, the birthday of Virginia's best-known renaissance man — U.S. President, Secretary of State, scholar, architect, collector and horticulturist.

FOXFIELD RACES
Charlottesville   *(804) 293-9501*

This popular steeplechase has also become one of Charlottesville's top social events. It's held the last Saturday in April.

CRESTAR 10-MILER
Charlottesville   *(804) 293-6115*

The city's largest foot race (fourth-largest in Virginia) is held the second week in April, commencing at University Hall.

DOGWOOD FESTIVAL
Charlottesville   *(804) 973-4121*

This popular community event features a queen's coronation and includes a fashion show, fireworks, a carnival and barbecue. It culminates in a grand parade that shows off Charlottesville at its springtime best. It's usually held for two weeks in mid-April.

EASTER TRADITIONS
Staunton   *(540)332-7850*

Rolling, tossing, dyeing and trundling eggs are just a few of the activities that take place on the historic farmsites at the Museum of American Frontier Culture mid-April.

VIRGINIA BEEF EXPO
Harrisonburg   *(540) 434-0005*

Sales of premium seedstock cattle and an agricultural trade show are high-

lights of this show the third weekend of April.

EASTER AT WINTERGREEN
Wintergreen   *(804) 325-2200*

On Easter weekend, Wintergreen Resort holds an Egg-Stravaganza of games for kids, a Ukrainian egg decorating workshop, a culinary workshop and an Easter morning worship service.

LEESBURG FLOWER
AND GARDEN FESTIVAL
Leesburg   *(540) 777-1262*

Downtown Leesburg is transformed into a botanical garden with plants, gardening equipment and supplies for sale, as well as entertainment and food. This festival takes place the third weekend in April.

SPRING GARDEN SHOW
Lynchburg   *(804) 847-1499*

This is a gardener's field day in early April at the Community Market, where landscapers, florists and nursery operators display their products and where gardening techniques are demonstrated. Entertainment and food add to the festivities.

SPRING BALLOON FESTIVAL
Bedford   *(540) 586-9401*

Hot-air balloons fill the Piedmont sky during this colorful spring festival.

FRANKLIN COUNTY SPRING
ARTS AND CRAFTS FESTIVAL
Rocky Mount   *(540) 483-9542*

Mountain crafts, food and music are the star attractions here.

BRUSH MOUNTAIN
ARTS AND CRAFTS FAIR
Blacksburg   *(540) 552-4909*

Quilters, potters, weavers, decoy carvers and other artists show their wares at the juried festival held in this art-loving college town.

ANNUAL ANTIQUE
SALE & QUILT SHOW

Blacksburg   *(540) 231-3812*

This annual event features a variety of antiques such as furniture, jewelry and china.

RIVER RUN AND BICYCLE RIDE

Narrows   *(540) 921-1544*

Athletes face off against the rugged terrain found near Breaks Interstate Park, on the Virginia and Kentucky border.

HONAKER REDBUD FESTIVAL

Honaker, Russell County   *(540) 889-8041*

This tiny community of 1,000 celebrates spring every year with a month-long festival of gospel singing, arts and craft shows, a canoe race down the Clinch River, car show, homecoming dinner, beauty pageant and parade. The redbud tree, indigenous to the Southwest Virginia county, blossoms this month.

LONESOME PINE
ARTS AND CRAFTS FESTIVAL

Big Stone Gap   *(540) 523-0846*

This community close to Kentucky is home to a wonderful annual celebration of mountain heritage. Here you will find craft-making demonstrations and the display and sale of homemade arts, crafts and food.

FOXFIELD RACES

Charlottesville   *(804) 293-9501*

Pack a picnic lunch and enjoy this central Virginia tradition, which features six steeplechase races and a lot of people-watching. It's the last Saturday of April.

ASH LAWN-HIGHLAND SPRING
GARDEN WEEK WINE FESTIVAL

Charlottesville   *(804) 293-9539*

In late April, take in the first major wine festival of the year at the historic home of James Monroe.

"THE WILD WINE WEST"
AT OASIS VINYARDS

Hume   *(540) 635-7627*

Nashville country stars perform live, and cowboys demonstrate Wild West skills during this celebration of Virginia wines in late April.

MONTPELIER WINE FESTIVAL

Montpelier Station   *(540) 832-2828*

Regional wines are showcased on the grounds of Montpelier in late April. The festival provides an opportunity to enjoy one of the state's premier products, as well as equestrian events, crafts, music and food.

HERITAGE TOURISM WEEKS

Lexington/Rockbridge County   *(540) 463-3777*

The focus is on the heritage of the community, Robert E. Lee, Stonewall Jackson, the colleges (Washington & Lee University and Virginia Military Institute), antiques, horse shows, downtown

Insiders' Tips

The cities of the Blue Ridge are great places to watch July Fourth fireworks. The flashing evening sky silhouettes the mountains for an unforgettable experience!

Lexington and the Maury River. At the Visitor Center, you'll receive a poster as a thank-you gift for visiting the community during Virginia Heritage Tourism Weeks. This event lasts two weeks and starts at the end of April.

MADISON HERITAGE WEEKS
Madison (540) 948-4455

The Kemper Mansion, home of former governor and general (C.S.A.) James Lawson Kemper, and the historic Arcade Building are open for viewing for two weeks, beginning at the end of April. Visitors can see items relating to the history of Madison County from 1700s to present, including historic quilts and agricultural and Indian artifacts, and can take a driving tour of historic churches in Madison County.

May

CULPEPER DAY
Culpeper (540) 825-7768

This community-wide festival is a tradition held the first Saturday of May.

POLO IN MIDDLEBURG
Middleburg (540) 777-0775

Kent Field (west of Middleburg on U.S. 50, south on Va. 624) is the venue for Sunday afternoon polo matches May through September. It isn't Palm Beach, so don't worry about dressing up to watch some good, fast sport in a beautiful meadow. By all means, pack a picnic and join the tailgating fun.

AIRSHOW
Bealeton (540) 439-8661

The first weekend in May is usually the opening airshow for The Flying Circus at Bealeton, southwest of Warrenton on U.S. 17 and Va. 644. Airshows, balloon rallies and car shows are held on the grounds through October.

VIRGINIA GOLD CUP
The Plains (540) 347-2612

The Old Dominion's premier steeplechase event is always held the first Saturday in May, the same day as the Kentucky Derby. Sometimes boisterous and oh, so preppy, this is a social event of major proportions in Virginia, attracting more than 50,000 onlookers during a typical year. The feature on the seven-event card is a grueling 4-mile test over fences.

OATLANDS SHEEP DOG TRIALS
Leesburg (540) 777-3174

This highly entertaining weekend fete (typically the second week of May) champions the herding instincts of border collies. It takes place at glorious Oatlands Plantation, just outside of Leesburg in the heart of the Virginia Hunt Country.

MAY DAY
Staunton (540) 332-7850

On the first Saturday in May, visitors help decorate the May Bush and take part in traditional games and festivities on the German, Ulster and English farms at the Museum of American Frontier Culture.

FOLK ARTS AND CRAFTS FESTIVAL
Weyers Cave (540) 886-2351

The focus here is on local artisans, many of whom exhibit solely at this festival, which is usually held in early May.

INTERNATIONAL SPRINGTIME CELEBRATION
Staunton (540) 332-7850

Four mini-festivals at the Museum of American Frontier Culture on the first or second Saturday in May coincide with Europe's traditional May Day celebrations. Activities at the museum's working German, Scotch-Irish, English and American farms include traditional dancing, music and foods.

OUTDOOR ART SHOW

Staunton (540) 886-2351

This downtown Staunton event features local and national artists, including a large number of wildlife painters.

ROAD TO ANTIETAM

Leesburg (540) 777-0099

The living history event the second weekend in May takes place on the closed streets of Leesburg, recreating the 1862 passage of Lee's army through Loudoun County.

NORTH-SOUTH SKIRMISH

Gainesboro (540) 888-7917

The national spring Civil War re-enactment by the North-South Skirmish Association is held at Ft. Shenandoah in Gainesboro.

SHENANDOAH
APPLE BLOSSOM FESTIVAL

Winchester (540) 662-3863

This four-day celebration is a salute to the area's apple-growing industry. You'll find high quality arts and crafts shows, numerous parades, live music, a 10-kilometer race and a circus.

SPRING FLY-IN

Winchester (540) 662-5786

On the Sunday of the Apple Blossom Festival, aircraft owners compete for prizes and share their aviation interests with the public at the Winchester Regional Airport.

ANTIQUE CAR SHOW

Winchester (540) 869-7475

This show, flea market and car corral draws hundreds of people to the Jim Barnett Park in Winchester.

WILDFLOWER WEEKEND

Strasburg (540) 253-9622

On the first weekend of May, hikes in the Blue Ridge Mountains to view the wildflowers are organized at the Hotel Strasburg.

VIRGINIA MUSHROOM FESTIVAL

Front Royal (800) 338-2576

This Main Street celebration highlights arts and crafts, food, wine tastings, live music, clogging and open-air theatrical performances. It's usually the second weekend in May.

VIRGINIA POULTRY FESTIVAL

Harrisonburg (540) 433-2451

The hoopla here, including cookouts, a parade and, yes, a poultry queen, celebrates Virginia's status as one of the largest chicken- and turkey-producing states.

WOOL DAYS

Staunton (540) 885-0897

Sharpen the shears, the sheep are ready! The Museum of American Frontier Culture does it the old-fashioned way, from shearing to washing, carding and spinning during the first week in May.

EXPLORING VIRGINIA'S
NORTHERN PIEDMONT

Paris (540) 592-3556

An organized driving tour of late 18th- and early 19th-century villages explores homes around Sky Meadows State Park, itself a preserved farm, during the first two weeks of May.

LIVESTOCK AUCTION

Marshall (540) 354-1566

On the second Saturday in May, a horse auction is held at the Fauquier Livestock Exchange. Such sales were once commonplace in rural America but are now a rarity.

WARRENTON FARMERS MARKET
Warrenton   (540) 347-1101

Local farmers sell vegetables, fresh pork, flowers, plants and freshly baked goods the first two Wednesdays and Saturdays of May.

A TASTE OF MIDDLEBURG
Middleburg   (540) 687-5528

Wine tasting, food, crafts and a tour of local wineries make for a festive time on the second weekend in May.

NEIGHBORHOOD ART SHOW
The Plains   (540) 253-5177

Collages, sculptures, ceramics and paintings by artists young and old are displayed at Grace Episcopal Church Parish House, usually the second weekend in May.

"POLO, WINE & TWILIGHT DINE"
The Plains   (540) 635-7627

Enjoy a day of horse sport, fine wine and food at Oasis Vineyard on the second Friday in May.

ANNUAL KITE DAY
Charlottesville   (804) 293-9539

At Ash Lawn-Highland, home of President James Monroe, the fields are open to children and the young at heart for kite flying. Both designs and flights are judged for prizes. The event is usually held in early May.

SPRING WILDFLOWER SYMPOSIUM
Wintergreen   (804) 325-2200

Every May Wintergreen Resort invites prominent specialists to lead workshops, lectures and other educational programs about wildflowers. The day includes guided hikes, wildflower sales, photography displays and entertainment.

MEMORIAL DAY CELEBRATION
Wintergreen   (804) 325-2200

Every year, the resort kicks off its summer season with the Stoney Creek Valley Parade, a kite festival, a Firemen's Ball and an opening day celebration at Lake Monocan.

WILDFLOWER WEEKEND
Shenandoah National Park   (540) 999-3482

The park celebrates the arrival of spring with guided walks, exhibits, slide programs and workshops during the third weekend in May.

NEW MARKET HERITAGE DAYS
New Market   (540) 740-3432

The Shenandoah Valley town salutes its German, Scottish and Irish heritage at this weekend festival capped by a large parade.

MEMORIAL DAY
HORSE FAIR AND AUCTION
Harrisonburg   (540) 434-4482

This annual tradition is the largest horse auction in the Shenandoah Valley.

THEATER AT LIME KILN
Lexington   (540) 463-3074

Memorial Day begins the summer season at Lime Kiln, an outdoor theater that's nationally recognized for presenting original plays and musicals relating to Virginia's culture and history. Plays and concerts take place under the stars in an enchanting setting, the ruins of an actual lime kiln built in the 1800s. Plays are performed Monday through Saturday until Labor Day. On Sunday nights, some of the best and brightest in the music business perform jazz, blues, folk and bluegrass music at Lime Kiln.

BONNIE BLUE NATIONAL HORSE SHOW
Lexington   (540) 463-3777

You'll see all breeds of horses at this major event at the Virginia Horse Center.

THE VIRGINIA CHILI COOK-OFF
Roanoke   (540) 342-2028

Thousands of connoisseurs pour into Roanoke's historic farmer's market the first Saturday in May to indulge themselves. Don't forget to head down the block for some homemade strawberry shortcake at Community School's Strawberry Festival.

DELAPLANE STRAWBERRY FESTIVAL
Sky Meadows State Park   (804) 786-1712

Crafts, hayrides, clowns, children's games, pony rides, a petting zoo are part of this celebration of the region's strawberry season. Entertainment includes a Civil War-style brass band, gospel singers and 18th-century dancing demonstrations. Food for sale will include strawberry sundaes, of course.

FESTIVAL IN THE PARK
Roanoke   (540) 342-2640

This two-week-long celebration beginning Memorial Day weekend includes one of the East Coast's largest sidewalk art shows, a river race, concerts, fireworks, children's games, ethnic foods, bike and road races and a children's parade. During the second week, a carnival is held at the Civic Center.

VINTON DOGWOOD FESTIVAL
                    (540) 983-0613

This community next to Roanoke celebrates spring in early May every year with a parade, band competition, an antique car show, music, food, crafts, bike races, a long-distance run, an evening of country music and more.

MAYFEST
Luray, downtown   (540) 743-3915

The normally serene Main Street and the town park are transformed into a frenzy of activity the third Saturday in May, reminiscent of the old-fashioned street festivals. The street is lined with crafters, antique dealers and vendors with flowers, plants and herbs. Food, live music, pony rides, llamas, art activities, go-cart rides, dancers and the performance of a traditional Maypole dance add to the fun. Historic buildings are open for tours too.

DOLLEY MADISON'S BIRTHDAY
Montpelier Station   (540) 672-2728

This is an annual celebration at Montpelier, 4 miles from Orange on Va. 20 S.

AN EVENING OF ELEGANCE
Lynchburg   (804) 847-8688

This annual fund-raiser for the Virginia School of the Arts is always held in early May. Internationally acclaimed dancers perform with local students at the E.C. Glass Auditorium.

CHILDREN'S DAY AT THE MARKET
Lynchburg   (804) 847-1499

In early May bring your kids to the Community Market to watch clowns and touch the animals at the petting zoo. You'll find a lot of entertainment, games, food and an annual poster contest.

INTERNATIONAL BASS BONANZA
Covington   (540) 962-2178

This fishing event is held every year at Lake Moomaw in the Allegheny Mountains. The elusive large-mouth bass is the featured attraction.

PIONEER DAY
Covington   (540) 962-8943

A downtown festival, Pioneer Day

pays tribute to the brave souls who settled this rugged corner of western Virginia.

MAY FEST

Stonewall Vineyards
Concord (804) 993-2185

This wine and food festival is held on a farm in the rolling hill country outside of Lynchburg.

ARTS AND CRAFTS FESTIVAL

Wytheville (540) 228-5541

This festival is usually held the first few days of May.

WINE AND CHEESE FESTIVAL

Wytheville (540) 228-3111

This Virginia wine sampler also includes an auction.

SOUTHWESTERN VIRGINIA PIONEER FESTIVAL

Tazewell (540) 988-6755

Learn how Southwest Virginia was colonized and developed at the Crab Orchard Museum and Pioneer Park. Demonstrations include basket weaving, wool spinning and blacksmithing.

PLUMB ALLEY DAY

Abingdon (540) 628-8141

This arts and crafts jamboree is always held the Saturday of Memorial Day weekend.

MOUNT ROGERS RAMP FESTIVAL

Whitetop Mountain (540) 388-3257

This tribute to the pungent wild mountain leek requires that you bring a bottle of mouthwash and a good supply of breath mints if you plan to try some of the many ramp-laden foods. There'll be ramps in stews and salads, fried with trout and roasted with bear meat. Mountain crafts and quilts are on display, and bluegrass music keeps things hopping on the mountaintop. This event is always held the third weekend in May.

MOUNT ROGERS NATURALIST RALLY

(540) 783-2125

This is a weekend retreat for discovering the natural history and wildlife of Southwest Virginia. It features a naturalist speaker and hikes led by college professors. It is usually scheduled in mid-May to coincide with the Ramp Festival.

APPALACHIAN TRAIL DAYS

Damascus (304) 535-6331

This three-day event in tiny Damascus draws Appalachian Trail hikers from far and wide, making it a standing reunion for many. The hikers stage an amusing parade and talent show. Arts and crafts shows, street dances, clogging demonstrations and live music keep little Damascus hopping for days. The celebration is usually held in mid-May.

RALPH STANLEY BLUE GRASS FESTIVAL

McClure (540) 395-6318

This foot stompin' event, featuring local native and bluegrass music legend Ralph Stanley, is held on Memorial Day weekend in this community along the edge of the Jefferson National Forest in the far reaches of South Virginia.

BIG STONE GAP COUNTRY FAIR

(540) 523-4950

A traditional affair, this event is always held on Mother's Day weekend at Bullit Park.

EXHIBITION OF SPORTING ART

Leesburg (540) 777-2414

This month-long event (1995 marks its 10th year) features the works of nearly 30 equine artists. It is held at

Morven Park's Museum of Hounds and Hunting.

ANNUAL HUNT
COUNTRY STABLE TOUR
Upperville (540) 592-3711

Some of the finest horse farms in Fauquier and Loudoun counties open their doors for this charitable event, including philanthropist Paul Mellon and Redskins football team owner Jack Kent Cooke. You can take tours both days of the weekend in late May. Tours originate at the big stone church in Upperville. Call for tickets.

June

UPPERVILLE COLT AND HORSE SHOW
Upperville (540) 347-2612

The oldest horse show in the country is held on beautiful showgrounds west of Middleburg on U.S. 50. From Tuesday through the first Sunday in June, some of the East Coast's best English riders compete in a variety of classes under the shade of towering oaks. On Sunday the main attraction is the Upperville Grandprix Jumper Classic, an exciting speed event over big, colorful fences.

SHENANDOAH VALLEY
FARM CRAFT DAYS
Middletown (540) 869-2028

This 28-year-old tradition takes place the first Saturday in June, featuring demonstrations, pottery, quilts, toys and other locally made items, as well as live music and tasty country fare. Belle Grove Plantation hosts the event.

VINTAGE VIRGINIA WINE FESTIVAL
The Plains (540) 253-5001

Thirty-five wineries take part in this early June weekend event on the grounds of Great Meadow. More than 75 vendors display their arts and crafts, and sidelights include food; jazz, reggae and pop music; rides; and children's entertainment.

BATTLE OF STAUNTON
RIVER BRIDGE REENACTMENT
Staunton (540) 572-4623

On the second Saturday in June, festivities begin at 11 AM, building to the battle re-enactment at 1 PM at Staunton River State Park.

SHENANDOAH VALLEY BACH FESTIVAL
Harrisonburg (540) 434-2319

The second week in June is filled with concerts and events celebrating the works of Bach and Mendelssohn. Noon concerts are free; admission is charged for major performances.

BLUEMONT CONCERT SERIES
Central and Northern
Virginia (540) 777-0574

Enjoy music under the stars during this summer concert series held in Warrenton, Leesburg, Orange, Winchester, Culpeper and Luray. Each town has a concert each week, beginning the third week in June.

MUSIC AT TWILIGHT
Charlottesville (804) 979-0122

Weekly musical performances are held under the stars at Ash Lawn-Highland, the home of fifth U.S. President James Monroe. Classical, folk, jazz and contemporary music are featured during the last two weeks of June.

CHAMBER OF COMMERCE
ALL-BREED HORSE SHOW
Harrisonburg (540) 434-3862

This is one of the biggest horse shows in the Shenandoah Valley, attracting exhibitors from several states to the

Rockingham County Fairgrounds during the third week in June.

MOWING DAY

Staunton   *(540) 332-7850*

Watch the staff at the Museum of American Frontier Culture compete in an old-fashioned mowing contest and learn the tools and techniques of mowing on the third Saturday in June.

JOUSTING HALL OF FAME TOURNAMENT

Mt. Solon   *(540) 350-2510*

Four levels of competitors vie for the jousting title at Natural Chimneys Regional Park. Induction ceremonies for the 1995 Jousting Hall of Fame follow the competition. Look for this event about the third Saturday in June.

MIDSUMMER EVE

Charlottesville   *(804) 293-4500*

The summer festival season opens with a gala benefit dinner performance by the festival opera company in late June. Call for reservations.

CELTIC FESTIVAL

Leesburg   *(540) 777-3174*

Celebrate the joint cultural heritage of Cornwall, Ireland, Scotland, Wales, the Isle of Man, Galacia and Brittany with music, games, food and language workshops. This event takes place the third weekend in June.

COLLECTOR CAR
FLEA MARKET AND CORRAL

Harrisonburg   *(540) 434-0005*

Classic cars are proudly displayed at the Rockingham County Fairgrounds during this collectors' weekend the end of June.

MARCH & BATTLE FOR PRESERVATION

Winchester   *(540) 662-4118*

Re-enactors march along roads used by armies during the Shenandoah Valley campaign of 1864. Activities include a battle at Hackwood Estate and a march past Jackson's and Sheridan's headquarters in Winchester. The march begins at the

Photo: Va Division of Tourism

The Bonnie Blue National, A-rated for all divisions, is one of the most prestigious events held at the Virginia Horse Center just north of Lexington.

Frederick County Fairgrounds on the last Saturday in June.

ANNUAL ANTIQUE AND CLASSIC CAR SHOW

Leesburg   (540) 338-5103

More than 30 categories of vintage and modified vehicles are on display at Oatlands Plantation during the last week in June.

APPALACHIAN TRAIL CONFERENCE

Harrisonburg   (540) 981-0693

Activities include hikes, workshops, children's activities and evening entertainment. The conference is held at James Madison University for a week in late June or early July.

CONFEDERATE MEMORIAL SERVICE

Winchester   (540) 662-1937

The more than 3,000 Confederate soldiers buried in the Stonewall Jackson Cemetery are honored in this service sponsored by the United Daughters of the Confederacy, Chapter 54.

BLUEMONT CONCERT SERIES

Winchester   (540) 665-0079

This free outdoor concert series draws hundreds to the lawn of the old Frederick County Courthouse in Old Town Winchester. You can hear folk, Cajun, bluegrass and other music under the stars on Friday evenings in June, July and part of August.

COURT DAYS FESTIVAL

Woodstock   (540) 459-2542

This event in mid-June re-creates the days when the old-time county judge came to town to settle cases. The festival features a dog show, pig roast, street dances, exhibits, live music, a bike-a-thon, 5-K run and more.

ANNUAL SUN AND SAND BEACH WEEKEND

Stuarts Draft   (540) 337-1911

You'll need plenty of energy for this one! Held at Shenandoah Acres Resort, this weekend is a nonstop summer festival of volleyball, mini-golf, sand-castle building contests, various water contests and a DJ dance on Saturday night. This is always held the third weekend in June.

CONSERVATION FESTIVAL

Roanoke   (540) 343-3241

Mill Mountain Zoo hosts this mid-June event every year.

ROANOKE VALLEY HORSE SHOW

Salem   (540) 586-7161

Held in mid-June, this is one of the top all-breed horse shows on the East Coast. It usually attracts about 1,000 entries from across the United States.

NELSON COUNTY SUMMER FESTIVAL

Va. 653   (804) 263-5392

Held in late June, this is a family-oriented, upscale festival on the lovely grounds of Oak Ridge Estate south of Lovingston.

SUMMER FESTIVAL OF THE ARTS AT ASH LAWN-HIGHLAND
Charlottesville   *(804) 293-4500*

This potpourri of music is highlighted by opera and musical theater productions, a Music at Twilight concert series with traditional and contemporary musical performances and a Summer Saturdays family entertainment series.

NELSON COUNTY SUMMER FESTIVAL
Va. 653   *(804) 263-5392*

This family-oriented, upscale festival takes place in late June on the lovely grounds of Oak Ridge Estate south of Lovingston.

BLUE RIDGE MUSIC FESTIVAL
Lynchburg   *(804) 948-1639*

A folk, classical or jazz concert is held every evening during this week-long event in mid-June at Randolph Macon Women's College.

DINNER AT DUSK
Lynchburg   *(804) 847-1459*

Dine with the crew members of the James River Bateau, the resurrected flat-bottomed boat that once hauled tobacco to Richmond and beyond before canals were built. Participants dress in full costume and tell tales of the river, perform folk music and celebrate the start of the Festival by the James.

FESTIVAL BY THE JAMES
Lynchburg   *(804) 847-1811*

This is a downtown festival that celebrates the James River and its significance to the Lynchburg area. Always held in mid-June, it includes a foot race, exhibitions and demonstrations by costumed artisans, Civil War re-enactments, horse pulls, canoe races and more.

TOURS OF HISTORIC AVENEL
Bedford   *(540) 586-4238*

At Historic Avenel, the home of the Burwells, you can see its original architecture and beautiful grounds as well as listen to many stories of past times.

SMITHFIELD PLANTATION DAYS
Blacksburg   *(540) 552-4061*

The Smithfield Plantation hosts this annual event the second Saturday in June.

CAMBRIA WHISTLESTOP ARTS FESTIVAL
Christiansburg   *(540) 382-4251*

This juried competition and festival showcases various Southwest Virginia artists.

FESTIVAL AROUND TOWN
Pearisburg   *(540) 921-1324*

This beautiful town near the Appalachian Trail hosts this all-day arts and music fete.

CIVIL WAR WEEKEND
Newbern   *(540) 674-4835*

Held usually the third weekend in June, this event features an afternoon tea, living history demonstrations, marches, a church service and lectures. A battle re-enactment happens Sunday afternoon at Tabor Farm. Other events are held at the Wilderness Road Regional Museum.

RENDEZVOUS
Radford   *(540) 639-3619*

Appalachian folkways and mountain storytelling are the focus of this all-day festival on the fourth Saturday in June. Events are held at the Long Way Home Outdoor Theater.

RAIL ROAD DAYS

Clifton Forge   (540) 862-2210

Celebrate the railroad heritage of the C&O with the Gandy Dancers, a train excursion, exhibits and all kinds of activities.

CHAUTAUQUA FESTIVAL IN THE PARK

Wytheville   (540) 228-6855

This is the biggest annual event in Wythe County, with nine days and nights of entertainment. In addition to arts and craft shows, you'll find antique sales, ballets and performances of big band, bluegrass and classical music.

GRAYSON COUNTY
OLD TIME FIDDLER'S CONVENTION

Galax   (540) 655-4144

This is a precursor to the Old-Time Fiddler's Convention held in August in Galax.

BEST FRIEND FESTIVAL

Norton   (540) 679-0961

This event features music, games, arts and crafts and is always held on Father's Day weekend.

CRAFTERS FAIR

Schuyler   (804) 325-2200

This fair is held in mid-June at the Walton's Mountain Museum in Schuyler, near Charlottesville, where Earl Hamner Jr. grew up and gained the inspiration for the wonderful family television series.

July

SAFE AND SANE
FOURTH OF JULY CELEBRATION

Winchester   (540) 465-5757

This midday party on the downtown pedestrian mall is spiced with patriotic speeches, cake, balloons, carriage rides, a bike-decorating contest and a parade.

HAPPY BIRTHDAY U.S.A.

Staunton

As corny as it sounds, this is an old-fashioned, flag-waving, apple-pie Fourth of July celebration spawned by Staunton's hometown heroes, the Statler Brothers. You can be sure to hear plenty of good country music at this event, held at Gypsy Hill Park.

FOURTH OF JULY CELEBRATION

New Market   (540) 740-3432

This Shenandoah Valley town hosts a big family celebration, with a lot of food, games, children's rides, a parade and fireworks.

INDEPENDENCE DAY CELEBRATION

Charlottesville   (804) 295-5191

Held every year at McIntire Park, the celebration includes softball and baseball games, band concerts, children's rides and games, a picnic and, of course, fireworks.

INDEPENDENCE DAY CELEBRATION

Charlottesville   (804) 295-8181

About 50 new citizens from the Charlottesville area are naturalized each Fourth of July on the grounds of Thomas Jefferson's Monticello. A fife and drum corps provides music at this moving event, attended usually by nearly 1,000 people.

FOURTH OF JULY JUBILEE

Wintergreen   (804) 325-2200

At Wintergreen Resort you'll find greased watermelon races, clogging demonstrations, an arts and crafts show and a grand fireworks display.

SHENANDOAH VALLEY
MUSIC FESTIVAL

Orkney Springs   (540) 459-3396

Classical music is performed live in a concert series from July to September.

Shows are performed in an outdoor pavilion next to the Orkney Springs Hotel, a massive pre-Civil War building. Get there early for the ice-cream socials held before every concert. Arts and crafts shows are also held those weekends.

FREDERICK COUNTY FAIR

Clearbrook   (540) 662-9002

An old-fashioned country fete is held at the county fairgrounds on U.S. 11 north of town.

SHENANDOAH VALLEY
BICYCLE FESTIVAL

Bridgewater   (540) 434-3862

Bikers of all levels congregate for a series of races ranging from five to 100 miles. Bridgewater College hosts the event, which usually happens the end of July.

ANNUAL RAFT RACE

Stuarts Draft   (540) 337-1911

At Shenandoah Acres Resort, folks of all ages race around a measured course in inflatable rafts. Winners receive cash prizes at the late July event.

MUSIC FOR AMERICANS

Roanoke   (540) 343-9127

At Roanoke's Victory Stadium, this Fourth of July celebration features a performance by the Roanoke Symphony Orchestra, the community chorus and fireworks.

MISS VIRGINIA PAGEANT

Roanoke   (540) 981-1201

This annual event produces the state's Miss America contestant.

VIRGINIA COMMONWEALTH GAMES

Roanoke   (540) 343-0987

Produced by Virginia Amateur Sports in Roanoke, this sport festival is for men and women of all ages and abilities. This Olympic-style competition includes such

sports as basketball, karate, tennis and chess as well as many others.

VINTON JULY 4TH CELEBRATION

Vinton   (540) 342-6025

The celebration is held every year at the Vinton War Memorial.

SALEM FAIR AND EXPOSITION

Salem   (540) 375-3004

This is an old-time country fair held at the Salem Civic Center, both indoors and outside. Carnival rides, games, food, concerts and livestock judging go on for two weeks. A bake-off attracts some of the best cooks in the Roanoke Valley.

PLANTATION DAYS FESTIVAL

Charlottesville   (804) 293-9539

At Ash Lawn-Highland, James Monroe's 535-acre estate, merchants, crafters, servants and soldiers are depicted in a celebration of early American life. More than 20 crafters and artisans in period costumes demonstrate and sell their work. Visitors can also enjoy 18th-century music and games and a dressage performance.

INDEPENDENCE CELEBRATION

Lynchburg   (804) 525-1806

This is not your typical Fourth of July party. At Poplar Forest, interpreters will portray the lives of local citizenry during Thomas Jefferson's time. The fun includes early 19th-century craft demonstrations and a lot of food.

JULY 4TH CELEBRATION

Bedford   (540) 586-7161

The Blue Ridge lights up under a blazing night sky.

BLUE RIDGE DRAFT
HORSE AND MULE SHOW

Ferrum   (540) 365-4416

Young and old alike enjoy seeing these

magnificent beasts show their beauty and strength at an old-time farm country setting at Ferrum College.

FOURTH OF JULY CELEBRATION
Radford   (540) 731-3677

At Radford's Bisset Park there will be gospel music, craft shows, food vendors and fireworks. All events take place along the New River.

RIVERFEST
Radford   (540) 639-2202

Celebrate the great outdoors with a raft race down the New River. Other highlights are a barbecue cooking contest, craft show and live music. It's always held the second Saturday following the Fourth of July.

NEW RIVER VALLEY HORSE SHOW
Dublin   (540) 980-1991

This is the largest such event in the New River Valley.

BLUE RIDGE HERITAGE FESTIVAL
Fort Chiswell   (540) 228-3111

Southwest Virginia's 19 counties show off their mountain music, arts and crafts, and the many attractions of the Blue Ridge and Highlands.

JULY 4TH CELEBRATION
Clifton Forge   (540) 862-4246

This is the largest Independence Day spectacle in the Alleghany Highlands.

HOTTEST FUN
IN THE SUN BEACH DAY
Wytheville   (540) 228-3111

The third Saturday of each July, this event draws sun worshipers and water enthusiasts for a great family fun day.

CHILI COOK-OFF
& INDEPENDENCE DAY CELEBRATION
Marion   (540) 783-3881

Cooks and revelers from throughout the Southeast head to Marion for this annual July Fourth party with spice.

HUNGRY MOTHER STATE PARK
ARTS & CRAFTS FESTIVAL
Marion   (540) 783-3161

This event is always held the third weekend in July.

August

RIVERFEST
Front Royal   (540) 636-4948

Sponsored by the Friends of the Shenandoah, this annual festival takes place at the confluence of the north and south branches of the Shenandoah River. Activities include canoe races, a fishing tournament and a river rodeo with a tug of war, centipede canoe race, obstacle course and a blindfolded canoe race. On shore are crafts, food and live music.

OLD TOWN HOE DOWN
Winchester   (540) 665-0779

Always held in August, this annual celebration of farming features displays of farm implements, live music, craft demonstrations, fresh produce and a petting zoo. It takes place in Old Town Winchester.

GREAT AMERICAN DUCK RACE
Winchester   (540) 662-4118

Held every August at Jim Barnett Park, this is an annual fund-raiser of the Winchester-Patrick County Chamber of Commerce. Games, music, refreshments and duck races attract a good crowd.

ROCKINGHAM COUNTY FAIR
Harrisonburg   (540) 434-0005

Virginia's largest agricultural county salutes its agrarian roots.

VIRGINIA MOUNTAIN PEACH FESTIVAL
Roanoke   (540) 342-2028

Come taste those delicious peach desserts, including shakes and cobbler, made from locally grown peaches. Also enjoy live entertainment, games and even a peach art contest.

VINTON OLD-TIME BLUEGRASS FESTIVAL AND COMPETITION
Vinton   (540) 983-0613

This event is held every year at the Vinton Farmers Market. Not only can you enjoy music by well-known musicians, but you can also listen to individual and band competitions. Don't forget to stop by and check out the crafts and carnival.

THOMAS JEFFERSON'S TOMATO FAIR
Lynchburg   (804) 847-1499

This early August agrarian festival starts at 6 AM with tomato and canned good competitions, live entertainment and handmade crafts. It's held at the downtown Community Market.

STEPPING OUT
Blacksburg   (540) 951-4200

This major downtown festival is always held the first weekend in August.

NEWPORT AGRICULTURAL FAIR
                                (540) 544-7469

One of the oldest agricultural fairs in Virginia, this Giles County community event has judged food and agriculture exhibits and livestock competitions, bluegrass music and horseshoe and jousting tournaments.

VIRGINIA HIGHLANDS FESTIVAL
Abingdon   (540) 628-8141

Beautiful, historic downtown Abingdon is the backdrop for this event that features one of the largest antique shows in the country. Historic tours, workshops and fine arts and crafts are added features. The festival is always held the first week in August.

OLD TIME FIDDLER'S CONVENTION
Galax   (540) 236-0668

This is the real McCoy — the oldest and largest old-time music festival in the country. It's always held during the second week in August. You'll find bluegrass and folk bands, clogging and flatfoot dancing day and night.

VIRGINIA KENTUCKY DISTRICT FAIR
Wise   (540) 328-9772

This country fair in rural Wise County features Appalachian music, games, folklife exhibits and rides.

APPALACHIA COAL AND RAILROAD DAYS
Appalachia   (540) 565-0361

This is a must-do for railroad and coal buffs. It's always held the second weekend in August.

NATURAL CHIMNEYS JOUST
Mt. Solon   (540) 350-2510

Here's an anachronism. "Knights" from several states congregate to joust for a shining ring. Bluegrass music fills the air, and the seven castle-like towers of Natural Chimneys form a spectacular backdrop. The event takes place the third Saturday in August.

AIRSHOW AND HOT AIR BALLOON FESTIVAL
Fauquier County

In mid-August, the Flying Circus near

Warrenton hosts a weekend of aerial fun. You can even take a ride in the open cockpit of a biplane before or after the show.

VINIFERA WINE FESTIVAL
The Plains   (540) 253-5001

The oldest wine festival in the Commonwealth is held on the grounds of Great Meadow, an event featuring 40 of the state's finest wineries, food, arts and crafts, music and wine lectures.

EASTERN WINE FESTIVAL
AT MORVEN PARK
Leesburg   (540) 537-0961

On the third weekend in August, more than 40 wineries offer tastings of their finest, along with music and special activities on the grounds of this historic estate.

September

VIRGINIA BLUES FESTIVAL
Charlottesville   (540) 296-8548

In early September the Downtown Foundation puts on a wonderful three-day show with national, regional and local performers, including workshops, videos and children's activities.

TASTE OF THE MOUNTAINS
MAIN STREET FESTIVAL
Madison   (540) 948-3645, 948-4455

This is a chance to watch craftsmen at work as they demonstrate basketweaving, woodcarving, glass blowing, chair caning, furniture making, quilting, spinning, bark-basket making and beekeeping. You'll want to tear yourself away to listen to Appalachian tunes played on dulcimers and harps and watch the footwork of the clog dancers. A petting zoo for the kids and plenty of mountain-inspired food add to the fun.

APPLE HARVEST
ARTS & CRAFTS FESTIVAL
Winchester   (540) 662-4135

This fall festival at Jim Barnett Park features apple butter-making and pie contests, live music and arts and crafts galore.

BOTTLE AND POTTERY
SHOW AND SALE
Harrisonburg   (540) 877-1093

This show and sale of antique bottles, pottery, postcards and small collectibles, sponsored by the Apple Valley Bottle Collectors Club, has been an annual happening for more than 20 years. It's held at the Rockingham Fairgrounds.

ANNUAL HARVEST FESTIVAL
Edinburg   (540) 984-8699

Shenandoah Vineyards hosts an all-day festival every September, giving visitors a chance to stomp grapes, munch barbecue, take a hayride, browse through an arts and crafts exhibit, dance and, of course, sample wine.

EDINBURG OLE' TIME FESTIVAL
Edinburg   (540) 984-8521

Bluegrass music and crafts are on tap at this Shenandoah County fest.

DRAFT HORSE AND MULE DAY
AT OATLANDS PLANTATION
Leesburg   (540) 777-3174

There was a time these big fellows did all the farm work, and pulled the family wagon to church on Sunday. This early September event, with its old-fashioned demonstrations, is a reminder of the horse's role in the shaping of the country.

NEW MARKET
ARTS & CRAFTS SHOW
New Market   (540) 740-3329

This is a show of high quality arts

and crafts from the Blue Ridge and Shenandoah Valley region. It happens in late September.

ALBEMARLE COUNTY FAIR
North Garden   *(804) 296-5803*

This event is usually held the first few days of September.

TRADITIONAL FRONTIER FESTIVAL
Staunton   *(540) 332-7850*

This is a good time to visit the Museum of American Frontier Culture, which hosts this festival the weekend after Labor Day every year. Come and enjoy traditional crafts, food and entertainment from Germany, England, Ireland and America at the museum's living-history farms.

"SPIRIT OF THE INDIAN" POW WOW
Crozet   *(804) 929-0334*

Claudius Crozet Park, 12 miles west of Charlottesville, is the venue for this gathering of Native Americans in early September. It's a wonderful opportunity to learn about their culture, past and present.

BUENA VISTA LABOR DAY FESTIVAL
(540) 463-5375

This is a huge event that usually attracts some of the state's leading politicians. There are band concerts, arts and crafts, tennis and horseshoe tournaments, amusement rides and more.

FINCASTLE FESTIVAL
(540) 473-3077

Historic Fincastle celebrates its Scotch-Irish roots at this day-long festival downtown. Arts, music, games and merchant open houses await visitors.

HENRY STREET AFRICAN AMERICAN HERITAGE FESTIVAL
Roanoke   *(540) 345-4818*

This is an annual celebration of African-American culture in a neighborhood close to downtown Roanoke. The day includes ethnic food, music, entertainment and children's activities.

FAIRFAX HUNT STEEPLECHASE RACES
Leesburg   *(540) 787-6673*

Historic Belmont Plantation (4 miles east of town on U.S. 7) is the setting for this afternoon of racing and outdoor socializing. The six-race program begins at 2 PM the third or fourth Saturday in September.

OLDE SALEM DAYS
Salem   *(540) 772-8871*

This is a downtown celebration held the second Saturday in September, the focus of which is antiques, crafts and health care.

VINTON FOLKLIFE FESTIVAL
Vinton   *(540) 983-0613*

This event is held at the Vinton War Memorial Grounds. Activities include exhibits, traditional music, storytelling and a children's area.

CONSTITUTION DAY CELEBRATIONS
Montpelier   *(540) 672-2728*

Enjoy free admission to tour Montpelier, the home of President James Madison, the father of the Constitution. This is an opportunity to better understand the man who contributed so much to the founding of our government.

LABOR DAY SPECTACULAR
Wintergreen   *(804) 325-2200*

Wintergreen Resort throws a huge

weekend party around Labor Day, with a boat race, cookout, bluegrass music, a goofy talent show and family scavenger hunts.

KALEIDOSCOPE
Lynchburg   (804) 847-1811

This is Lynchburg's big annual fall festival that lasts nearly three weeks. It includes a children's festival on the third Saturday, a major antique show with 100 dealers, a riverfront music jamboree with barbecue, a craft show, bike race and teddy bear parade. Thousands of runners participate in the 10-mile race.

FALL FOOD FESTIVAL
Lynchburg   (804) 847-1499

Held on a mid-September weekend, this fest features the best in regional and seasonal fare.

BOONES MILL APPLE FESTIVAL
Boones Mill   (540) 483-9542

This tiny community rallies enormous resources to stage a major parade and social event along U.S. 220. Look for major politicos among the common folk.

WINE FESTIVAL
Smith Mountain Lake   (540) 721-1203

On the last Sunday in September, nearly a dozen of Virginia's best wineries converge at Bernard's Landing and Resort for a festival on the beautiful lake. Chamber music, wine tastings and good food make this one of the area's more sophisticated festivals.

HOME TOUR GALA
Smith Mountain Lake   (540) 772-6677

This national award-winning fundraiser for Multiple Sclerosis showcases the grandest homes on the lake. Homes are accessible by either land or water. Don't miss this event for show-and-tell for a good cause.

SEPTEMBERFEST
Radford   (540) 731-3656

This is a two-day downtown festival with jazz, wine tastings, sidewalk sales and competitions with a variety of bands. Septemberfest always happens the second Friday and Saturday in September.

CLAYTOR LAKE
ARTS AND CRAFTS FAIR
Pulaski County   (540) 980-7363

This a popular Labor Day weekend event for the whole family.

DOCK BOGGS MEMORIAL FESTIVAL
Wythe County   (540) 328-0100

This music fest is always held the second weekend in September.

SALTVILLE LABOR DAY CELEBRATION
                             (540) 496-7038

The day includes an 1800s fashion show and Civil War re-enactment. There will also be salt-making demonstrations, a street dance, parade and live entertainment.

CEDAR BLUFF HERITAGE FESTIVAL
Cedar Bluff   (540) 964-4889

In this town square during the middle of May, you can find many activities like cake walks, crafts and tasty food.

GRAYSON HIGHLANDS FALL FESTIVAL
Mouth of Wilson   (540) 579-7092

Held at the Grayson Highlands State Park, this is an old-time festival with apple butter and molasses-making demonstrations and presentations by a blacksmith. There is bluegrass and gospel music, barbecue chicken and other foods.

ANNUAL ORANGE STREET FESTIVAL
Orange   *(540) 672-5216*

On the second Saturday of the month, the streets of Orange are filled with crafts, food, children's rides and live entertainment.

ANNUAL INTERNATIONAL STREET FESTIVAL
Winchester   *(540) 665-0079*

Usually held in late September, this festival features costumes, native gourmet dishes and crafts and entertainments from around the world.

FOXFIELD RACES
Charlottesville   *(804) 293-9501*

The fall race meeting, held in late September, showcases some of the best steeplechase horses in the country — and some famous owners. Charlottesville's horsey set throws champagne parties on the backs of Rolls-Royces and Bentleys, but there are plenty of beer-and-hot dog feasts as well.

CHILHOWIE APPLE FESTIVAL
Chilhowie   *(540) 646-8213*

This Smyth County celebration is always held the last weekend in September.

WARRENTON HORSE SHOW
Warrenton   *(540) 347-2612*

There's a homey feel to the Warrenton Show, which is still held in one ring (unlike the three-ring circuses of other shows) so that you can take a seat and not miss a thing. The atmosphere is relaxed and cordial but the competition is of the highest quality. The show is always Labor Day weekend at the showgrounds north of town on U.S. 29 Business.

October

VIRGINIA FALL RACES AT GLENWOOD PARK
Middleburg   *(540) 687-5662*

Glenwood Park is one of the few steeplechase courses where spectators can see every fence — if they're not too busy celebrity watching. After the races, stroll through the town. Middleburg's shopkeepers and restaurants go all out to make visitors welcome on race day.

ANTIQUE SHOW AND SALE
Winchester   *(540) 662-4996*

This show is held in early October at the War Memorial Building.

NORTH-SOUTH SKIRMISH ASSOCIATION FALL NATIONALS
Gainesboro   *(540) 666-7917*

Civil War re-enactors fire old weapons at breakable targets in the 45th installment of this event at Ft. Shenandoah. There's also a ladies' dress competition.

BATTLE OF CEDAR CREEK LIVING HISTORY AND REENACTMENT
Middletown   *(540) 869-2028*

This re-enactment is held on the original Civil War Battlefield. It takes place at Belle Grove Plantation on the weekend closest to October 19, the anniversary of the Battle of Cedar Creek of 1864.

HERITAGE FESTIVAL
Luray   *(540) 778-3230*

This festival brings to mind the old-time county fairs. There's country music, clogging shows, wagon rides, apple cider, home-cooked food, a steam and gas engine show and a Saturday Chili Cook-Off. More than 100 crafters display their wares.

ELKTON AUTUMN DAYS
ARTS & CRAFTS FESTIVAL
Elkton   (540) 298-9370

This is an outdoor festival that's usually held during the best weekend for enjoying the brilliant colors of autumn.

LEESBURG HAUNTINGS
(540) 777-0099

For four nights on the eve of Halloween, the town offers guided tours of historic haunted houses and places. Actors re-enact spooky happenings of days gone by. Groups of 25 leave the Town Hall every 10 minutes between 5 PM and 9 PM.

ALDIE HARVEST FESTIVAL
(540) 327-4246

This 182-year-old village bursts with life in mid-October with a festival centering around the restoration of the town's 1810 mill. More than 132 craftsmen and artists take part in the day's activities, which include a Civil War encampment, food and music.

VIRGINIA FALL FOLIAGE FESTIVAL
Waynesboro   (540) 949-6505

This happens usually the first two consecutive weekends in October. This major event features a 10K run, an arts and crafts show with more than 200 exhibitors, a chili cookoff and a lot of good foods made with apples. It also includes a gem and mineral show.

OKTOBERFEST
Staunton   (540) 886-2351

German beer, Virginia wine, food and an oompah band playing traditional German music make this a special festival. There's also a Bach Bash presented by the Mid-Atlantic Chamber Orchestra, as well as arts and crafts displays.

FALL FIBER FESTIVAL
& SHEEP DOG TRIALS
Orange   (540) 672-2935

The stars are the sheep, llamas, angora and cashmere goats and angora rabbits who provide the raw materials for the spinning, weaving and shearing demonstrations. Sheep dog trials take place both days of the event, which is usually held the first weekend in October.

HARVEST FESTIVAL ON THE MARKET
Roanoke   (540) 342-2028

Every October, folks pour into the streets of Roanoke's historic City Market for horse-drawn carriage rides, lessons in scarecrow-building, hot cider and live bluegrass.

ROANOKE RAILWAY FESTIVAL
(540) 342-2028

The city celebrates its railroad heritage every year with a Columbus Day festival all weekend. There's also nostalgic entertainment, a car show and a huge rail-related crafts show at the nearby Civic Center.

ANNUAL ZOO BOO
Roanoke   (540) 343-3241

It's a Halloween party at the Mill Mountain Zoo.

AFFAIR IN THE SQUARE
Roanoke   (540) 342-5708

This event combines entertainment, food, beverages and dancing on every level of Center in the Square and has become an annual custom for many residents of Southwest Virginia.

HAUNTED CAVERNS
Dixie Caverns   (540) 380-2085

This Halloween tour of Dixie Caverns will make your hair stand on end.

Grinding chain saws, shrieks and a lot of fake blood make this event a blast for those who thrive on horror.

APPLE BUTTER MAKING FESTIVAL

Nelson County   *(804) 277-5865*

This festival is held both at the beginning of October and in the middle of the month.

BACCHANALIAN FEAST

Charlottesville   *(804) 296-4188*

This evening feast at the Boar's Head Inn includes a seven-course meal with Virginia wines and entertainment. It's usually held on one of the first Fridays in October to kick off the Monticello Wine and Food Festival.

MONTICELLO WINE
AND FOOD FESTIVAL

Charlottesville   (804) 296-4188

Held at the Boar's Head Inn, this festival is a chance to taste many of the wines made in Virginia and view exhibits of the state's many wineries and vineyards.

VIRGINIA FESTIVAL
OF AMERICAN FILM

Charlottesville   *(804) 924-FEST*
                              (800) UVA-FEST

Film-makers, scholars, movie stars and the public explore trends in American film-making at this event, which usually happens around the end of October. In the past, such stars as Gregory Peck and Sissy Spacek have graced the festival (see our Arts and Culture chapter).

VIRGINIA HERITAGE WEEKEND

Wintergreen   *(804) 325-2200*

Wintergreen Resort hosts this event the first weekend of October. There will be a country cookout and an outdoor bluegrass concert, Appalachian heritage crafts workshops, clogging demonstrations, folklore and storytelling.

NATIONAL JOUSTING CHAMPIONSHIP

Leesburg   *(301) 371-4924*

Culminating the jousting season in mid-October is this all-important competition at Oatlands Plantation. Don't expect knights in armor trying to spear each other. It's a bit tamer but nevertheless exciting to watch a horseman try to spear a succession of tiny rings at a dead gallop.

DAYTON AUTUMN CELEBRATION

Dayton   *(540) 879-9538*

This Rockingham County town greets fall in mid-October with music, food, antique cars, 250 arts and crafts exhibits, children's games and open house at historical sites such as Ft. Harrison, the Shenandoah Valley Heritage Museum and Research Center and Cromer-Trumbo House. The Dayton Farmer's Market nearby will have 20 food and specialty shops under one roof.

INTERNATIONAL GOLD CUP

The Plains   *(540) 253-5001*

Great Meadow is a wonderful venue for this race meeting, which takes place at the height of the fall foliage season on the third Saturday in October.

HALLOWEEN WEEKEND

Wintergreen   *(804) 325-2200*

Take the eerie Ghost Express chair lift then share hair-raising stories around the campfire. There's also a children's haunted house, a costume contest and opportunities for families to carve pumpkins, plus the many regular activities of this four season resort.

VIRGINIA GARLIC FESTIVAL

Amherst (804) 946-5168

The five-acre Rebec Vineyards hosts this mid-October celebration. Several Virginia wineries participate; the wonderful food will please epicures. A Garlic Queen dressed in a giant bulb with sprouts shooting from her head has been known to make an appearance.

ELKTON AUTUMN DAYS

(540) 298-9370

Food, crafts, entertainment and a car show are features of this Rockingham County celebration in late October.

HARVEST FESTIVAL

Lynchburg (804) 847-1499

This end-of-October festival features Virginia-made products and crafts, square dancing and country music. Children go crazy with the costume contests and community pumpkin-carving.

SEDALIA COUNTRY FAIR

Big Island (804) 299-5080

At this fair you can find animal events, antique and new farm machinery, exhibits and food, glorious food.

JAZZ ON THE LAWN

Concord (804) 993-2185

Just east of Lynchburg is another winery, Stonewall Vineyards, which hosts this relaxing weekend event in mid-October. Enjoy live jazz, gourmet food and local wines.

SORGHUM MOLASSES FESTIVAL

Clifford (804) 946-5063

This little town east of the Blue Ridge salutes the dark, gooey sweet substance in October with a festival that includes a jousting tournament, country music, arts and crafts and a flea market. You can also watch molasses and apple butter being made.

SMITH MOUNTAIN LAKE FALL FESTIVAL

Moneta (540) 721-1203

Also on Columbus Day weekend, Smith Mountain Lake's six or so communities all host festivals, forming a virtual ring of festivals around the lake. There are arts and crafts shows, an antique car show, a flea market, traditional folkway demonstrations and more.

BLUE RIDGE FOLKLIFE FESTIVAL

Ferrum (540) 365-4416

Ferrum College hosts this annual event the last Saturday in October. Widely attended, the festival showcases regional traditions, with crafts workers showing time-honored skills, old-time musicians and traditional Appalachian competitions.

NEWBERN FALL FESTIVAL OF ARTS & CRAFTS

Newbern (540) 674-4835

Held at the Wilderness Road Museum, this event is filled with the Appalachian Mountains through and through. Square dancing, antiques, crafts and stagecoach rides are just a few of the activities you can find here.

PULASKIFEST

Pulaski (540) 980-1000

The Jackson Park is the sight for this fest, which is always full of entertainment and food and features a parade, street dance and even a model railroad show.

FALL FOLIAGE FESTIVAL

Clifton Forge (540) 862-4969

The autumn glory of Alleghany

County serves as an incredible backdrop for this arts, craft and food festival.

WHITETOP MOUNTAIN SORGHUM AND MOLASSES FESTIVAL
(540) 388-3294

This festival at Mount Rogers National Recreation Area features molasses and apple butter made the old-fashioned way. There are games, bake sales, arts and crafts and old-time gospel and bluegrass music.

MECC HOME CRAFTS DAYS
Big Stone Gap   (540) 523-2400

Two days of arts and crafts at Mountain Empire Community College feature whittling, broom-making and other mountain heritage displays, as well as bluegrass and country music and clogging.

November

CHRISTMAS IN THE COUNTRY
Winchester   (540) 722-6367

Special activities are held in various locations from early November through Christmas.

MONTPELIER HUNT RACES
                    (540) 672-2728

These famous races have been taking place on the beautiful grounds of the former James Madison estate since 1934. The race card will feature two flat races and five over fences, as well as Jack Russell terrier races and the Dolley Madison tailgate competition. This event is usually the first Saturday in November.

FESTIVAL OF TREES
Roanoke   (540) 344-0931

Local charities and businesses benefit the Mental Health Association by erect-ing and decorating large themed Christmas trees at the Jefferson Center. This annual event delights everyone who loves Christmas decorations on beautiful trees.

THANKSGIVING AT WINTERGREEN
                    (804) 325-2200

If cooking for a crowd is not what you want, spend the weekend at Wintergreen. They'll deliver turkey and all the trimmings to the door of your rented condo. Or you can partake of traditional buffets and dinners at all the resort's restaurants. There's also a turkey trot square dance, a hayride sing-along and a musical revue cabaret.

BLESSING OF THE HOUNDS
Keswick   (804) 293-3549

Before the start of the Thanksgiving Day foxhunt, members of the local hunt gather at Grace Church for the traditional blessing of the foxhounds. It's a colorful ceremony, with hounds and horses milling about in anticipation of the day's sport.

THRESHING TIME
Staunton   (540) 332-7850

Workers at the Museum of American Frontier Culture show how farmers in different parts of the world harvest grain.

OAKENCROFT HOLIDAY OPEN HOUSE
Charlottesville   (804) 296-4188

Oakencroft Vineyard and Winery entertains visitors the weekend after Thanksgiving.

CHRISTMAS AT THE MARKET
Lynchburg   (804) 847-1499

This colorful event is always held at the end of November at the downtown Community Market.

SANTA AT THE LAKE

Smith Mountain Lake   (800) 676-8203

Where else would Santa arrive by parasail? It's a real thrill when the boat pulls in and the rosy-cheeked man with the white beard descends from the skies over Smith Mountain Lake and onto the dock at Hales Ford Center — truly a unique experience for the youngsters.

FRANKLIN COUNTY FALL ARTS AND CRAFTS FESTIVAL

Rocky Mount   (540) 483-9542

This festival is usually held the weekend before Thanksgiving.

ARTS AND CRAFTS BAZAAR

Wytheville   (540) 228-3111

This bazaar is usually held the weekend before Thanksgiving.

December

TRADITIONS OF CHRISTMAS

Museum of American Frontier Culture
Staunton   (540) 332-7850

Throughout the month opportunities abound for you to tour the museum's living farms by lantern at night and to learn about how America's early settlers and their kin prepared for Christmas. Children may attend gift-making workshops.

CHRISTMAS AND FLOWER SHOW

Big Stone Gap   (540) 523-1235

The show is held on the first weekend in December.

ABRAM'S DELIGHT CANDLELIGHT TOUR

Winchester   (540) 662-6550

See Abram's Delight, Winchester's oldest home, in a different, magical light early in December.

CHRISTMAS OPEN HOUSE AT STONEWALL JACKSON'S HEADQUARTERS

Winchester   (540) 662-6550

Members of the United Daughters of the Confederacy are costumed hostesses at this Confederate Christmas celebration.

CHRISTMAS CANDLELIGHT TOUR

Middletown   (540) 869-2028

Belle Grove Plantation decked out in its holiday splendor is a grand way to celebrate the season.

CHRISTMAS AT THE MANSE

Staunton   (540) 886-2351

The holidays add a special glow to the Woodrow Wilson Birthplace.

CHRISTMAS OPEN HOUSE AT MORVEN PARK

Leesburg   (540) 777-2414

The mansion is decorated with turn-of-the century ornaments, the fireplaces are ablaze, and a 12-foot-tall Christmas tree fills the Great Room with its pine fragrance. It looks as if the late Virginia governor Westmoreland Davis and his wife might walk through the door at any moment. The open house is usually early in the month.

MONTICELLO HOLIDAY OPEN HOUSE

Charlottesville   (804)984-9828

In early December, visitors are treated to candlelight tours of the mansion, which is decorated in period ornaments. There's music every evening, and refreshments are served in the gift shop.

CHRISTMAS BED AND BREAKFAST TOUR

Loudoun County   (540) 777-1806

This self-guided tour of selected bed and breakfast and country inns is a good way to review places you may want to stay during another visit. After seeing these beautiful places by candlelight with all their holiday decorations, you'll have a tough time making a choice.

HOLIDAY IN LEXINGTON

Lexington   (540) 463-3777

Visiting Lexington during the year is always nice, especially when it is the Christmas season. Activities range from a 10K road race to possibly a visit from a celebrity.

ROANOKE CHRISTMAS PARADE

(540) 981-2889

This is a festive outing for the whole family; it's always held the first Saturday in December.

DICKENS OF A CHRISTMAS

Roanoke   (540) 342-2028

Roanoke's City Market is the place for carriage rides, chestnut roasting, ice carvings, hot cider and holiday music on the second Saturday in December.

FIRST NIGHT ROANOKE

(540) 342-2640

This is a nonalcoholic New Year's celebration in the downtown City Market area. The fun includes ice-skating for kids, holiday music, hot cocoa and a "Resolution Wall" where you can write your New Year's resolutions for the world to see.

ANNUAL YULETIDE TRADITIONS

Charlottesville   (804) 977-1783

These special events at Ash Lawn-Highland, historic Michie Tavern and Monticello are held throughout December. Included in the activities are Christmas By Candlelight evening tours and historic re-enactments at Ash Lawn-Highland, as well as Gingerbread and Lace, a celebration with caroling, ornament-making, tree-trimming and refresh-ments. At Michie Tavern, an array of Christmas delicacies is served in the Ordinary for a Yuletide feast. Monticello holds a candlelight open house several evenings before Christmas, with refreshments and music. There's also a holiday wreath workshop at the Monticello Visitors Center. After Christmas you can attend afternoon holiday concerts at Ash Lawn-Highland.

MERRIE OLDE ENGLAND CHRISTMAS FESTIVAL

Charlottesville   (804) 296-2181

During the holidays the Boar's Head Inn hosts a feast with a sampling of medieval dishes.

FIRST NIGHT VIRGINIA

Charlottesville   (804) 296-8269

This is a family-oriented New Year's celebration of the arts in the downtown area from 6 PM to midnight.

APPALACHIAN MOUNTAIN CHRISTMAS

Wintergreen   (804) 325-2200

During Christmas week, the resort celebrates with horse-drawn carriage rides, ornament and Appalachian craft workshops, wandering minstrels, jugglers and clowns and an old-fashioned carol sing. You can also enjoy a candlelight Christmas buffet and grand lighting ceremony.

CHRISTMAS AT POINT OF HONOR

Lynchburg   (804) 847-1459

This is a celebration of the joyous season as it would have been in the 1820s. Held at Point of Honor, a mansion built by Patrick Henry's doctor, George Cabell, the event is an opportunity to revel in the color and aroma of festive greens and sing along with a local group performing 19th-century carols.

SCROOGE DAY

Lynchburg   (804) 847-1499

Always the last Saturday before Christmas, this is the day to take care of last-minute shopping at the downtown Community Market. You'll find handmade gifts, stocking stuffers, home-baked treats, wreaths, greenery and trees.

DIAMOND HILL CHRISTMAS CANDLELIGHT TOUR

Lynchburg   (804) 845-4014

Come tour four homes in Lynchburg during the Christmas season. Each will have music and a candlelight dinner. Don't forget to make your reservations.

PATRICK HENRY WOMEN'S AUXILIARY CHRISTMAS TEA

Red Hill   (804) 376-5216

Enjoy Christmas tea at Red Hill, Colonial style. Patrick Henry's home is decorated with period trimmings. Refreshments and holiday music add to the holiday mood.

CHRISTMAS LIGHTS AT ELKS NATIONAL HOME

Bedford

Retired Elks work all year to get ready for one of the grandest displays of Christmas lighting in Virginia every December. Drive through and see years of innovative decorations by these retired fraternal associates.

DECK THE HALLS OPEN HOUSE

Newbern   (540) 674-4835

Visit the Wilderness Road Regional Museum for a rustic Christmas to remember.

CHRISTMAS CANDLELIGHT TOUR OF HOMES

Abingdon   (540) 676-2282

In mid-December, Abingdon's loveliest homes are open for tours. There are also holiday music parties, carolers and horse-drawn carriage rides.

FIRST NIGHT WINCHESTER

Winchester   (540) 662-3884

The town's annual New Year's Eve celebration of the arts features more than 40 different artists entertaining the public at sites throughout Winchester. It's a family-oriented, alcohol-free celebration.

Inside
Arts and Culture

Whew! For a relatively sparsely populated region, the Blue Ridge of Virginia offers abundant and diverse opportunities for arts and cultural experiences. Listing the best and brightest is a difficult task, since they're all backed by energetic people who believe strongly in the cause they promote.

Fine arts, folk art, history and pop culture blend well in these Blue Ridge counties. Elvis Presley lives on in Roanoke, where he is honored by a private citizen at Miniature Graceland, while maple sugar is celebrated at its own museum in Highland County. Also in Highland, you can attend Bear Mountain Outdoor School and learn Blue Ridge country survival skills such as building a log cabin.

Alleghany County has one of the largest railroad archives in the United States, the province of the C&O Railroad Historical Society.

If music is your leisure choice, try Friday night flat-footing at Cockram's General Store in Floyd County, where fiddles, autoharps and a 1940 juke box hold forth. Or, you can attend chamber music fests at Garth Newel Music Center in Bath County, where you'll probably rub elbows with jet-setters who patronize The Homestead Resort.

Historically speaking, the Charlottesville area is one of the country's best-known tourist cities, with such attractions as Montpelier, Monticello and Ash Lawn-Highland, the former homes of three of our

Photo: Virginia Division of Tourism

Poplar Forest, Thomas Jefferson's summer retreat, is in Bedford County near Lynchburg.

greatest presidents. A half-million visitors a year make the trek to the neoclassical mansion designed by the third president of the United States, Thomas Jefferson. Farther south is Jefferson's summer getaway at Poplar Forest in Bedford County. In the hills of Pulaski County, visitors stroll through an 1810 village in Old Newbern and see what life was like nearly two centuries ago.

History buffs will find the region's libraries an important source of information. In Lynchburg, Jones Memorial is one of the nation's foremost genealogical libraries and offers research and lending services by mail. Virginia Tech's Carol Newman Library has the fifth-largest microfilm collection in the United States and Canada.

Theater opportunities range from movies to live performances. Worldly chic Charlottesville, home to numerous movie stars and directors, hosts the biggest names in the movie business during its annual Virginia Festival of American Film. More than 20,000 people show up to view film classics and hobnob with celebrities, who usually attend the closing bash.

If historical drama is more to your liking, you can attend Virginia's only outdoor drama, *The Long Way Home*. This stirring true saga of Mary Draper Ingles' capture by Indians and escape home through nearly 1,000 miles of wilderness to Radford has riveted audiences for 22 years.

No matter how small, nearly every community in the Blue Ridge has its own performing theater group, some comprised of as few as a dozen people, as in sparsely populated Giles County. In small-town Lexington, Lime Kiln Theater enjoys a national reputation for its open-air plays and musical performances in a magical setting. Staunton residents Robin and Linda Williams of public radio's *A Prairie Home Companion* with Garrison Keillor are regulars. Middletown's Wayside Theater, just south of Winchester, attracts patrons from Washington, D.C., to its summer performances, which often include name actors who love the area.

Museum buffs will find a surprising range and quality of offerings in the Blue Ridge. The works of world-famous artist P. Buckley Moss, "the people's artist," whose annual revenues have been estimated at $11 million, can be seen in her private retreat and museum at Waynesboro.

There's probably not a small town in the United States with as many military museums as Lexington, with its VMI Museum, George C. Marshall Museum, Stonewall Jackson House and Lee Chapel.

The Roanoke Valley Museum houses an international tribute to the millions of lives touched by the volunteer rescue squad movement, To the Rescue, which honors the father of the movement, Julian Stanley Wise.

Some museums honor forgotten geniuses, such as the Cyrus McCormick Museum in Rockbridge County, dedicated to the inventor of the first successful reaper. Every county seat seems to have its own museum for recording local history. One, in Botetourt County, records the history of a county seat that once was an English land grant stretching the whole way to the Mississippi River.

Not to be underestimated for the role they play in the region's arts and culture are the diverse programs underwritten by colleges and universities. The contributions of academic giants such as Virginia Tech in Blacksburg and the University of

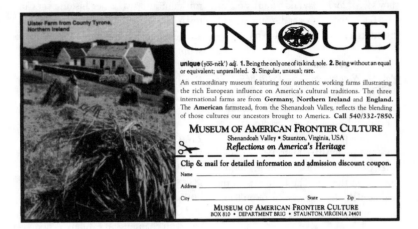
Virginia in Charlottesville are immeasurable.

The largest colony of artists in residence in the country, the Virginia Center for the Creative Arts (affiliated with Sweet Briar College), is in the remote foothills of the Blue Ridge in Amherst County. And tiny Ferrum College in Franklin County is the nation's most important repository of Blue Ridge culture through its Blue Ridge Farm Museum, Institute and Folk Life Festival.

Education in the arts doesn't begin on the college level. In culturally rich Lynchburg is the Virginia School of the Arts, one of the few secondary schools in the nation tailored for these pursuits.

The cultures of many ethnic groups are celebrated in the Blue Ridge. In Roanoke, the Harrison Heritage Museum for African-American Culture exists to celebrate and remind western Virginia of the rich contributions of its black citizenry. In her day, African-American poet Anne Spencer was a celebrity in Lynchburg, entertaining a steady flow of world dignitaries at her home and grounds, which are now open to the public by appointment. In her meticulous garden, she chatted with Martin Luther King, Paul Robeson, Marion Anderson, Thurgood Marshall, Dr. George Washington Carver and Jackie Robinson. Congressman Adam Clayton Powell even honeymooned there.

Enjoy making your choices from the attractions listed. Hours and prices may change, so be sure to call ahead. Good luck if you're trying to see it all!

Shenandoah Valley Region

Winchester and Frederick County

Theater

SHENANDOAH SUMMER MUSIC THEATRE
Shenandoah University, 1460 University Dr.
Winchester   (540) 665-4569

Student actors, singers and dancers perform four lively musicals during June and July, Wednesday through Sunday, at the university. A subscription to all four shows is $51 for Friday and Saturday nights, $47.60 for other nights and matinees, with discounts for seniors and children.

WAYSIDE THEATRE
Main St., Middletown   (540) 869-1776

The second-oldest professional theater in the state brings the best of Broadway to the valley from May to December. The company's professional actors from New York and around the country perform comedies, dramas and mysteries in an intimate downtown theater. The theater is in the middle of this little town, which you'll find by taking Exit 302 from I-81.

Dance

PLAINS PROMENADERS
SQUARE DANCE GROUP
Luray   (540) 743-6792

This group of about 60 dancers meets for classes and workshops every Tuesday night September through May at the Plains Elementary School in Timberville. Some of the more advanced dancers also perform at special events around the area. The group's been around for about 25 years.

Museums

ABRAM'S DELIGHT MUSEUM
1340 Pleasant Valley Rd.
Winchester   (540) 662-6519

This is the oldest house in Winchester, built in 1754 of native limestone with walls two feet thick. There's also a restored log cabin on the lawn from the same period. Abram's Delight is beautifully restored and furnished with period pieces. It's open daily from 10 AM to 4 PM April 1 through October. Admission is $3.50 for adults, $3 for seniors and $1.75 for children ages 6 to 12. You can save by buying a block ticket for entrance to this

museum and two other historic sites in town, Stonewall Jackson's Headquarters and George Washington's Office Museum. Block tickets cost $7.50 for adults, $6.50 for seniors and $4 for children. Family tickets are $20. Groups of more than 20 are $7 adults, $6 seniors.

KURTZ CULTURAL CENTER
2 N. Cameron St.
Winchester   (540) 722-6367

Just a short walk from the downtown pedestrian mall is this historic building housing the Old Town Welcome Center and Gift Shop, several displays and a gallery with changing art exhibits. A permanent interpretive exhibit called "Shenandoah — Crossroads of the Civil War" details the Shenandoah Valley's major battles. A Patsy Cline display contains records, photos, belongings and videos of the Winchester-born country singer. The cultural center is open Monday through Saturday from 10 AM to 5 PM and Sunday noon to 5 PM.

WASHINGTON'S OFFICE MUSEUM
Braddock and Cork Sts.
Winchester   (540) 662-4412

Part of this old log and stone building was used by Washington when he was colonel of the Virginia Regiment protecting the 300-mile-long frontier to the west. It's open daily from 10 AM to 4 PM, noon to 4 PM Sunday, April 1 through October. Admission is $2 for adults, $1.50 for seniors and $1 for children ages 6 to 12.

Other Cultural Attractions

BELLE GROVE PLANTATION
U.S. 11, Middletown   (540) 869-2028

Belle Grove (c. 1794) is an 18th-century plantation, working farm and center for the study of traditional rural crafts. It was the home of Maj. Isaac Hite Jr. and his family for more than 70 years. Hite was a grandson of one of the first permanent settlers in the Shenandoah Valley. Thomas Jefferson was actively involved in Belle Grove's design, thanks to some family connections. Hite married the sister of James Madison, who was a close friend of Jefferson. In fact, James and Dolley Madison spent part of their honeymoon visiting the Hites at Belle Grove.

Belle Grove hosts a variety of special activities throughout the year, from the Shenandoah Valley Farm Craft Days in early June to the Battle of Cedar Creek Living History Weekend in mid-October. There's also a very nice gift shop and quilt shop at the site.

The plantation is open to the public mid-March through mid-November from 10:15 AM to 3:15 PM daily and Sunday from 1:15 to 4:15 PM. Admission is $3.50 for adults, $3 for seniors and $2 for children ages 6 through 12. Belle Grove is a mile south of Middletown on U.S. 11; take Exit 302 from I-81, then head west on Va. 627 to U.S. 11.

STONEWALL
JACKSON'S HEADQUARTERS
415 N. Braddock St.
Winchester   (540) 667-3242

Jackson used the private home of Lt. Col. Lewis T. Moore as his headquarters during the Civil War from 1861 to 1862. Jackson's office is much as it was during his stay, and the house contains artifacts of

Jackson, Turner Ashby, Jed Hotchkiss and other Confederates. The house is open daily from 10 AM to 4 PM April 1 through October. Admission is $3.50 for adults, $3 for seniors and $1.75 for children.

Front Royal

Museums

WARREN
RIFLES CONFEDERATE MUSEUM
95 Chester St.   (540) 636-6982

Mosby's Rangers, Stonewall Jackson, Robert E. Lee, Jubal Early, J.E.B. Stuart and Confederate spy Belle Boyd all saw action in Warren County. Uniforms, flags, pictures and other relics of their feats are displayed here. The museum and gift shop, which is owned and operated by the Warren Rifles Chapter of the United Daughters of the Confederacy, is open from mid-April to November 1, weekdays 9 AM to 5 PM and Sunday noon to 5 PM.

Shenandoah
and Page Counties

Music

SHENANDOAH VALLEY
MUSIC FESTIVAL
Woodstock   (800) 459-3396

This 33-year-old outdoor summer music festival features symphony pops,

---

Lights! Action! Camera! The Blue Ridge has been the setting for many television programs and movies, including *Lassie*, *What About Bob?*, *Dirty Dancing*, *Sommersby* and *The Waltons*, a TV series based on the Nelson County upbringing of its creator, Earl Hamner.

Insiders' Tips

classical masterworks, folk, jazz and Big Band music — all performed on the grounds of the grand, historic Orkney Springs Hotel, a popular spa and mineral springs resort at the turn of the century. Evening concerts are held on weekends from April through Labor Day in a rustic open-air pavilion. Arts and crafts shows featuring regional artisans take place on the hotel's front lawn on the symphony concert weekends.

Another festival tradition is the old-fashioned ice cream social held next to the pavilion prior to each concert. Admission prices and concert times vary. For information and a free season brochure contact the Festival's Woodstock headquarters.

By the way, the Orkney Springs Hotel serves country-style buffet dinners on all concert nights. Reservations are required and can be made by calling (540) 856-2141. Many guests picnic on the grounds before concerts.

LURAY SINGING TOWER
(540) 743-3915

Across from the Luray Caverns is a tower containing a carillon of 47 bells, the largest weighing 7,640 pounds. Free recitals are given on weekends at 2 PM during March, April, May, September and October. From June through August, the bells peal at 8 PM every day except Monday and Wednesday.

Museums

BEDROOMS OF AMERICA MUSEUM
9386 Congress St.
New Market   (540) 740-3512

This sounds like a sleeper of a museum, but actually it's a fascinating place if you like old furniture and want to learn more about American antiques. Eleven

rooms of authentic furniture represent every period of America's bedrooms, from William and Mary (c. 1650) through art deco (c. 1930). The rooms are also furnished with period accessories, bed coverings, curtains and wall coverings.

The museum is housed in a restored 18th-century building used for a time by Confederate general Jubal Early as his headquarters during the Civil War. It's open daily from 9 AM to 8 PM Memorial Day to Labor Day and 9 AM to 6 PM the rest of the year (closed Christmas Day). Admission is $2 for adults, $1.50 for seniors and $1.25 for children ages 7 to 14.

NEW MARKET BATTLEFIELD HISTORICAL PARK AND HALL OF VALOR MUSEUM
(540) 740-3101

In the spring of 1864, a wavering Confederate line was reinforced with teen-age cadets from Virginia Military Institute. This museum chronicles their brave but tragic stand, and has some interesting displays of VMI grad Stonewall Jackson (see our Civil War chapter).

MUSEUM OF AMERICAN CAVALRY
(540) 740-3959

On the New Market Battlefield in the home of Maj. Christiona Shirley CSA is an unusual collection chronicling the development of the cavalry. Full-scale mounted figures are among the displays. The museum is open daily 9 AM to 5 PM. Admission is $4.50 for adults and $2.50 for children.

STRASBURG MUSEUM
King St.   (540) 465-3175

This museum was originally a steam pottery (c. 1891) and is a registered historic landmark. Strasburg was once famous for its pottery, and its old nickname,

Pottown, can still be seen around town on various business signs. The museum displays blacksmith, copper and pottery shop collections and artifacts from Colonial farms, homes, barns and businesses. You can also view Civil War and railroad relics. The museum is open daily from 10 AM to 4 PM May through October. Admission is $2 for adults and 50¢ for children.

TUTTLE & SPICE
GENERAL STORE MUSEUM
4 miles north of New Market on U.S. 522 at
Shenandoah Caverns   *(540) 477-9428*

The museum features nine shops set up to resemble a 19th-century country village. These include a tobacco store, doctor's house, haberdashery, millinery, apothecary shop and ice-cream parlor. The items in the shops are museum pieces and not for sale, but you can buy mementoes in the large gift shop. Admission is $2 for adults and $1 for children ages 6 to 12, and the museum is open daily from 9 AM to 6 PM.

WOODSTOCK MUSEUM
137 W. Court St.   *(540) 459-5518*

This downtown museum displays artifacts of country life in Shenandoah County, including tools, pottery, hardware, linens and handmade furniture. Admission is free. Hours vary.

Visual Arts

JOHN SEVIER GALLERY
Congress St. and Old Cross Rd,
New Market   *(540) 740-3911*

Set in a little log cabin in the heart of the downtown, this gallery specializes in watercolors and oil paintings by three local artists. It also sells locally made crafts such as woodwork, ornaments, stained-glass windows and fine photographs. One wall is set aside for an Artist of the Month display.

Other Cultural Attractions

LURAY CAVERNS CAR AND
CARRIAGE CARAVAN
U.S. 211 Bypass,
Luray   *(540) 743-6551*

This museum next to Luray Caverns grew from the car-collecting hobby of the caverns' president, H.T.N. Graves. Among the vehicles are Rudolph Valentino's 1925 Rolls Royce, a Conestoga wagon, an ornate sleigh and an 1892 Benz, one of the oldest cars in the country. All 140 items — cars, coaches, carriages and costumes — are fully restored. Admission is included in your ticket to Luray Caverns. The caravan is open every day from 9 AM until 1 hour after the last cavern tour.

Harrisonburg and
Rockingham County

Theater

JAMES MADISON UNIVERSITY
DINNER THEATER
Gibbons Hall   *(540) 568-6740*

Every summer the drama department puts on three plays seven nights a week. You can munch on a nice spread of food while you're watching the light dramas.

LATIMER-SHAEFFER THEATRE
James Madison University   *(540) 568-6260*

Dance, live music and plays fill the playbill throughout the academic year and in the summer. The 325-seat single-level theater is especially comfortable, with ample leg room and good acoustics. In May the Blue Ridge Dinner Theatre serves a sump-

Photo: To the Rescue National Exhibition

A photograph from the To the Rescue Exhibition at Tanglewood Mall.

tuous feast before the show; call (540) 434-1776.

Museums

JAMES MADISON UNIVERSITY
LIFE SCIENCE MUSEUM
Burruss Hall   (540) 568-6378

This museum displays Native American relics, seashells, birds and butterflies from around the world. It's open during the academic year, and the hours vary, de-pending upon the schedules of student volunteers.

REUEL B. PRITCHETT MUSEUM
Bridgewater Community College (804) 828-2501

A collection of rare artifacts here includes a three-volume Bible printed in Venice in 1482 and a medieval book of Gregorian chants made and hand-copied by a monk. Admission is free; the museum is open Tuesday through Thursday 2 to 4 PM.

SHENANDOAH VALLEY HERITAGE MUSEUM

115 Bowman Rd., Dayton   *(540) 879-2681*

This museum has a 12-foot electric relief map of Stonewall Jackson's Valley Campaign of 1862. The map fills an entire wall and lets you see and hear the campaign battle by battle. The museum also displays many artifacts of the Shenandoah Valley's history. It is open Monday through Saturday from May 1 through October 9 AM to 4 PM and Sundays 1 to 4 PM. The rest of the year it is open only on weekends. Admission is $4 for adults and $2 for children ages 6 to 12.

Visual Arts

SAWHILL GALLERY

James Madison University   *(540) 568-6407*

This free gallery exhibits five or six shows of diverse art during the year. It's open seven days a week during the academic year, weekdays only during the summer. Call ahead to confirm hours.

Other Cultural Attractions

THE DANIEL HARRISON HOUSE (FORT HARRISON)

Dayton   *(540) 879-2280*

This historic stone house (c. 1749) just north of Dayton was a natural fort to which Daniel Harrison added a stockade and an underground passage to a nearby spring. What appear to be loopholes set in the house's stone walls for firing rifles at Indians gave rise to the name Fort Harrison. Free guided tours are available. The house is open 1 to 5 PM on weekends from late May through October, and for special events November to April. The house also hosts community events such as a Family Craft Weekend in June and the Dayton Autumn Festival in October.

LINCOLN HOMESTEAD

U.S. 42, Harrisonburg

Abraham Lincoln's father, Thomas Lincoln, was born in Rockingham County, and his ancestors were buried here in a little cemetery 7.5 miles north of Harrisonburg. The house now standing at the old Lincoln homestead is privately owned, so please respect that when you visit the cemetery.

Staunton, Waynesboro and Augusta County

Theater

FLETCHER COLLINS THEATER

Deming Hall, Mary Baldwin College
Staunton   *(540) 887-7189*

Every academic year, the theater department at this women's college produces five plays, from musicals such as Gilbert and Sullivan to Shakespeare and modern plays.

OAK GROVE PLAYERS

232 W. Frederick St.
Staunton   *(540) 885-6077*

This amateur theater company produces five plays every summer in the middle of a grove of oak trees 2 miles west of Verona. Founded in 1954 by Fletcher Collins, the retired head of Mary Baldwin College's theater department, Oak Grove Players is one of the oldest outdoor theaters in the country. A lot of patrons picnic on the grounds before the plays, which are mainly comedies. Admission is by season subscription only, although patrons are allowed to buy tickets for their out-of-town guests. The Oak Grove Players were the first to perform *The Nerd*, a play by the late Larry Shue, a native of Staunton.

SHENANARTS INC.
Staunton   *(540) 248-1868*

ShenanArts is a not-for-profit performing arts company that produces a variety of plays and musicals and hosts a retreat for playwrights every summer at the Pennyroyal Farm (c. 1808), just north of Staunton. Performances take place at the Pennyroyal Farm in warm weather and at McCormick's Cabaret at Frederick and Augusta streets in downtown Staunton in the winter. The arts corporation also offers theater programs for youth, one of which led to a full-blown production of a rock opera, *The Wall*, in 1992. A touring company performs throughout Virginia and West Virginia. One of the traveling shows is a play about AIDS geared for teens and performed entirely by teen-age actors. The annual Shenandoah Valley Playwrights Retreat has been going on for 19 years and hosts writers from all over the world.

WAYNESBORO PLAYERS
Waynesboro   *(540) 885-4668*

This is a nonprofit amateur theater group made up of actors from Waynesboro, Staunton and Augusta County. They perform three plays a year, in addition to some dinner theater offerings at Waynesboro-area restaurants. Most of the plays are performed at the Waynesboro High School auditorium. Contact Bill Robson at the above phone number.

Dance

SHENANDOAH CLOGGERS
Staunton Parks
and Recreation Dept.   *(540) 245-5727*

This group of about 26 dancers practices every Thursday night at Staunton's Gypsy Hill Park. They teach lessons to children and adults from about 6 to 6:45 PM, then practice until 9 PM. The cloggers perform for a variety of audiences, including nursing homes, civic meetings, arts festivals and parades.

Music

MID-ATLANTIC CHAMBER ORCHESTRA
Staunton   *(540) 885-1232*

This Washington, D.C.-based orchestra of professional musicians performs three or four times a year at the Robert E. Lee High School auditorium. Contact Bob Link at the above number for more information.

SHAKIN'
Staunton

All kinds of bands, from rock 'n' roll to country, perform downtown at Mary Baldwin College every other Friday during summer months from 5:30 to 7:30 PM. This is another freebie.

STONEWALL BRIGADE BAND
Gypsy Hill Park, Staunton

This is reportedly the oldest continuously performing band, having given its first concert before the Civil War. The local musicians perform every Monday at 8 PM during the summer months. There's no admission charge.

Museums

MUSEUM OF AMERICAN FRONTIER CULTURE
Exit 222 off I-81, then U.S. 250 W.
Staunton   *(540) 332-7850*

Somehow, "museum" doesn't seem an appropriate word for the living, breathing outdoor Museum of American Frontier Culture. Authentic farmsteads have been painstakingly brought from the Old

World and reconstructed here. Original gardens, hedges, pastures and even road layouts have been duplicated, along with the old ways of survival. You can tour Scotch-Irish, 17th-century German, early American and English farmsteads with a staff of knowledgeable, articulate interpreters. Also authentic are the farm animals, from lambs and chickens to cows and kittens, making this a fine attraction for children.

Throughout the year, the museum hosts dozens of special events, such as Lantern Tours at Christmas and the Traditional Frontier Festival in mid-September, with crafts, food and entertainment. The museum is open 9 AM to 5 PM daily for most of the year, and 10 AM to 4 PM December 1 through March 15. The facility is closed Thanksgiving, Christmas and New Year's days. Admission is $5 for adults, $4.50 for seniors and $2.50 for children. Special rates for groups of 15 or more are available.

P. Buckley Moss Museum

2150 Rosser Ave., Waynesboro (540) 949-6473
The museum dedicated to this former resident of Augusta County resembles many of the large houses built by early 19th-century settlers. Since the early 1960s, Moss has found her inspiration and much of her subject matter in Shenandoah Valley scenery and in the area's Amish and Mennonite people. Although the artist was born in New York, she moved here in the mid '60s.

Born with what later was diagnosed as dyslexia into a family of high achievers, Moss was ridiculed and taunted as a child for her lack of academic prowess. She hid her childhood sorrow in her painting, and eventually her family recognized her artistic genius. As a result, she now uses her foundation profits,

guided by the worldwide Moss Society, to help needy children. Whenever she travels, she makes it a point to visit pediatric hospital centers to encourage children.

The museum's displays examine the symbolism in her work and her sources. The museum and shop are just south of I-64 at the Waynesboro West Exit. The hours are 10 AM to 6 PM Monday through Saturday and 12:30 to 5:30 PM Sunday. Admission is free.

Woodrow Wilson Museum and Birthplace

18 to 24 N. Coalter St.
Staunton   (540) 885-0891
This museum is a tribute to our nation's 28th president, who was born here in 1856. The museum chronicles his life as a scholar, Princeton University president, governor and statesman. Seven exhibit galleries include rare artifacts, photographs, personal possessions and a replica of Wilson's study at Princeton. The displays do not shy away from the controversies Wilson generated in his lifetime, from the way in which he alienated wealthy trustees and alumni as Princeton's president to his lack of support for women's suffrage as America's president. Of course, the displays also highlight the reforms Wilson brought about as the nation's leader.

The museum houses Wilson's beloved Pierce-Arrow automobile, which is brought out yearly in the Happy Birthday USA parade down Main Street and also travels to the Pierce-Arrow Convention in California. His birthplace has been carefully restored to appear as it would have when he lived there as a child. Throughout the Greek Revival-style house are furniture, silver and other personal items belonging to the Wilsons and period pieces typical of Presbyterian manses in the antebellum era.

The museum and birthplace are open 9 AM to 5 PM daily in the summer months. Hours are 10 AM to 4 PM Monday through Saturday December through February except Thanksgiving, Christmas and New Year's days. Admission is $6 for adults and $2 for ages 6 to 12, with AAA and Seniors discounts.

Visual Arts

SHENANDOAH VALLEY ART CENTER
600 W. Main St.
Waynesboro   *(540) 949-7662*

This nonprofit cultural center, an affiliate of the Virginia Museum of Fine Arts, provides a forum for artists of all diversities to exhibit their works. Housed in a beautiful, old downtown former residence, the center holds art exhibits, music and drama performances, workshops and classes for children and adults. You'll also find readings of prose and poetry and even music appreciation lectures. The galleries are open 10 AM to 4 PM Tuesday through Saturday and 2 to 4 PM Sunday. Admission is free.

STAUNTON-AUGUSTA ART CENTER
I Gypsy Hill Park   *(540) 885-2028*

An old pump house at the entrance to the beautiful Gypsy Hill Park in Staunton is headquarters for this art center, an affiliate of the Virginia Museum. It puts on 10 exhibitions every year, some of which are shows on tour from the Virginia Museum. It also displays art by area elementary and high school students every May and exhibits works of local artists. In addition, the art center offers classes and workshops for children and adults throughout the year. It's open 9 AM to 5 PM weekdays and 10 AM to 2 PM Saturday. Admission is free.

VALLEY FRAMING STUDIO & GALLERY
328 W. Main St.   *(540) 943-7529*
Waynesboro   *(800) 821-7529*

Valley Framing Studio is the area's most comprehensive art gallery, carrying the largest inventory of art and artists' work in the Shenandoah Valley. The gallery specializes in limited edition prints and represents nearly 100 percent of the major print publishers in the art world. Work from artists such as Bev Doolittle, Robert Bateman, Steve Lyman, Charles Wysocki and Charles Frac is available here. Civil War or aviation art lovers will recognize works by Troiana, Kuntsler, Gallon, Harvey, Phillips and Kodera. Valley Framing also has an extensive inventory of local and regional artists' prints, bronzes and ceramics. The gallery is open year round from 10 AM to 5 PM Monday through Friday and 10 AM to 3 PM Saturday and by appointment.

Other Cultural Attractions

STATLER BROTHERS COMPLEX
501 Thornrose Ave.
Staunton   *(540) 885-7297*

The Statler Brothers, the world-famous country singers, make their home in Staunton and have their own museum and office complex in town. On display are mementos collected by the band in 25 years of performing. The museum is open 10:30 AM to 3:30 PM weekdays only. Free tours are given at 2 PM. A gift shop sells albums, cassettes, compact discs, T-shirts, sweaters and other souvenirs. A tip from those in the know: If you really want to see the Statler Brothers in the flesh, hang out until after the museum closes. That unusual tour time does serve a purpose. The band is on the road two weeks, then working at home two weeks. You may catch them leaving the building.

SWANNANOA
Afton Mountain, Waynesboro   (540) 942-5161

The romantic history behind the Swannanoa Marble Palace and Sculpture Garden is only one reason to visit this mountain-top estate, which was created by a railroad executive as a monument to his wife. More than 300 artisans used the best materials of their time (c. 1905) to create this palace as a replica of the Villa de Medici in Rome. The gardens and artwork (including a 4,000-piece Tiffany stained-glass window) have been faithfully maintained.

Today, Swannanoa is also headquarters of a New Age school of transcendental thinking, The University of Science and Philosophy, founded by Walter and Lao Russell, who rented the mansion in the late '40s. The Russells believe the estate was perched atop a sacred mountain and reopened the estate as a center for their belief in the Science of Man. The center offers correspondence courses and seminars.

The garden and palace are open to the public 9 AM to 5 PM daily. Admission is $5 per person.

Lexington

Visual Arts

ART FARM GALLERIES
Va. 39, near the Virginia
Horse Center   (540) 463-7961

Chinese artist and teacher I-Hsiung Ju started the Art Farm in 1975 as a "farm to raise young artists." A retired professor of art at nearby Washington and Lee University, Dr. Ju conducts summer workshops in the traditional Chinese method of painting. Students come from all over the country to live for a week at the farm and learn from Dr. Ju. The gallery is on the first floor of a rambling house and displays the artist's paintings. Many are reasonably priced; all are beautiful.

ARTISTS IN CAHOOTS
1 Washington St.   (540) 464-1147

This well-filled gallery is run by a cooperative of local artists and crafters who somehow manage to put out beautiful works of art at reasonable prices. The collection encompasses paintings, prints, etchings, photographs, ceramics, jewelry, decoys, sculpted art glass, wood and metal crafts. New in 1995 are more Sandage jewelry designs, the extraordinary metal sculptures of Milenko Katic, Virginia clay jewelry by Maureen Worth, Margaret Carroll's stained glass, works by photographer Nathan Beck and paintings by Ellie Penn and Anne Weed. New shorebird carvings and heron decoys by John Owen complete the array. The artists staff the shop themselves and extend a warm welcome, chatting with patrons as they create. The shop gift wraps for free, ships purchases and accepts most major credit cards.

Museums

GEORGE C. MARSHALL
MUSEUM AND LIBRARY
VMI Parade Grounds   (540) 463-7103

The Marshall Foundation was founded in 1953 at the suggestion of President Harry Truman to honor the memory of Gen. George C. Marshall, the only military hero to win a Nobel Peace Prize, for his plan to reconstruct Europe following World War II. Winston Churchill said of Marshall, "Succeeding generations must not be allowed to forget his achievements and his example." Marshall also was former Army Chief of Staff and Secretary of State and Defense.

Presidents Johnson and Eisenhower dedicated the museum in 1964. Visitors can see a stirring movie and striking photographic display, including the hauntingly stark, black and white photos of the faces of children of war-torn Europe. The museum is open from 9 AM to 5 PM March 1 through October 31 and closes one hour earlier November 1 through March 1. Admission is $3 for adults and $1 for children ages 7 to 18; a senior citizen discount is available. School groups and college students with a valid school I.D. are admitted free.

LEE CHAPEL AND MUSEUM
Washington and Lee University
Main St. (540) 463-8400

Civil War buffs won't want to miss the beautiful Lee Chapel and Museum, the focal point of the campus where the great Confederate served as president for five years after the war. Lee's remains are buried here, and you can see the famous Edward Valentine statue of a recumbent Lee. The museum is open 9 AM to 5 PM Monday through Saturday from April through October and closes one hour earlier October through April. Sunday hours are 2 to 5 PM.

STONEWALL JACKSON HOUSE
8 E. Washington Ave. (540) 463-2552

Stonewall Jackson House is the only home the famous Confederate general ever owned. Restored in 1979 by the Historic Lexington Foundation, the house is furnished with period pieces, including many of Jackson's personal possessions. The house, which is listed on the National Register of Historic Sites, is open to the public daily for guided tours of the rooms. In addition to tours and exhibits, the Stonewall Jackson House sponsors a variety of educational programs through the

Garland Gray Research Center and Library, on the office level of the museum. Educational activities include in-school programs, internships, lectures, workshops and scholarly symposia.

It is open 9 AM to 5 PM Monday through Saturday and 1 to 5 PM Sunday. Hours extend to 6 PM in June, July and August. The museum is closed on major holidays. Admission is $5 for adults and $2.50 for children ages 6 to 12.

VMI MUSEUM
VMI Parade Ground
N. Main St. (540) 464-7232

The VMI Museum, on the lower level of Jackson Hall on the VMI Campus, brings nation's history to life. Stonewall Jackson's horse, Little Sorrel, a taxidermist's work of art, probably is its most curious and popular display. Other exhibits tell American history through the lives and service of VMI faculty. Both Gen. Stonewall Jackson and Gen. George W. Custis Lee taught at VMI.

Open 9 AM to 5 PM Monday through Saturday and 2 to 5 PM Sunday, the museum is closed holidays.

Music

LENFEST CENTER
FOR THE PERFORMING ARTS
Washington and Lee Univ. (540) 463-8000

W&L's Lenfest Center is the cultural heart of Lexington, offering lively arts, including national performers in concert, W&L's own University-Rockbridge Symphony Orchestra and other music department performances. The center offers a Concert Guild Series, Theater Series and Lenfest Series featuring performances to appeal to all artistic tastes.

Theater

LIME KILN THEATRE

Lime Kiln Rd.
Box Office, 14 S. Randolph St.   (540) 463-3074

The Roanoke Times called it "one of the most agreeable spots in the Western World." Performances at the outdoor Theater at Lime Kiln celebrate the history and culture of the Southern mountains. What makes the place unique — even enchanting — is its setting in what was once a limestone quarry. Lime Kiln is best known for its annual musical, *Stonewall Country*, a rollicking tribute to local Civil War hero Thomas "Stonewall" Jackson. Robin and Linda Williams, favorites of Garrison Keillor's *A Prairie Home Companion* and longtime friends of Lime Kiln, wrote the music for *Stonewall Country* and audiences return year after year to experience this Shenandoah Valley summer tradition.

Also to be performed is *Glory Bound*, by local playwright Tom Ziegler, who also wrote *Apple Dreams*, which debuted to rave reviews at Lime Kiln in 1993. You can also catch the Family Folk Tale Festival, wholesome entertainment for the whole family, from August 22 to September 2, plus special matinee performances on August 20 and 27 at 2 PM.

Lime Kiln's popular Coors Concert Series always offers an eclectic slate of musicians. The schedule for the summer of 1995 includes Leo Kottke, Robin and Linda Williams, John McCutcheon and Mike Cross.

Lime Kiln has picnic areas with tables and grills and sells some food and drinks. The site is handicapped-accessible and has a Big Top Tent in case of bad weather, so performances take place rain or shine. Group rates are available.

The organization began sponsoring a Regional Playwriting contest two years ago to encourage the creation of plays relevant to this region and as an outreach to the community. During the fall, winter and spring, Lime Kiln's resident artists go to area schools, clubs and civic and senior groups and, when schedules permit, accept bookings throughout the summer as well.

Performances begin at 8 PM nightly. Plays run Tuesday through Saturday, and concerts are performed on Sunday.

Other Cultural Attractions

HISTORIC GARDEN WEEK
(540) 463-3777

History and garden aficionados flock to Lexington in the spring for its incomparable Historic Garden Week. Each April (the date changes yearly), civic-minded residents open their historic homes and gardens to an appreciative public. Many of the residences are furnished with family heirlooms and gorgeous antiques and have ornate gardens.

HOLIDAY IN LEXINGTON
(540) 463-3777

For one weekend in December, this 19th-century college town welcomes you to its historic downtown district sparkling with minilights and white candles. Events include tours of historic properties and homes, music, galas, theater and overall festivity. If you like Christmas in Williamsburg in eastern Virginia, try it western Virginia style.

HULL'S DRIVE-IN THEATRE
Va. 5   (540) 463-2621

One of the last auto drive-in theaters left in Virginia, Hull's is worth a visit for a dose of nostalgia. From the well-groomed grounds to the syrupy snowballs, Hull's Drive-In is one of the premier mom 'n' pop operations anywhere. Nothing's changed since 1950. It's open weekends at dusk mid-March through November.

McCormick Farm

Steeles Tavern   **(540) 377-2255**

This place, 20 miles north of Lexington, is the home of Cyrus McCormick, who invented the first successful mechanical reaper. McCormick Farm is part of the Virginia Tech College of Agricultural and Life Sciences and a Virginia Agricultural Experiment Station. Visitors may tour the blacksmith shop, gristmill, museum and McCormick family home.

McCormick was 22 when he invented the reaper in 1831. The invention launched a new era in agriculture, an age of mechanization that not only changed life on the farm but also made it possible for millions of people to leave the land and enter an industrial society.

The site is open 8:30 AM to 5 PM daily.

Mock Convention

Washington and Lee Univ.   **(540) 463-8460**

This is an event worth waiting for every four years. It's a tremendous party featuring a long, incredible parade straight from the '50s. Students try to outdo each other with outlandish floats. The 1992 extravaganza included an Elvis float with live donkeys in tow! It should be a mandatory event for all civics students.

Held only during presidential election years, W&L's nationally known Mock Convention in spring attracts national politicians and celebrities. It is written up internationally as "the nation's foremost and most-accurate predictor in presidential politics." The convention has earned this reputation by correctly predicting the presidential nominee 14 times in 19 attempts since its inception in 1908. It has been wrong only once since 1948 (predicting Edward Kennedy as the 1992 Democratic nominee). New York Gov. Mario Cuomo and former Speaker of the House Tip O'Neill were among the speakers of the 1992 convention.

The next convention is March 1 and 2, 1996.

Botetourt County

Museums

Botetourt Museum

Court House Complex
Fincastle   **(540) 992-8223**

Botetourt County (pronounced BOT-uh-tot), named in 1770 for Lord Botetourt of England, once stretched to the Mississippi River, encompassing what is now parts of West Virginia, Kentucky, Ohio, Indiana and Illinois. Fincastle was the

Insiders' Tips

Charlottesville is Virginia's prose and poetry capital, where the literati like symposiums and lectures sponsored by UVA's English department, visits to Edgar Allan Poe's restored UVA dormitory room and hanging out at the nearby Kafkafe with other budding Flannery O'Conners and William Faulkners.

The Elks' National Home in Bedford.

historic county seat. The museum, which attracts thousands of visitors annually, is sponsored by the Botetourt County Historical Society. Programs, especially those dealing with genealogy, are open to the public. The museum plays an important role in Historical Fincastle's annual fall Old Fincastle Festival, one of the largest festivals in the Roanoke Valley. Museum hours are 10 AM to 2 PM Tuesday and Thursday, 2 to 4 PM Sunday and upon request.

Craig County

Museums

CRAIG COUNTY MUSEUM
Main and Court Sts.
New Castle   No Phone

Dedicated Craig County residents are lovingly restoring this c. 1910, three-story brick hotel as a repository for Craig County's past. They've already restored a bedroom to just as it was in the old hotel and have established a genealogy library for those tracing their roots in this rural, scenic town. Operated by the Craig

County Historical Society, which also sponsors the Craig County Fall Festival in October, the museum's potential as a first-class attraction is just beginning to be fulfilled. It is open Monday through Wednesday 1 to 4 PM.

Roanoke

Visual Arts

THE ARTS COUNCIL OF THE BLUE RIDGE
Center in the Square, Center
on Church, Level I
20 E. Church Ave.   (540) 342-5790

The heart and soul of the cultural community in the Roanoke region, this council provides services and information to its 75 member organizations and artists throughout the Blue Ridge region. Programs include a quarterly newsletter; the City Art Show, a regional juried art exhibition held annually; Center Scholars, an arts program for high school students; Art in the Window, which offers free display space for artists and children; and the Perry Kendig Award for outstanding support of the arts.

In 1994 the Council published "Blueprint 2000," the first community-wide cultural plan in the region. Office hours are Monday through Friday 9 AM to 3 PM.

ART MUSEUM OF WESTERN VIRGINIA
Center in the Square, Levels 1 and 2
1 Market Square   *(540) 342-5760*

The Art Museum of Western Virginia is a gathering place for the large colony of Valley artists who migrate here both for the beauty and for the artistic opportunities. Permanent galleries emphasize American art of the 19th and 20th centuries. The sculpture court holds impressive works, and the folk art gallery features works by artisans of the southern mountains. Museum education programs feature dialogues, family days, tours, films, performances, classes and workshops. Its rotating exhibitions are of regional, national and international significance. Art Venture is an interactive art center for children. You can purchase regional American crafts and folk art in the museum store.

The museum is open 10 AM to 5 PM Tuesday through Saturday and 1 to 5 PM on Sunday. Art Venture is open Saturday 10 AM to 2 PM. Admission to all galleries is free.

Museums

HARRISON MUSEUM OF AFRICAN AMERICAN CULTURE
523 Harrison Ave. N. W.   (540) 345-4818

A Roanoke showcase for African-American culture, the Harrison Museum is on the Virginia Historic Landmarks Register as the first public high school for black students in western Virginia.

The museum's stated mission is to research, preserve and interpret the achievements of African Americans, spe-

cifically in western Virginia, and to provide an opportunity for all citizens to come together in appreciation, enjoyment and greater knowledge of African American culture.

Since its opening in 1985, the museum has offered art and historical exhibits in its galleries and the Hazel B. Thompson Exhibition Room. The permanent collection of local artifacts and memorabilia has grown from a few objects to several thousand. Thanks to the generosity of donors, Harrison Museum owns an impressive African collection, which includes masks, bronze sculptures, paintings, furniture and textiles. Several traveling exhibits and displays may be borrowed by schools and organizations.

One of its most popular undertakings is the annual Henry Street Heritage Festival held on the last Saturday in September. It's a festive celebration of African-American heritage; it was held on the Henry Street site for its first four years, then relocated to Elmwood Park in downtown Roanoke in 1994.

The Museum store and gift shop offers Afrocentric art, books, cards, jewelry and African art. Museum hours are 10 AM to 5 PM Tuesday through Friday and 1 to 5 PM Saturday and Sunday. For group tours, contact the curator.

ROANOKE VALLEY HISTORICAL SOCIETY AND MUSEUM
Center in the Square, Level 1 and 3
1 Market Square   (540) 342-5770

The rich heritage of Roanoke unfolds before you in the galleries of the Roanoke Valley Historical Society and Museum, run by a dedicated group of preservationists. Prehistoric artifacts acquaint you with life in the Valley before Colonial settlement, through the frontier era and boom days of the Norfolk & Western Railroad and into the present. You will see a re-creation of an 1890 country store and fashions from the 1700s to the 1990s.

A permanent World War II exhibit opened in August 1995. It illustrates the impact of the war on Roanoke and the role of the Virginia National Guards, 116th Infantry 29th Division, which landed on Omaha Beach on D-Day and fought through to the end of the war in Europe.

Museum members conduct tours of historic sites offered to the public. Its shop, Past Presents, on the first floor, sells hand-made quilts, historical maps, genealogi-cal charts and vintage toys. You can also buy the dogwood pattern china used at Hotel Roanoke.

Hours of operation are 10 AM to 4 PM Tuesday through Friday, 10 AM to 5 PM Saturday and 1 to 5 PM Sunday. Ad-mission is $2 for adults, $1 for seniors and children ages 6 to 12 and free for those younger than 5.

THE SALEM MUSEUM
801 E. Main St., Salem   (540) 389-6760
The Salem Museum is in the Williams-Brown House. That's easy. What was a little difficult for awhile was finding the Williams-Brown House, c. 1840, which was slated to be torn down until a group of Sa-lem residents towed it from its original lo-cation to a safer destination just a quarter of a mile away.

Run by volunteers of the Salem His-torical Society, the museum focuses on a range of topics, from adventures and hardships of the Civil War to the leisure of a summer sojourn at the Lake Spring Resort Hotel. A gift shop and a gallery for rotating historical exhibits are also on the premises.

Hours are 10 AM to 4 PM Tuesday

through Friday and noon to 5 PM Satur-day. Admission is free.

SCIENCE MUSEUM OF WESTERN VIRGINIA AND HOPKINS PLANETARIUM
Center in the Square, Levels 1, 4 and 5
1 Market Square   (540) 342-5710
The Science Museum is a fun place for adults and children to explore the wonders of science through such hands-on experiences as broadcasting a weather report and seeing yourself on TV, or vis-iting the touch tank and Tot and Parent Learning Center. You can touch light-ning in the Physics Arcade and see the stars in Hopkins Planetarium, where you'll explore the reaches of the universe and then come back down to Earth for lectures, movies and special events such as technology expos and wildflower pil-grimages. Children also like the first-floor Science Museum Shop, which sells edu-cational toys that are so much fun kids don't have a clue that they're learning while they play.

Exhibits change frequently, ranging from roaring mechanical dinosaurs and real sharks to animated life-size animals of the future. The first-class planetarium has hosted dancing laser shows and imagina-tive narratives on the creation of Earth and the stars. It's a great place to spend an af-ternoon in Roanoke.

The museum is open 10 AM to 5 PM Monday through Saturday and 1 to 5 PM Sunday. Admission is $5 for adults, $4 for senior citizens and $3 for ages 3 to 12. With exhibits the Planetarium is an ad-ditional $1.25 and without it's only $2.50.

CATHOLIC CHURCH MUSEUM
624 N. Jefferson St.   (540) 362-2245
The history of the Catholic Church in the Roanoke area is depicted in artifacts and memorabilia in this three-room

museum in the former Saint Vincent's Orphan Asylum and Convent on the grounds of Saint Andrew's Church, a landmark structure built in 1900. The impressive Gothic-style building looms above the downtown commercial landscape. The museum facilitates research into the history of the Roanoke area through cemetery and orphanage records and files maintained on the Catholic churches and their members in the region, as well as through its library collection. You can buy religious articles and books here.

Operated by the Catholic Historical Society of the Roanoke Valley, the museum is open 10:30 AM to 2 PM Tuesday or by appointment.

FIFTH AVENUE
PRESBYTERIAN CHURCH WINDOW
301 Patton Ave. N. W.   *(540) 342-0264*

In 1903 the Rev. Lylburn Downing, pastor of Fifth Avenue Presbyterian, an African-American church, commissioned a stained-glass window to honor Confederate general Stonewall Jackson. The Rev. Mr. Downing had been a member of the Sunday School class Jackson had established for slaves at his own church in Lexington. Although the church burned down in the 1920s, the unusual window was spared and then included in the rebuilt church, where it serves today as a symbol of racial harmony.

The window may be viewed Tuesday and Thursday from 10 to 11 AM.

TO THE RESCUE
NATIONAL EXHIBITION
Tanglewood Mall
430 Electric Rd. S.W.   *(540) 776-0364*

To the Rescue, the only permanent national exhibition dedicated to volunteer lifesaving, brings an international spotlight to Roanoke as the birthplace of the rescue squad movement. As a nine-year-old Roanoker, Julian Stanley Wise never forgot standing helplessly by as two men drowned when their canoe capsized on the Roanoke River. He vowed then that he would organize a group of volunteers who could be trained in lifesaving. He did. In 1928 he and his crew of NW Railway workers became the first volunteer rescue squad in America to use both medical techniques and transport on victims. Later, they were the first to use iron lungs during the polio epidemics that struck the country. They pioneered the Holger method of lifesaving and modern day cardiopulmonary resuscitation.

The creation of the exhibit, which includes dramatic hands-on interactive videos and displays, was overseen by famous museum expert Conover Hunt, a Virginia native whose last project was The Sixth Floor, the JFK Museum in Dallas. The quality and brilliance shows. The exhibit includes artifacts from 31 states and three countries. To the Rescue also houses the National Rescue Hall of Fame, which recognizes Emergency Medical Services heroes during National EMS Week each May. Additionally, the exhibit includes the National EMS Memorial, recognizing 38 men and women from 14 states who gave their lives while saving others.

Hours of operation are 10 AM to 4 PM Tuesday through Friday, 10 AM to 5 PM Saturday and 1 to 5 PM Sunday. Admission is $1.

VIRGINIA'S EXPLORE PARK
3900 Rutrough Rd.   *(540) 427-1800*

Virginia's Explore Park, a living history museum and nature center at Mile

115 on the Blue Ridge Parkway, allows visitors to experience the rich cultural heritage and natural beauty of western Virginia just minutes from Roanoke. The park features authentic homes, barns, a schoolhouse, a blacksmith/wheelwright shop and other structures in the Blue Ridge Settlement where living history interpreters demonstrate the lifeways of 19th-century settlers while encouraging visitor participation. Attractions also include a live exhibit on regional American Indian culture and an 18th-century frontier life exhibit. In addition, 6 miles of hiking trails are available that wind through beautiful river gorge scenery and wooded areas.

Special events, such as Fort Days, 18 century Militia Days, the Fall Foliage Festival, Christmas at Explore, classes and workshops take place throughout the year. Call for details on upcoming events and a Explore Events Calendar.

The park is open 9 AM to 5 PM Saturday through Monday from April through October. Admission is $4 for adults and $2.50 for students ages 6 to 18. Group rates are available.

VIRGINIA MUSEUM OF TRANSPORTATION
303 Norfolk Ave. (540) 342-5670

Roanoke displays its railroad heritage at this museum in a restored freight station next to the Norfolk & Southern mainline. Exhibits chronicle the formation of transportation over several generations, putting you face to face with steam engines, vintage electronic locomotives and classic diesels. You can climb on board a caboose and stroll through a railway post office car. The J611 Steam Locomotive is on permanent display at the museum.

Inside, walk down Main Street to see early autos, freight trucks, fire engines and carriages. You'll see the way passenger cars looked at their peak in the '40s, before the automobile took over as king of the highways. Don't miss the carved wooden miniature circus with thousands of figurines and the largest collection of museum rolling stock on the entire East Coast. The gift shop sells prints, books and toys for railway buffs. The museum hosts special events including the Roanoke Railway Festival.

The site is open 10 AM to 5 PM Monday through Saturday and noon to 5 PM Sunday. It's closed on Monday in January and February. Admission is $4 for adults, $3 for senior citizens, $2 for students and $1.75 for children ages 3 to 12.

Music

OPERA ROANOKE
541 Luck St.
The Jefferson Center (540) 982-2742

Standing ovations are the norm for Opera Roanoke, Southwest Virginia's professional opera company. Led by general director Craig Fields, the company engages up-and-coming singers in innovative productions. Opera Roanoke presents its productions at Roanoke's Mill Mountain Theatre and at Roanoke College's Olin Theater in Salem. Favorites such as Mozart's *The Marriage of Figaro*, Verdi's *Rigoletto* and Puccini's *Madam Butterfly* are showcased with top talent, who portray the passion, humor, beauty and tragedy of life. Breaking away from the tried and true at times, the company recently presented the world premiere of former artistic director Victoria Bond's composition *Travels*.

Opera Roanoke goes an extra step by projecting English translation supertitles over the stage to be sure that opera goers can follow every turn of the plot. "What's Opera, Doc?", Opera Talk and Director's

Photo: Ferrum College

Items from the Blue Ridge Folk Instruments and their Makers exhibit at Ferrum College.

Notes enlighten, education and entertain both the novice and opera buff.

THE ROANOKE SYMPHONY ORCHESTRA
541 Luck Ave., Ste. 200   (540) 343-6221
Quality performances, superb musi-

cians, innovative programs and exceptional guest artists are the hallmarks of the Roanoke Symphony Orchestra, founded in 1953 and the only professional orchestra in Virginia west of the Blue Ridge Mountains. In addition to the standard classical repertoire, programs include country-western, rhythm and blues, and jazz. Regional and national grants allow the orchestra to reach a younger audience, and the Symphony also gives concerts and programs designed especially for families and students.

The RSO has welcomed a diverse roster of guest artists, including Marian McPartland, Liona Boyd, Awadagin Pratt, Billy Taylor, Leontyne Price, Chet Atkins, Roberta Flack, Tony Bennett, Willie Nelson and Leon Bates. Each year, the Symphony invites the winner of the prestigious Naumberg Competition to perform with the orchestra. In 1994 the orchestra performed with the Moody Blues on their 25th Anniversary Days of Future Passed Tour in Roanoke. The *New York Times, The Wall Street Journal, NBC Today Show, ABC Evening News* and *NPR's Performance Today* have featured the RSO.

The RSO is preparing to hire a new music director/conductor. Finalists for the position will lead the orchestra at home and on tour on the 1995-96 season. September 1996 will mark the debut season with a new maestro.

Theater

GRANDIN MOVIE THEATRE
1310 Grandin Rd.   (540) 345-6177

Yes, you *can* see a movie in a gorgeous cinematic theater like the ones that prevailed years ago throughout America before being doomed to the wrecking ball. Julie Hunsaker and the Lindsey family have rescued this fine structure, one of Roanoke's greatest cultural treasures. Comedian Bill Murray of *Saturday Night Live* and *Ghostbusters* fame did a benefit for the Grandin, remarking that places

like the Grandin should never be forgotten or destroyed. You can see classics and newer movies for the best prices in town, often 99¢ specials. This cavernous, popcorn-scented architectural masterpiece will thrill its guests, especially children who have never seen anything quite like the tiled floors, mahogany candy cases and ornate decor of the Grandin.

MILL MOUNTAIN THEATRE
Main State and Theatre B
Center in the Square, Level I
Box Office   (540) 342-5740

"New York quality in the Blue Ridge" is how this year-round professional theater has been characterized. Operating under a letter of agreement contract with Actor's Equity Association, the Theatre has become known as one of the best regional theaters in the country based upon its new and original works, lavish musicals, innovative classics, creative children's plays and musicals, and dramas.

Each October, the annual New Play Competition culminates in the finalists' plays being presented in the Theatre B facility as part of the Norfolk Southern Festival of New Works. A family-oriented musical is scheduled for the winter holiday season, followed by a classic later in the winter. Spring ushers in a comedy or drama followed by two musicals in the summer. Tickets are reasonably priced and vary according to performance date and time.

In addition, once a month from October through June, the Theatre presents a free script-in-hand reading of a new play at a "bring-your-lunch" noon series. Educational and drama enrichment programs round out the offerings.

Mill Mountain Theatre recently celebrated its 30th anniversary. It now attracts performers such as Donna

McKechnie, the Tony Award-winning star of *A Chorus Line*, who chose the Theatre for a pre-New York tryout. Others, such as Robert Fulghum (who worked with the Theatre to develop a dramatization of his books), Sheldon Harnick and Stephen Schwartz have all been in residence at MMT.

Other Cultural Attractions

CENTER IN THE SQUARE

1 Market Square   *(540) 342-5700*

This complex is the home of Art Museum of Western Virginia, the Arts Council of the Blue Ridge, Mill Mountain Theatre, Roanoke Valley History Museum and the Science Museum of Western Virginia and Hopkins Planetarium. Resident organizations' hours vary.

Roanoke's Center in the Square, visited by nearly 400,000 annually, is unique in America. It is the best-attended cultural center in western Virginia, attracting even more patrons than Richmond's Valentine Museum. Five resident organizations coexist in a restored 1914 warehouse anchoring Roanoke's historic city market. A sculptural spiral staircase symbolizes how these five organizations have come together to create a richer cultural life in western Virginia. A confetti-like sculpture, a gift by the famed Dorothy Gillespie, hangs on one wall. In the heart of shops, galleries and restaurants, Center in the Square is the binding cultural tie in the life of a growing, vibrant downtown and a "must see" while in Roanoke. You can make some great buys on items with a science, art or history theme in the Center's three member stores.

JEFFERSON CENTER

540 Campbell Ave. S.W.   *(540) 343-2624*

The Jefferson Center opened its doors in August of 1993, the result of the Center Foundation's fund-raising efforts to refurbish Roanoke's grand old Jefferson High School, which had stood empty for years. Within its walls is a wide variety of tenants: a Police Academy, Opera Roanoke, the Roanoke Symphony offices, Habitat for Humanity and others. The "J" Room is full of memorabilia, such as trophies, awards and annuals from Jefferson High's alumni. The Foundation even revived the school's old newsletter, the "Jefferson News," to carry information about reunions and events.

MINIATURE GRACELAND

605 Riverland Dr.   *(540) 56-ELVIS*

The King lives! You'll find him in miniature in this Southeast Roanoke neighborhood beneath the Mill Mountain Star, rockin' — revolving, actually — in perpetual glory on the stage of a miniature auditorium before an audience of adoring Barbies. Kim and Don Epperly's private collection has attracted visitors from 14 countries. In the spring of 1995, it seemed as if the entire community turned out to help the Epperlys spruce the place up, since both have been ill. We're pleased to say everything looks great again.

Kim Epperly, editor of the international "The Wonder of You" newsletter, dedicated to the late Elvis Presley, is the heart and soul behind keeping the memory of the entertainer alive. Her husband has crafted replicas of Presley's estate, which fill their side yard. The display is lighted nightly and fans are invited to stroll through the grounds and hear an Elvis song wafting over the loudspeaker.

In 1994, the Epperlys consented to show their private collection at an opening on January 10, Presley's birthday, at the Roanoke Valley History Museum. It was a blockbuster!

Inside the basement of her home, Epperly maintains her own personal museum of Elvis artifacts, including "Love Me Tender" shampoo and conditioner, full-size mannequins sculpted with auto body compound to look like Elvis' features and newspaper clippings of when the King first visited Roanoke. Each year, the Epperlys add something new to the yard. Don Epperly has done most of the construction from scrap wood, based on pictures or descriptions from his wife. They just finished up his airport and a privacy fence. Soon, Sun Studios will be added and the Civic Center will be moved to the back. Visitors are welcome anytime.

East of the Blue Ridge

Leesburg

Other Cultural Attractions

MORVEN PARK
(540) 777-2414

The Greek Revival mansion and estate, which was once the home of Virginia governor Westmoreland Davis, stands just to the west of Leesburg. The house is furnished with fine antiques and curios that the Davises collected on their travels around the world. On the grounds are gardens, an extensive carriage museum and a Museum of Hounds and Hunting, which contains foxhunting memorabilia from Colonial days.

The estate, maintained through a trust established by the late Mrs. Davis, is one of the country's finest equestrian centers, staging fall and spring steeplechase races, horse shows, three-day events, foxhunts

and carriage competitions. Morven Park's mansion, gardens, Museum of Hounds and Hunting and Mrs. Robert C. Winmill Carriage Collection are open to visitors Tuesday through Sunday noon to 5 PM from April 1 to October 31 (weekends only in November). There is a small admission fee to the mansion (see the Horse Country Activities section in our Other Attractions chapter for more information).

OATLANDS
U.S. 15 S.
Leesburg   *(540) 777-3174*

This magnificent Federal/Greek Revival-style house was built in 1803 by a descendent of Robert "King" Carter using bricks molded on the property and wood from a nearby forest. The 261-acre estate has historic formal gardens in which something always seems to be blooming. Oatlands is a striking venue for spring and fall steeplechases, the popular Oatlands Sheepdog Trials in May and other events. Hours are 10 AM to 4:30 PM Tuesday through Saturday and 1 to 4:30 PM Sunday. Admission to the mansion is $6 for adults, children younger than 12 free; gardens, $3 for adults, children free. Special events are slightly more, but include the mansion and garden fees.

Washington and Sperryville

Theater and Music

THE THEATRE AT WASHINGTON
Gay and Jett Sts.
Washington   *(540) 675-1253*

This is the site of cultural activities ranging from high-quality films to plays and performances by gospel choirs, chamber music ensembles, folk rockers and other musical groups.

THE OLD TOWN HALL

Gay St., Washington   *(540) 675-1616*

This is actually a performing arts center that serves as home to two touring groups: the music group Trapezoid and the Ki Theatre, a multimedia performance troupe made up of leaders in the fields of theater, dance, music, storytelling and the visual arts. The artists create and perform original theatrical productions.

The building, formerly an old Methodist church, draws the entire community the first weekend in December, when Christmas nativity plays are performed by more than 30 locals.

Old Town Hall hosts a popular exchange program in which artists from across the country (and sometimes from other parts of the world) perform January through April on the third Sunday of the month. At the end of each show, the audience has an opportunity to converse with the performers.

Visual Arts

MIDDLE STREET GALLERY

Corner of Gay and Middle Sts.
Washington   *(540) 675-3440*

This nonprofit artists' cooperative features museum-quality paintings, photography and sculpture. Exhibitions change monthly, and classes are offered for adults and children. The gallery is open Friday through Sunday from 11 AM to 6 PM and by appointment.

Charlottesville and Surrounding Area

Theater

COMMUNITY CHILDREN'S THEATRE

(804) 971-5671

For 40 years this company has brought affordable family theater to the Charlottesville community. Performances often sell out well in advance, but individual tickets, when available, are sold at the door an hour before curtain and at other locations. The Theatre offers free children's workshops in the winter. Performances are held at the Charlottesville Performing Arts Center.

FOUR COUNTY PLAYERS

(540) 832-5355

This theater company out of Barboursville produces Shakespearean plays, full-scale musicals and children's productions. In August Shakespeare productions are staged in a most magical setting: the ruins of what was once the estate of James Barbour, governor of Virginia (1812 to 1814), Secretary of War and ambassador to the Court of St. James. Thomas Jefferson, a friend of Barbour's, designed the house, but it was destroyed by fire on Christmas Day, 1884. Overgrown boxwoods tower over the ruins, adding to the air of enchantment about the place. The award-winning Barboursville Vineyards are within walking distance.

In cooler months, Four County Players operates a dinner theater in conjunction with Toliver House in Gordonsville.

HERITAGE REPERTORY THEATRE

1 Culbreth Rd., UVA
Charlottesville   *(804) 924-3376*

This highly praised theater produces a series of plays every summer at the University of Virginia.

LIVE ARTS

609 E. Market St.
Charlottesville   *(804) 977-4177*

Live Arts, one block off the downtown mall, is home to a resident theater company, the Live Arts Theater Ensemble. LATE are produces everything from original avant-garde plays to well-known

Broadway musicals. LATE began several years ago in Charlottesville and aims to become a professional theater. The center hosts theater, dance, poetry readings and music events and provides a space in which other groups may perform.

THE OLD MICHIE THEATRE
609 E. Market St.   (804) 977-3690

This is home to theater and puppetry arts for children and teens in Central Virginia. A summer theater school offers weeks of instruction in drama, music, storytelling, puppetry and clowning. The theater also produces summer musicals.

UNIVERSITY OF VIRGINIA
DEPARTMENT OF DRAMA
(804) 924-3376

This is UVA's main student theater group, producing six major stage shows every academic year. The UVA Spanish Theater Group also performs plays entirely in Spanish every spring. Productions have included *All My Sons* by Arthur Miller, *My Three Sisters* by Anton Chekhov and *Top Girls*, a contemporary satire by Cary Churchhill.

Dance

CHIHAMBA
(804) 296-4986

The Chihamba of Dancescape celebrates and educates people about African cultures through music and dance. Ongoing programs include concerts, lecture demonstrations, workshops and African craft sessions in beading, weaving, tie-dying, leather work, mask making and sand painting.

DANCESCAPE
(804) 296-4986

Dancescape not only offers instruction in various African art forms (see Chihamba, above), it also gives classes in flatfoot clogging, modern dance and jazz to adults, teens and children. One of the instructors hails from Guinea, West Africa. Mohammed Dacosta danced for several dance companies before moving to Charlottesville. Another instructor, Sheila Stone, apprentices with a 78-year-old flatfooter who lives near Elkins, West Virginia.

THE MIKI LISZT DANCE COMPANY
(804) 973-3744

Based at the McGuffey Art Center, this nonprofit company performs annual dance concerts, conducts workshops with guest artists and offers lectures and demonstrations in nursing homes, schools, hospitals, libraries and museums. The company also sponsors the annual Community Children's Dance Festival.

Music

ASH LAWN-HIGHLAND
(804) 293-9539

The restored home and gardens of President James Monroe host a chamber music series every summer, as well as three light operas. Other special events throughout the year bring pianists, singers and dancers who perform to 18th-century music.

CHARLOTTESVILLE AND
UNIVERSITY SYMPHONY ORCHESTRA
112 Old Cabell Hall   (804) 924-6505

Seventy musicians form this volunteer orchestra, which has received rave reviews. Professional principal musicians perform alongside outstanding student and community players. Concerts are held in the Cabell Hall auditorium on the historic lawn at UVA.

CHARLOTTESVILLE GAMELAN ENSEMBLE
(804) 979-4818

This group performs traditional Javanese music, as well as more contemporary American Gamelan, using various bronze gongs and xylophone-type instruments.

OLD CABELL HALL
UVA *(804) 924-3984*

Situated at the south end of the famous college lawn, this auditorium is the scene of concerts throughout the year, from avant-garde jazz to chamber music. The Tuesday Evening Concert Series, a Charlottesville tradition for more than four decades, has presented such artists as Yo Yo Ma, the Tokyo String Quartet and the Juilliard String Quartet.

ORATORIO SOCIETY OF CHARLOTTESVILLE-ALBEMARLE
(804) 286-2150

Central Virginia's largest community chorus performs major classical choral works in at least one concert annually.

THE PRISM COFFEEHOUSE
214 Rugby Rd. *(804) 97-PRISM*

This nonprofit volunteer organization presents folk, traditional and acoustic concerts in a casual smoke-free, alcohol-free setting. Formed in 1966, the Prism is one of America's oldest surviving coffeehouses. The first Thursday of every month is devoted to jazz with different guest performers at each session. Every second Thursday brings a fast-moving In-the-Round performance in which four musicians share the stage, taking turns playing original songs. The Coffeehouse hosts concerts each weekend, and local songwriters meet here for jam sessions. It's a happening place; call for advance tickets.

THE SWEET ADELINES
(804) 973-7203 night, 924-0276 day

This a four-part harmony barbershop chorus for women only. They perform around town and compete in barbershop events nationally. All women interested in barbershop harmony are invited to attend.

THE WESTMINSTER ORGAN CONCERT SERIES
(804) 293-3133

Held every year at Westminster Presbyterian Church, this series of concerts offers organ music combined with other instruments and singers. Concerts are free.

YOUTH ORCHESTRA OF CHARLOTTESVILLE-ALBEMARLE
(804) 924-6505

This orchestra has been around for more than a decade, providing the best in musical direction and coaching for elementary and high school musicians. It includes a youth orchestra, jazz ensemble, string ensemble and the Evans Orchestra for younger musicians.

Museums

BAYLY ART MUSEUM
Rugby Rd. *(804) 924-3592*

The University of Virginia's own modern museum has a permanent collection of ancient pottery, sculpture and some paintings, along with special, short-term exhibitions. String quartets and other classical music groups perform here at certain times during the year. Admission is free, and the museum is open Tuesday through Sunday from 1 to 5 PM.

JAMES MADISON MUSEUM

129 Caroline St.
Orange   *(540) 672-1776*

The downtown museum offers four permanent exhibits celebrating the life and times of Madison and his important contributions to the American political system. Artifacts include furnishings from his nearby home, Montpelier, some of his presidential correspondence and a few of Dolley Madison's belongings. The museum is open year round on weekdays from 9 AM to 4 PM and weekends from 1 to 4 PM, March through November. There's a nominal admission fee.

THE VIRGINIA DISCOVERY MUSEUM

Downtown Mall   *(804) 977-1025*

On the east end of the mall is a dynamic place for children and their families, filled with hands-on exhibits, science programs, costumes in which the children can play dress-up and a real cabin from Rockingham County. Special exhibits change every few months. An art room with an array of materials invites children to create at their own pace, and a gallery space displays their creations for about three weeks. The facility is open Tuesday through Saturday from 10 AM to 5 PM and Sunday 1 to 5 PM. Admission is $4 for adults and $3 for seniors and children younger than 13.

WALTON'S MOUNTAIN MUSEUM

Schuyler Community Center, Va. 617
Schuyler   *(804) 831-2000*

Earl Hamner, whose early years were chronicled in the popular television series, grew up in tiny Schuyler. The museum dedicated to Hamner and the Waltons opened to great fanfare several years ago in the same school where the Hamner youngsters learned their ABCs. The museum, made possible by a state grant and support from Hamner and community leaders, is actually a series of former classrooms that recreate sets from the television program. You'll find copies of actual scripts, photo displays that juxtapose Hamner's real family with the television actors, and all manner of memorabilia. Visitors can also watch a video documentary of interviews with Hamner, former cast members and episodes from one of the most endearing television series ever. The school is a stone's throw from the old Hamner homestead.

Schuyler is between Charlottesville and Lynchburg, a few miles off U.S. 29. From the first Saturday in March through the last Sunday in November (excluding major holidays), museum hours are 10 AM to 4 PM. Admission is $4 for adults and $3 for seniors and groups of 20. Children 12 and younger are admitted free.

Visual Arts

BETH GALLERY AND PRESS

Barboursville   *(540) 832-3565*

Artist Frederick Nichols Jr. has his studio and gallery here just off U.S. 33 in a renovated general store across from the railroad tracks. He calls his work "photo-impressionism." He does enormous colorful landscapes of Blue Ridge scenes using either oil paint or a silk-screen process. A friendly fellow, Nichols will give tours through the gallery and studio on the weekends and during the week when he's open. Nichols' career took off a few years ago when he won top honors at an international print exhibition in Japan.

FAYERWEATHER GALLERY

Rugby Rd.   *(804) 924-6122*

This university gallery next to the Bayley Art Museum has regular exhibits by faculty and student artists, so it's naturally where the staff of the UVA Art Department likes to hang out. Admission is free, and it's open Monday through Friday from 9 AM to 5 PM.

FRANCES CHRISTIAN BRAND GALLERIES
111 Washington Ave.   *(804) 295-5867*

Call before you drop by this eclectic gallery, which is actually a private home containing the art collection of Frances Christian Brand, now deceased. Cynthia Brand, her granddaughter, lives here and likes to have people over for coffee while they admire the rooms full of pre-Colombian pottery, Mexican art, African masks and sculptures, and paintings done by Frances Brand.

McGUFFEY ART CENTER
201 Second St. N.W.   *(804) 295-7973*

This center, in a renovated elementary school within walking distance from historic Court Square and the downtown pedestrian mall, is an arts cooperative that began in 1975 with city support. Its light, airy rooms have been transformed into more than 40 studios where you can some-

times watch artists work. There are also three galleries and a gift shop. Exhibits, tours and gallery talks are available to the public year round. The center offers classes in children's art, printing, painting and drawing.

NEWCOMB HALL ARTS SPACE
University of Virginia   *(804) 924-3601*

This student-run gallery in the UVA Student Union building is open daily from noon to 9 PM and admission is free. The ever-changing variety of art on display has included the heartbreaking AIDS quilt.

PIEDMONT VIRGINIA COMMUNITY COLLEGE
Va. 20 and I-64   *(804) 977-3900, Ext. 203*

An art gallery here has regular exhibits by student and professional artists. Admission is free, and the gallery is open from 8 AM to 10 PM weekdays.

Photo: Va. Division of Tourism

Point of Honor in Lynchburg shows visitors what it was like in the days of Dr. George Cabell Sr., Patrick Henry's physician.

JORDAN ART GALLERY

Greenwood   (540) 456-8465

Exhibits, which change every two months, include the work of award-winning national and international artists and some local folk too. The gallery is part of an upscale shop specializing in antiques and quality reproductions. It's on U.S. 250 W., 16 miles from Charlottesville, at the foot of the Blue Ridge Mountains. The gallery is open seven days a week, 9 AM to 5 PM year round.

Other Cultural Attractions

ASH LAWN-HIGHLAND

Charlottesville   (804) 293-9539

This 535-acre estate was the home of James Monroe, our nation's fifth president, who fought in the American Revolution under George Washington and went on to hold more offices than any other U.S. president.

As ambassador to France, Monroe negotiated with Napoleon for the Louisiana Purchase, which doubled the size of the country. During his presidency, Monroe established the nation's first comprehensive foreign policy, later called the Monroe Doctrine, to prevent further European colonization of the Americas.

Ash Lawn-Highland is about 2 miles from Thomas Jefferson's Monticello, off I-64. Many of Monroe's possessions are in the mansion, and his boxwood gardens, now occupied by magnificent peacocks, are carefully tended. Livestock, vegetable and herb gardens, and Colonial craft demonstrations depict life 200 years ago on the plantation.

Special events include summer operas performed in English, an early American festival, Plantation Days on the Fourth of July weekend and Christmas candlelight tours.

The Monroe estate is owned and maintained as a working farm by Monroe's alma mater, the College of William and Mary. Ash Lawn-Highland is open daily 9 AM to 6 PM March through October and 10 AM to 5 PM daily from November through February. Admission is $6 for adults, $5.50 for seniors and $3 for children ages 6 to 11. A special President's Pass costing $17 (seniors $15.50) includes Ash Lawn-Highland, Monticello and Michie Tavern.

MICHIE TAVERN

Charlottesville   (804) 977-1234

Historic Michie Tavern (pronounced "micky") is one of the oldest homesteads remaining in Virginia and was originally set along a well-worn stagecoach route near Earlysville, about 17 miles away. To accommodate the many travelers seeking food and shelter at their home, the Michie family opened it as a tavern in 1784. The tavern was dismantled piece by piece and reassembled on its present site in 1927.

Today, visitors to Monticello and Ash Lawn-Highland can still stop by the tavern for a hearty Southern-style meal. The tavern museum offers continuous tours of rooms decorated with 18th-century Southern furniture and artifacts. Next door, a 200-year-old converted slave house called The Ordinary offers a Colonial buffet of fried chicken, black-eyed peas, stewed tomatoes, cole slaw, potato salad, green bean salad, beets, homemade biscuits, cornbread and apple cobbler from 11:30 AM to 3 PM for about $10.

Michie Tavern also features 18th-century craft demonstrations every weekend from April through October and houses the small Virginia Wine Museum in its basement. Next door in the Meadow Run Grist Mill is a general store where visitors can buy Virginia wines, specialty foods and crafts.

The Michie Tavern Museum is open year round from 9 AM to 5 PM except Christmas and New Year's Day. Admission to the museum is $5 for adults, $4.50 for seniors and $1 for children ages 6 to 11.

MONTICELLO

Charlottesville   *(804) 295-8181*

Thomas Jefferson's home, one of the country's finest architectural masterpieces, is such a popular tourist attraction that long lines are inevitable during the peak season of summer and early fall. Start early; you can always grab a snack at the lunch stand, which is open from 10:30 AM to 3:30 PM daily April through October.

Jefferson began construction of Monticello in 1769 when he was just 26, and he often longed to retire there during the most active part of his political career. Work on Monticello continued for 40 years, during which Jefferson made many alterations.

Jefferson's wide-ranging interests made him an avid collector of sculpture, maps, paintings, prints, Native American artifacts, scientific instruments and fine furniture — and these objects kept his house quite cluttered. Today, Monticello is filled with original furnishings and many of Jefferson's other possessions. It gives one the feeling that he'll return from Washington at any moment.

Though he was our nation's third president, the author of the Declaration of Independence and an international statesman, Jefferson apparently disliked politics. He wrote to his daughter Martha in 1800, "Politics is such a torment that I would advise every one I love not to mix with it."

Though he did not shirk his duty to his country and its fragile democratic system, he indulged his other interests at

Monticello, especially horticulture and garden design. Ornamental and vegetable gardens, two orchards, a vineyard and an 18-acre ornamental forest. He experimented with more than 250 varieties of vegetables and herbs, many of which are grown today in his 1,000-square-foot vegetable garden. Monticello's Thomas Jefferson Center for Historic Plants, the first of its kind in the nation, sells historical plants and seeds in the garden shop from April through October.

Monticello is on Va. 53, 3 miles southeast of Charlottesville. Take Exit 121 off I-64 and follow the signs. The mansion and grounds are open daily from 8 AM to 5 PM March through October and 9 AM to 4:30 PM the rest of the year (closed Christmas Day). Written tour information is available in foreign languages.

Admission is $8 for adults, $7 for senior citizens and $4 for children ages 6 to 11. As mentioned earlier, it's possible to save on the cost of adult admission to Monticello, Ash Lawn and Michie Tavern by buying a $17 President's Pass at the Charlottesville/Albemarle Convention and Visitors Bureau at Va. 20 S. and I-64 near Monticello.

THOMAS JEFFERSON VISITORS CENTER

Va. 20 S.   *(804) 293-6789*

This permanent exhibition shows aspects of Jefferson's domestic life at Monticello. Nearly 400 objects and artifacts, from his pocketknife to a porcupine quill toothpick, are on display, many for the first time. You can view an award-winning film, *Thomas Jefferson: The Pursuit of Liberty*, daily at 11 AM and 2 PM in the exhibition theater. The center is open from 9 AM to 5:30 PM daily March through October and 9 AM to 5 PM the rest of the year. Admission is free. The museum shop is a great source of brass, porcelain, crystal, pewter and silver pieces, as well as reproductions made exclusively for Monticello.

MONTPELIER

Montpelier Station   *(540) 672-2728*

The gracious home of President James Madison and his beloved wife, Dolley, opened for public tours in 1987. The restoration of Montpelier, which changed hands six times after Dolley Madison was forced to sell it to settle debts, is a work in progress. The archeological work and architectural research are ongoing, which makes Montpelier an exciting place to visit. You may hear from the enthusiastic staff about a new discovery on the 2,700-acre property the same day it happens!

Unlike Jefferson, Madison did not document the fine details of his everyday existence. The uncovering (and literally, in some cases, unearthing) of what Montpelier was like in Madison's time is painstaking. Also unlike Monticello, where lines form for hours and tours are rather regimented, you can dally at Montpelier and even brainstorm with a tour guide.

Montpelier was first settled by Madison's grandparents in 1723. After the completion of Madison's second presidential term, Dolley and James retired to the estate, where their legendary hospitality kept them in touch with world affairs. Madison was the primary author of the Constitution and one of the authors of the *Federalist Papers*. He was a proponent of freedom of religion and education in Virginia and served as second rector of the University of Virginia. His public life spanned 53 years and included services as a delegate to the Continental Congress, member of the Virginia House of Delegates, U.S. congressman, Thomas Jefferson's Secretary of State, and U.S. president for two terms.

Montpelier was owned by the duPont family for decades before it was bequeathed to the National Trust for Historic Preservation in the 1980s. The duPonts built major additions to the home and planted elaborate formal gardens. The biggest challenge for Montpelier's new owners, the National Trust, was what to do about all the new rooms and interior changes. They considered doing away with the duPont imprint and restoring the property to its original Madisonian form. But a compromise was struck, with the exterior and landscape keeping their 20th-century appearances, along with three duPont rooms in the house. The rest of the mansion's museum is being reconfigured as Madison-period rooms, based on the results of research.

Guided tours cover the main floor of the 55-room mansion and visitors are encouraged to stroll throughout the grounds and see the barns, stables and bowling alley and the garden temple Madison built over his ice house. Dolley and James Madison lie in a cemetery on the grounds, along with a number of Madison family members.

One of the legacies of Marion duPont Scott, who made her home at Montpelier from 1928 until her death in 1983, is the annual Montpelier Hunt Races, which take place on the first Saturday in November.

Montpelier is about 25 miles north of Charlottesville off U.S. 15 near Orange. It is open daily from 10 AM to 4 PM, except Thanksgiving, Christmas, New Year's Day and the first Saturday in November. During January and February, the site is only open on weekends. Admission is $6 for adults and $1 for children ages 6 to 12.

THE ROTUNDA/
THE UNIVERSITY OF VIRGINIA
(804) 924-7969

Free tours of Mr. Jefferson's "academic village" are offered daily from the rotunda, which Jefferson designed in the style of the Pantheon. Since 1825 the university has been renowned for its unique architectural design. In 1976 the American Institute of Architects voted Jefferson's design for the university the most outstanding achievement in American architecture.

Along with his authorship of the Declaration of Independence and the Statute of Virginia for Religious Freedom, the university was an achievement for which Jefferson wished to be remembered. He called it the "hobby of his old age" — quite an understatement. Not only was he the principal architect, Jefferson helped select the library collection, hire faculty and design the curriculum. He was one of the

Photo: Lexington Visitors Bureau

Lee Chapel at Washington and Lee University was built at the request and under the supervision of Robert E. Lee.

major financial contributors and succeeded in securing public funding for the school.

It was his ardent lobbying for public education in Virginia that led to the establishment of the university in the first place. Jefferson had studied at the College of William and Mary in Williamsburg, but he felt the state, which then encompassed West Virginia, needed a major university. He accomplished all this during his retirement at Monticello, from which he often watched the university's construction with his telescope. The rotunda was completed in 1826, the year Jefferson died.

You can take a free tour from the rotunda at 10 and 11 AM and 2, 3 and 4 PM daily, except for three weeks at Christmas. The tour includes Edgar Allan Poe's dorm room, which appears much the same as it did when Poe was a student in 1825. Poe, by the way, left the university prematurely after running up a huge gambling debt that he couldn't pay.

THE VIRGINIA FESTIVAL
OF AMERICAN FILM
University of Virginia
Charlottesville   *(800) UVA-FEST*
This eight-year-old festival held at UVA is dedicated to celebrating and exploring the unique character of American film. It lasts for four days, bringing leading actors, film-makers, scholars and the public together to discuss American film in a serious way.

The event has attracted national attention by featuring special events that honor the history of American film. These have included a 50th anniversary "encore premiere" of *Mr. Smith Goes to Washington*, with its star, James Stewart, in attendance.

Other renowned actors and film-makers who have participated in the festival include Gregory Peck, Sissy Spacek, Charlton Heston, Sidney Poitier, Robert Duvall, John Sayles and Robert Altman.

This is a stimulating, exciting event, well worth factoring into your fall vacation. Special discount hotel-and-event package rates are available.

SCOTTSVILLE ON THE JAMES
The Albemarle County seat until 1762, Scottsville is an old river town on the James River, about 20 miles from Charlottesville on Va. 20. In and around the town are 32 authentic Federal buildings, one of the four or five largest concentrations of Early Republic architecture in the state. The town also has a museum, originally a Disciples Church built in 1846.

Lynchburg

Visual Arts

ARTS COUNCIL OF CENTRAL VIRGINIA
Greater Lynchburg Chamber
of Commerce   *(804) 847-1597*
The Arts Council serves as a clearinghouse for information about area artists, musicians, actors and dancers and compiles calendars of their performances. Its stated mission is to make Lynchburg a model cultural center.

LYNCHBURG FINE ARTS CENTER
1815 Thomson Dr.   *(804) 846-8451*
An affiliate of the Virginia Museum of Fine Arts in Richmond, the Lynchburg Fine Arts Center serves the region with live theater performances in

its 500-seat theater; classes and work-shops in drama, art, dance and music; and exhibits by area artists in the Center's two galleries. The Lynchburg Regional Ballet Theatre is the Center's resident dance company, performing two ballets each season, as well as offering classes in ballet, tap and jazz for all ages and levels. The costume shop has more than 5,000 costumes, which the public may rent.

VIRGINIA CENTER
FOR THE CREATIVE ARTS

Amherst   *(804) 946-7236*

This surprising artistic treasure just outside of Lynchburg in Amherst County is the nation's largest working retreat for professional writers, artists and composers. Artists who visit from abroad are often the leading creative forces in their own countries, and some of the most important exchanges between artists worldwide take place here. The Virginia Center for the Creative Arts is supported in part by the National Endowment for the Arts and the Virginia Commission for the Arts, and is affiliated with Sweet Briar College, a private woman's college.

The V.C.C.A. is not frequently open to the public but does have exhibits at Camp Gallery, in the renovated barn that also houses the artists' studios. There are exhibitions each summer, which include meet-the-artists receptions. Many public events, such as poetry readings with Russian writers-in-residence, are cosponsored with Sweet Briar.

Camp Gallery hours are 2 to 4:30 PM Sunday during the summer only.

MAIER MUSEUM OF ART

Randolph-Macon Woman's College
1 Quinlan St.   *(804) 947-8136*

Known for its collection of 19th-and 20th-century American paintings, the Maier Museum at prestigious Randolph-Macon Woman's College displays works by Winslow Homer, James McNeill Whistler, Mary Cassatt and Georgia O'Keeffe. This is a tremendous community asset well worth the visit for arts lovers. The museum is open September through May from 1 to 5 PM, Tuesday through Sunday.

Museums

LYNCHBURG MUSEUM
AT OLD COURT HOUSE

Fifth St.   *(804) 847-1459*

The Lynchburg Museum, housed in one of Virginia's outstanding Greek Revival civil buildings, is the headquarters for Lynchburg's fine museum system. The courtroom was restored around 1855. It traces Lynchburg's history and is an outstanding collection for both scholars and history buffs, especially of the Civil War period.

The museum is open from 1 to 4 PM daily and closed holidays. Admission is $1.

PEST HOUSE MEDICAL MUSEUM
AND CONFEDERATE CEMETERY

Old City Cemetery
Fourth and Taylor Sts.   *(804) 847-1811*

In the 1800s Lynchburg residents who contracted contagious diseases such as smallpox or measles were quarantined in the Pest House. Medical care and cleanliness were virtually nonexistent then, and most patients died and were buried a few yards away. By 1861 the Pest House was used for Confederate soldiers. Dr. John Jay Terrell, 33, who volunteered to assume responsibility for the soldiers, changed these wretched conditions by emphasizing antiseptic practices. His restored office shows the state of medicine during that era, including an 1860s hypodermic needle and one of the first chloroform masks ever used.

Open sunrise to sunset, the facility offers guided tours by appointment.

Music

BLUE RIDGE MUSIC FESTIVAL
Randolph-Macon Woman's
College (804) 947-8000
The Blue Ridge Music Festival was begun as a celebration of musical diversity. Now in its sixth season, the Blue Ridge Music Festival continues to inspire and challenge music lovers of all ages and tastes with concerts of the world's great chamber music, jazz improvisation and folk music from Tex-Mex ballads to Appalachian melodies.

POINT OF HONOR
112 Cabell St. (804) 847-1459
In the afternoons you can usually find Lynchburg's history elite, some of whom are from historical families themselves, at this 19th-century mansion, which was lovingly restored by the Lynchburg Historical Foundation, the Garden Club of Virginia and the Katharine Garland Diggs Trust. Point of Honor shows today's families what life was like in the days of Dr. George Cabell Sr., Patrick Henry's personal physician. It also was home to Mary Virginia Ellet Cabell, one of the founders of the Daughters of the American Revolution. Its name comes from the gun duels fought on its lawn.

Point of Honor is open daily 1 to 4 PM; closed holidays. Admission is $3 for adults and $1 for students.

Theater

CHERRY TREE PLAYERS
4925 Boonsboro Rd. (804) 384-4577
A new theater, the Players is a group of artists, musicians, business people, directors, technicians and others who came together to advance the arts and theater in the Lynchburg area. There is an active children's and youth theater as well. Admission is $10 for adults. No children younger than 6 may attend.

Other Cultural Attractions

ANNE SPENCER HOUSE AND GARDEN
1313 Pierce St. (804) 846-0517
Anne Spencer was an internationally recognized African-American poet of the Harlem Renaissance period of the 1920s. Her poems are included in the *Norton Anthology of Modern Poetry*. Behind her home is the garden and accompanying cottage, Edan Kraal, built for her by her husband as a place where she could write. The garden has been beautifully restored by Hillside Garden Club. Revered the world over for her intellect, Spencer entertained many great leaders and artists of her day, including Dr. Martin Luther King, Supreme Court Justice Thurgood Marshall, scientist Dr. George Washington Carver, sports legend Jackie Robinson, Congressman Adam Clayton Powell (who honeymooned there) and the legendary singers Paul Robeson and Marion Anderson. Her son, Chauncey, still lives in the family home, so hours are by appointment only.

JONES MEMORIAL LIBRARY
2311 Memorial Ave. (804) 846-0501
The second-oldest library in Virginia, Jones Memorial is also one of Virginia's

foremost genealogical libraries. The Jones is known for its vast records: 30,000 volumes specializing in genealogical, historical and Lynchburg holdings. These include Revolutionary War records, family histories, enlistments and Virginia county and state court records. Records from England, Ireland and Scotland include heraldry information. The library offers research and lending services by mail. This gem is probably one of the most under-utilized treasures of the Blue Ridge.

The library is open 1 to 9 PM Tuesday, noon to 5 PM Wednesday through Friday and 9 AM to 1 PM Saturday; it's closed Sunday and Monday.

RED HILL
PATRICK HENRY NATIONAL MEMORIAL
Brookneal (804) 376-2044

Who can forget Revolutionary War hero Patrick Henry's speech, "Give me liberty or give me death!" Red Hill is the last home and burial place of the famous orator, first governor of Virginia and champion of individual rights. The Red Hill museum/visitors center and historic buildings showcase the world's largest collection of Patrick Henry memorabilia, including the famous Peter Rothermel painting, "Patrick Henry Before the Virginia House of Burgesses." You can visit Henry's house, law office and other plantation buildings, and the grounds contain the Henry family cemetery and the national champion Osage orange tree. Red Hill, which Mr. Henry called "one of the garden spots of Virginian," offers a breathtaking view of the Staunton River Valley.

The memorial is open 9 AM until 5 PM daily except November through February, when it closes at 4 PM. It is closed holidays. Admission is $3 for adults, $1 for students and children.

VIRGINIA SCHOOL OF THE ARTS
Columbia and Rivermont Ave. (804) 847-8688

Virginia School of the Arts, a private residential secondary school, is dedicated to preparing young people for careers in dance, theater and the visual arts. It is one of only six such schools for the arts in America, and students come from throughout the United States. Its arts faculty includes prominent professional performers and artists who contribute greatly to Lynchburg's culture.

Bedford County

Museums

BEDFORD CITY/COUNTY MUSEUM
201 E. Main St.
Bedford (540) 586-4520

Visitors can see a collection of artifacts and memorabilia showing the story of Bedford, a charming city at the foot of the Peaks of Otter, a Blue Ridge Parkway attraction. The exhibits begin with early natives of the region and progresses through the mid-20th century. Here, you'll see Native American relics, Revolutionary War and Civil War artifacts, clothing, flags, quilts and more. Research assistance is available for genealogists outside Bedford.

Hours are 10 AM to 5 PM Monday through Saturday. Admission is $1 for adults and 50¢ for children.

Other Cultural Attractions

ELKS NATIONAL HOME
Bedford (540) 586-8232

A spacious retirement home used as a set in the Disney movie *What About Bob?*, the Elks National Home for retired members of this fraternal organization is best-known for its annual Christmas light display. Men from every state work all year to give western Virginia's children a Christmas show worth driving to see. The rest of the year, the beautiful grounds are open for visitors.

HOLY LAND
USA NATURE SANCTUARY

Va. 6, Bedford   *(540) 586-2823*

This 400-acre nature sanctuary where visitors can imagine the journey and deeds of Jesus Christ is in the beautiful Blue Ridge close to the Peaks of Otter. You have to use your imagination to envision the biblical scenes outlined for Bible research and study, but many find inspiration from the visit.

POPLAR FOREST

Va. 661, Forest   *(804) 525-1806*

Poplar Forest, Thomas Jefferson's summer home, has been under renovation for several years now, and visitors are invited to watch the painstaking excavations and historical restoration. During Jefferson's time, Poplar Forest was a working plantation of nearly 5,000 acres tended by slaves who grew corn and tobacco. Although Monticello was Jefferson's pride and joy, Poplar Forest was where he came to get away from it all, riding three days from Charlottesville by horseback to reach it. As Mikhail Gorbachev said when he visited in the spring of 1993, "This is the first Camp David!"

Jefferson himself designed the unusual building. History and Jefferson buffs will be fascinated with seeing his office, library and even two domed necessaries that were part of day-to-day life. July 4 is the best time to visit, since actors staff the home in period attire and speak the language of the day, transporting you back to 1815. The

event is free and takes place from noon to 5 PM. Picnicking is encouraged. Poplar Forest's huge, ancient boxwoods are incredible to see on the beautiful grounds. The staff's enthusiasm for this cultural treasure is highly contagious.

Open 10 AM to 4 PM Wednesday through Sunday April through November, Poplar Forest is open on major holidays except Thanksgiving. (Please note that the last tour begins at 3:45 PM.) You can arrange a group tour any time of the year. Admission is $5 for adults, $4 for senior citizens, $3 for college students and $1 for children ages 12 to 18. Younger children are admitted free.

SEDALIA CENTER

Va. 638, Big Island   *(804) 299-5080*

The Sedalia Center, "for the art of living and the living arts," is a regional, nonprofit organization offering programming in the arts, culture, environmental awareness, health and inner development. It offers classes, workshops, seminars and special events which, the Center mission states, ignites and nourishes the creative process in each person.

The Center's modern building is set on seven acres at the foot of Flintstone Mountain near Big Island. Special events include dance, storytelling, music festivals and a country fair. The Sedalia Coffeehouse is held every fourth Saturday, and contra dancing is every second Friday. At least once a quarter, you'll find the Coffeehouse serving as an open jam, in keeping with Sedalia's mission.

Among the classes are Cajun cooking, Tai Chi, and an introduction to the mountain dulcimer and instrument construction. Lecture titles may include "How Native American Indians Lived with Nature and How Some of Their Approaches Might Work for Us." A small but dedicated group of creative people makes the Sedalia Center the heart of a special culture for people of the Blue Ridge foothills.

Franklin County

Museums

BLUE RIDGE INSTITUTE MUSEUMS
Ferrum College, Ferrum   *(540) 365-4416*

The Blue Ridge Institute of Ferrum College, the State Center for Blue Ridge Folklore, presents the folkways of the region and Virginia as a whole through two unique museum facilities.

The Blue Ridge Farm Museum, which presents the history and culture of early Southwest Virginia settlements, features an 1800s German-American farmstead with log house, outdoor oven, outbuildings, pasture and gardens revealing the daily life of Colonists who came from the German settlements of Pennsylvania and the Shenandoah Valley. All buildings are authentic and were moved from their original Blue Ridge locations. Heirloom vegetables flourish in the gardens, vintage breeds of livestock shelter by the barn, and costumed interpreters work at farm and household chores true to early life in the region.

Both historical and contemporary folkways engage the visitor to the Institute's Museum Galleries. Two rotating exhibits showcase the rich texture of Virginia folklife in music, crafts, art and customs. The Museum galleries are the only facilities in the Commonwealth dedicated exclusively to the presentation of traditional culture.

The Farm Museum is open weekends from mid-May through mid-August, Saturday 10 AM to 5 PM and Sundays 1 to 5 PM. Admission is $3 for adults and $2 for children and senior citizens. Museum Galleries are open year round Monday through Saturday 10 AM to 4 PM. Admission is free.

Theater

BLUE RIDGE DINNER THEATRE
Ferrum College, Sale Theatre
Schoolfield Hall, Ferrum   *(540) 365-4335*

The Blue Ridge Dinner Theatre operates on the three guiding principles of theater: discovery, wholesome family entertainment and celebration. It also serves up a great luncheon or dinner in combination with everything from murder mysteries to great historical masterpieces. Adjacent to the Blue Ridge Institute, the Dinner Theatre also offers theater-goers tours of the facility. The Ferrum's theater group, the Jack Tale Players, continues the legacy through acting out legends of the South.

Performances are varied, with hours at 12:15 PM and 6:45 PM.

Other Cultural Attractions

BOOKER T. WASHINGTON NATIONAL MONUMENT
Hardy   *(540) 721-2094*

Booker T. Washington was born into the legacy of slavery, spending the first nine years of his life in bondage on this small tobacco farm. It was from this unlikely beginning that Washington achieved international recognition as an educator, orator, unofficial presidential advisor, founder of Tuskegee Institute and African-American leader. Begin your tour of his birthplace by watching the slide show and seeing the exhibits at the visitors center.

This is the most famous attraction in

Franklin County and with good reason. From the beautiful, restored farm and its animals to the hike up Plantation Trail, this monument offers a scenic, historic sojourn into a time in America when slavery was a way of life.

The site is open daily 9 AM to 4:30 PM, except for Thanksgiving, Christmas and New Year's Day. Admission is free.

BLUE RIDGE FOLKLIFE FESTIVAL
Ferrum College, Ferrum   (540) 365-4416

On the fourth Saturday of October, Ferrum College showcases regional folklife with this blockbuster festival, now in its 22nd year. Visitors can experience the tastes, sights and sounds of western Virginia folk culture as demonstrated by local residents. More than 40 Blue Ridge crafters demonstrate and sell rugs braided by hand, baskets, shingles and other folk arts. The South's thriving auto culture is featured along with vintage steam and gas-powered farm machinery. Among the most popular events for spectators are the horse pulling contests and coon dog water races. Many of these demonstrations are getting to be extinct as the old-timers die, so if you want to see the Blue Ridge as it was make it a point to go to the festival. It's crowded, but a lot of fun.

The festival is held from 10 AM to 5 PM. Admission, which includes a tour of the Farm Museum, is $4 for adults and $3 for students.

BLUE RIDGE INSTITUTE
Ferrum College, Ferrum   (540) 365-4416

Visitors are often astounded that a small Methodist-related college in Franklin County, Virginia, has taken on the role of preserving a cultural heritage to the extent and level of visibility that Ferrum College has done. The result, the

Blue Ridge Institute, along with the Blue Ridge Farm Museum and its Folklife Festival, places Ferrum among the nation's most important colleges culturally. Its archives contain thousands of photos, videotapes, phonograph records, vintage books and manuscripts, all treasures troves of Appalachian scenes and people, Shenandoah Valley beliefs, Southwest Virginia folktales and African-American and Caucasian folk music from throughout Virginia.

BRI Records, which presents the diverse musical heritage of Virginia's folk culture, has been nominated for two Grammy awards.

People of English, Scot, Irish, African and German descent will be especially interested in the distinct identities reflected in Blue Ridge music, crafts, foods, beliefs and customs formed after their forebears came to America.

The institute is open Monday through Friday 8 AM to 4:30 PM. Archives are open by appointment.

New River Valley Region

Blacksburg

Visual Arts

Virginia Tech features several art galleries with good reputations that are worth visiting.

ARMORY ART GALLERY
201 Draper Rd.   (540) 231-4859

Virginia Tech's Department of Art and Art History operates the Armory Art

Gallery as an educational and outreach program. The 1,000-square-foot gallery, in the Old Blacksburg Armory, has a year-round rotation of exhibits by national or regional artists, work by student artists and other shows of community interest.

PERSPECTIVE ART GALLERY

Squires Student Center   (540) 231-5200

Perspective Gallery offers a range of artistic styles and media by artists ranging from internationally known professionals to students. The gallery, a facility of the University Unions and Student Activities, also offers talks and receptions where the public can meet featured artists.

XYZ COOPERATIVE GALLERY

223 N. Main St.
above College Inn   (540) 953-3435

A lively exhibit gallery, XYZ sponsors continuing shows that are characterized by their vitality and unique range.

Theater

THEATRE ARTS DEPARTMENT

Virginia Tech   (540) 231-5335

The New River Valley's cultural richness comes in great part from Virginia Tech's presence, and theater is no exception. The only theatre arts department in Virginia to have both its graduate and undergraduate programs accredited by the National Association of Schools of Theatre, Virginia Tech's has received more awards from the American College Theatre Festival than any other college or university in the Southeast. The Theatre Arts Department at Tech stages about 20 productions each year, including comedies, dramas, musicals and new plays.

Virginia Tech hosts four subscription shows during the academic year. The school has three theaters: Haymarket Theatre at Squires Student Center, Black Box Theatre in the Performing Arts Building and Squires Studio Theatre. All productions are open to the public. Don't miss Tech's Summer Arts Festival.

Other Cultural Attractions

CAROL M. NEWMAN LIBRARY

Virginia Tech Campus   (540) 231-6170

Virginia Tech's Carol M. Newman Library has nearly 5 million microforms, making it the fifth-largest such collection in the United States and Canada. Contained within this store of information are rare books and magazines, government documents, newspapers, Virginia Confederate Service Records and issues of the campus newspaper back to 1903.

SMITHFIELD PLANTATION

Virginia Tech campus, off U.S. 460 Bypass
onto Va. 314   (540) 951-2060

Built by Col. William Preston in 1772, Smithfield Plantation has been extensively restored and is a Virginia Historic Landmark. It was the birthplace of two Virginia governors, James Patton Preston and John Buchanan Floyd, and was briefly the home of a third, John Floyd Jr.

Hours are 1 to 5 PM Thursday through Sunday April 1 through November 1. Admission is $4 for adults and $1.50 for children 12 and younger.

VIRGINIA TECH DUCK POND

Virginia Tech campus

If you took a poll of where many people went on their first date or fell in love in the New River Valley, it would be the Virginia Tech Duck Pond, hands down! It's a Tech landmark beside the golf course, where mothers take their babies, couples hold hands and picnic and